IMAGES
of America

ANNA MARIA ISLAND

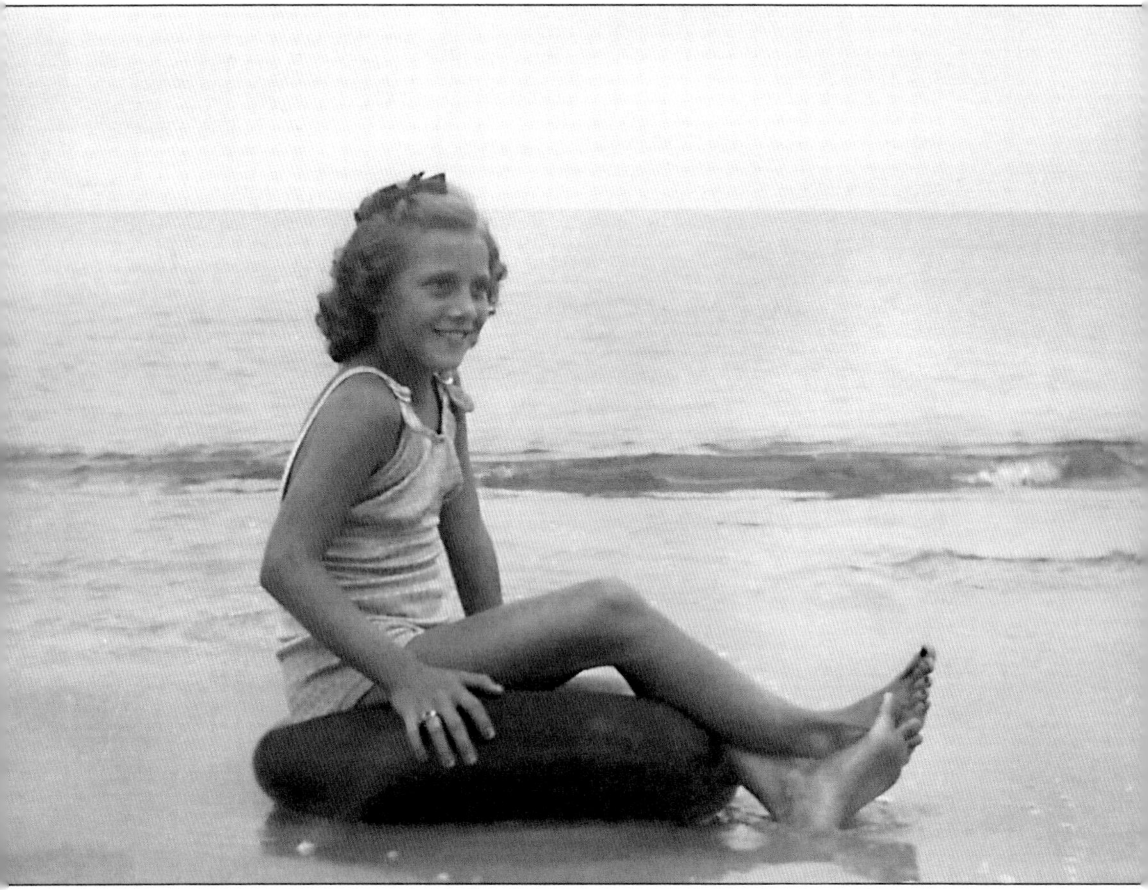

Pictured here in a photograph dated September 8, 1940, ten-year-old Sybil Joyce Hankin rests on an inner tube at the shoreline at Virginia Beach. Joyce, as she was known, grew up loving the beach and instilled her passion early on in her daughter, Bonner Joy, with many day trips to the beach where she grew up. Joyce (Hankin) Eller, married with three more children, moved in 1972 to Florida, near Anna Maria Island, and soon after died. (Author's collection.)

ON THE COVER: A Sarasota circus performer and member of the famed Wallenda family walks over the waters of Longboat Pass in 1955 as a crowd of spectators and celebrants gathers onshore and in boats to celebrate the beginning of a new bridge to link Anna Maria Island to Longboat Key. Some of the commercial fishing boats in the pass hold support lines for the high wire. (Courtesy of the Anna Maria Island Historical Society.)

IMAGES
of America

ANNA MARIA ISLAND

Bonner Joy

ARCADIA
PUBLISHING

ISBN 978-1-4671-1507-0

Published by Arcadia Publishing
Charleston, South Carolina

Printed in the United States of America

Library of Congress Control Number: 2015943774

For all general information, please contact Arcadia Publishing:
Telephone 843-853-2070
Fax 843-853-0044
E-mail sales@arcadiapublishing.com
For customer service and orders:
Toll-Free 1-888-313-2665

Visit us on the Internet at www.arcadiapublishing.com

In November 1992, I launched a new newspaper, the Islander, *covering the people and three city governments on Anna Maria Island. It was then I came to know Jean Blassingame, Snooks Adams, Ellen Marshall, Birdie Tebbetts, John Holmes Jr., John Bacich, Bill and Peg Blassingame-Diamant, and* Islander *editor-columnist June Alder, who all came to share remembrances of the early days on Anna Maria Island. Wyatt Blassingame came to Anna Maria Island in the late 1940s, and while I did not know him, his inspiration came to me through his words and the stories and poetry shared with me by way of his wife, Jean, and daughter Peggy. They all inspired a love for history in me with their gifts—tales of life on Anna Maria Island. Another writer and photographer, my partner at the newspaper, inspired and taught me the skills I would need to publish a newspaper and this book. I have much for which to thank Paul M. Roat, born and raised in Bradenton Beach, and many fond memories of him. We shared great times on the beach, reading Travis McGee stories. But it was my mother, Joyce, who instilled in me my love for the beach and introduced me to Anna Maria Island. Thank you all.*

Contents

Acknowledgments

In 2014, I started sending the *Islander*'s original photography archives—the photographs used in the newspaper from 1992 up to the digital years—to Tallahassee and the State Archives of Florida. The *Islander*'s contribution to the state archives will soon be available for viewing on select "Islander" pages by everyone with Internet access at the website Floridamemory.com.

It will be an exciting day for me when it goes live, because perusing old pictures and putting places and names together is great joy for me.

Which brings me to the tremendous archive of photographs available in the Manatee County Public Library Digital Collection. Many thanks go to library services manager Eva Ehde and staff members Ericka Dow and Daniel Bradley for assisting with access to this valuable collection. The majority of images in this pictorial history collection were selected from the library's website. Unless otherwise noted, images appear courtesy of the Manatee County Public Library. The library's collection was made possible through funding from the Library Foundation, located at 1301 Barcarrota Boulevard West in Bradenton, Florida.

Thanks also go to the late Paul Roat for entrusting me with his parent's family photo albums that date back to the early years when Jeanne and Maynard Roat moved to Anna Maria Island.

The late June Alder also entrusted the *Islander* with a bevy of original photographs and notes that date back to the early 1900s.

Thanks also go to Melissa and Frank Williams of SteamDesigns in Holmes Beach for technical support with the *Islander* photograph collection.

Introduction

A jewel in the Gulf of Mexico, Anna Maria Island was once inhabited by members of the Seminole tribe of Native Americans, but once the beauty was known to its first homesteader, George L. Bean, Anna Maria Island's destiny was as a beacon to paradise. In spite of thickets of mangroves, people came by boat, steamer, and ferry to enjoy the white sands, the turquoise waters of the Gulf of Mexico, and the calm bays and to feel the cool onshore breezes as the sun set in a blaze of colors. And fishing. The *Islander* newspaper of the early 1950s heralded, "Where life is peaceful, and the fishing is good." Anglers came from afar to test their skills against the world's greatest game fish, the tarpon, hunt a goliath grouper in the depths of Tampa Bay, and gather some of the finest seafood anywhere to their tables.

A long pier and a small church at the north end anchored a small community of stalwart residents and sea captains in the 1900s—and yes, developers. Sales for beach cottages were brisk in the 1920s, and their prospects came on steamers and ferries from Tampa to dock at the Anna Maria Pier, built in 1910. They strolled a long walkway—Pine Avenue—westward from the pier to a wide expanse of sugar-sand beach on the calm waters of the Gulf of Mexico, a bathhouse, and community building where sales were conducted.

The pier still stands and serves visitors who walk the 750-plus planks from the shore to the T-end to fish and dine. The bathhouse evolved to become the Sandbar Restaurant. And the sales office has served for 67 years as a community theater.

As the north end of the island grew and incorporated in 1925 as the City of Anna Maria, Bradenton Beach grew on the south end of the city thanks to the opening of the first wooden bridge to the island in 1921, connecting the fishing village of Cortez and mainland Manatee County to Bradenton Beach. But mid-island, the city of Holmes Beach began to develop, and sharp-eyed settlers invested their earnings into expanses of land—and soon came housing, grocers, gas stations, a school, banks and small shopping centers. Holmes Beach incorporated in 1950, and with three new modern bridges opening in 1957, connecting Holmes Beach and Bradenton Beach to the mainland, as well as a link from the south end to Longboat Key, the island cities—and Anna Maria Island—were well on their way to becoming the jewel of Manatee County.

I first came to Anna Maria Island in 1972, and it still seems like yesterday. It hardly seems like history, but I followed my mother's footprints in the sand more than 40 years ago.

I knew just where to go. She had sent me a snapshot of the beach she frequented—a view through a sea grape tree that shaded the northern end of the Manatee Public Beach where the white sand and the aqua waters of the Gulf of Mexico looked like a postcard. On the side, she had written, "my beach."

She parked her car in the shade of that sea grape and carried her beach gear to the shore as many days as she could in the short six months she lived in Bradenton before her death. Her letters to me were filled with hope that I would soon make the move to Florida.

And so I did in January 1975, with two young children, a career in hospitality, and a job at the El Conquistador Country Club, now IMG.

Life led me to a sales job at the former *Islander* newspaper, then owned by Don Moore. Next for me was work at a magazine and 13 years or so managing my own advertising agency.

Many of my contemporaries were what we jokingly called "smug drugglers," or their friends and family, and it was an interesting time. The children went to Anna Maria Elementary School. We hung out in Cortez and, from time to time, Key West, and heard many tall tales, some likely true. I quickly came to love my new sense of place on Anna Maria Island.

From those early settlers in the 1900s, there now are many generations of memories—my own included—and many more people to call it home. Also, there are visitors—snowbirds and day visitors. Vacationers arrive to Anna Maria Island from all over the world to call paradise theirs for a day or a lifetime.

I hope this collection of photographs helps them feel at home on "my beach."

One

The Early Years

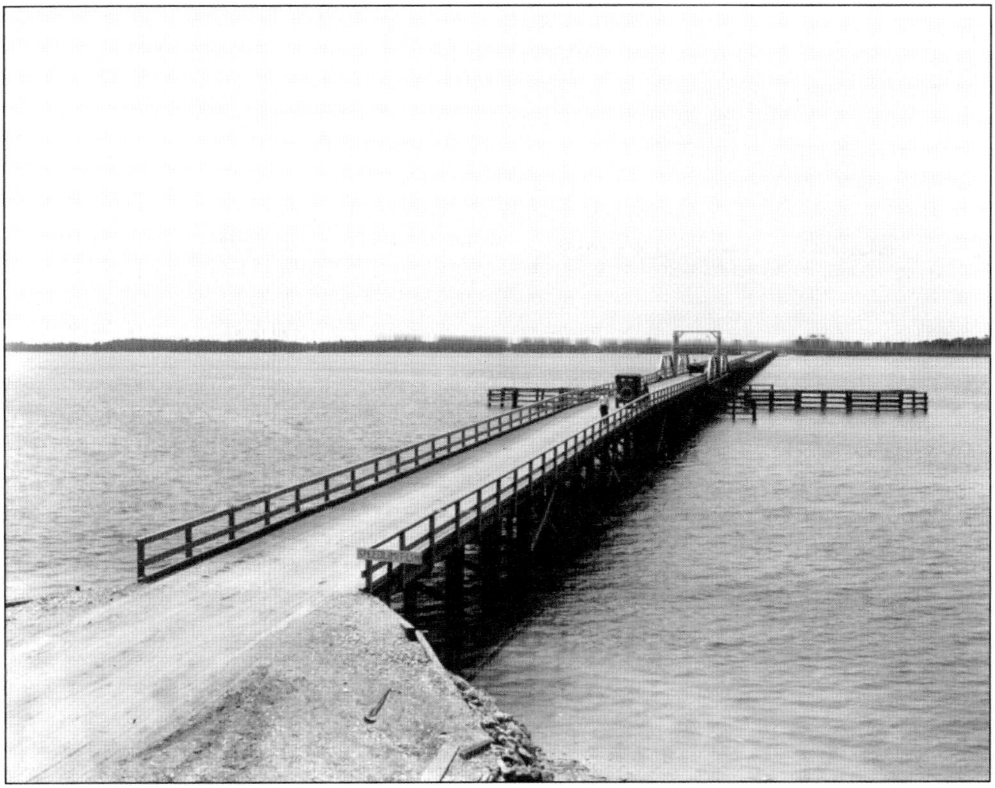

Linking the fishing village of Cortez to Anna Maria Island and what would become Bradenton Beach, the first bridge to Anna Maria Island was built of wood in 1921. There is a sign on the bridge indicating the speed limit, 15 miles per hour, and traffic was limited to one direction at a time. The automobiles on the bridge are heading to the island, where the roof of the bathing pavilion is visible.

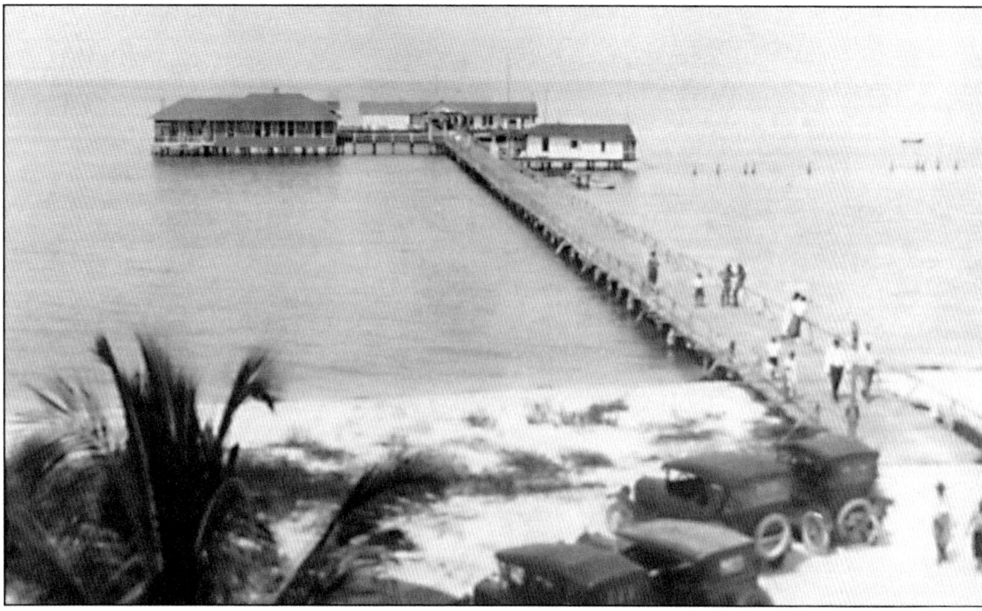

Visitors arrive at the Anna Maria Pier around 1924. The pier opened in 1911, a decade before the first bridge was built to the island and 14 years before the city incorporated. It was the focus of commerce for the small community at the north end, where steamers brought goods and visitors, many of whom paraded with their umbrellas to a bathhouse on the Gulf of Mexico at the opposite end of Pine Avenue. May 13–14, 2011, marked a celebration of the 100th anniversary of the city-owned pier.

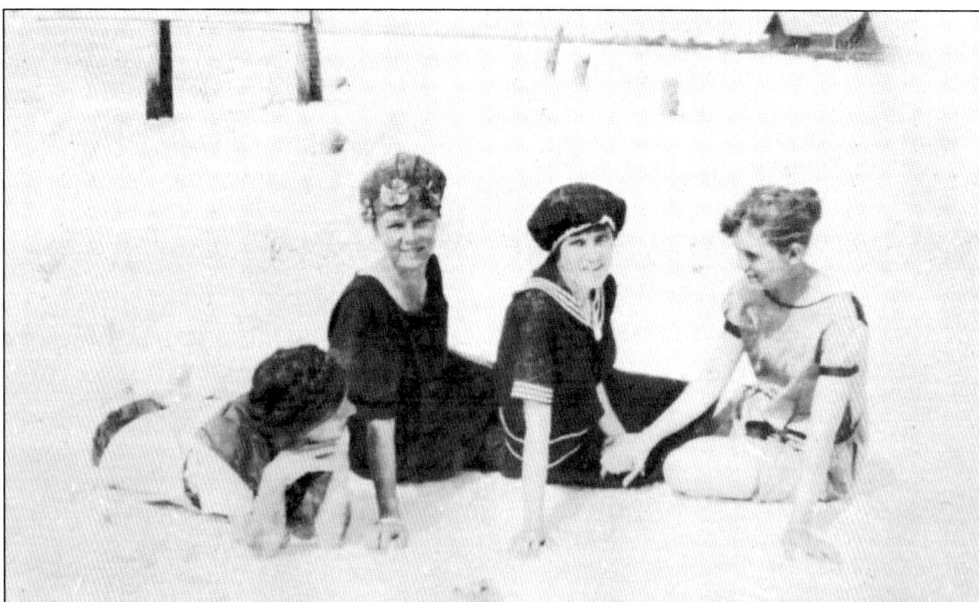

Four women pose on the beach in Anna Maria in typical 1920s swim attire. In the background, a beach home is under construction, and at the water's edge, pilings are evident. They may be seated on the bayfront beach near the Anna Maria Pier, judging from the surroundings. Most development on the island began on the bayfront around the pier landing.

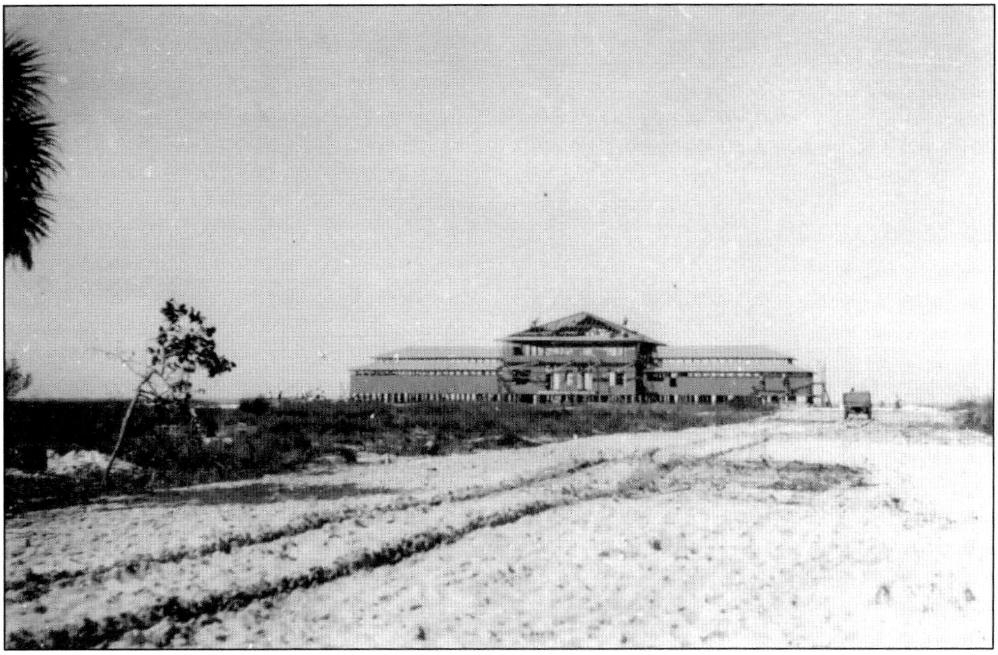

Construction workers are pictured here erecting the Bradenton Beach Pavilion and Bathhouse. This two-story elevated wooden building had a large porch on the main floor and a stairway leading down to the beach level. Dimly seen in the shade under the porch are picnic tables on the beach level. The pavilion's center portion had a dance hall and dining room. The owners had luxury apartments on the top floor.

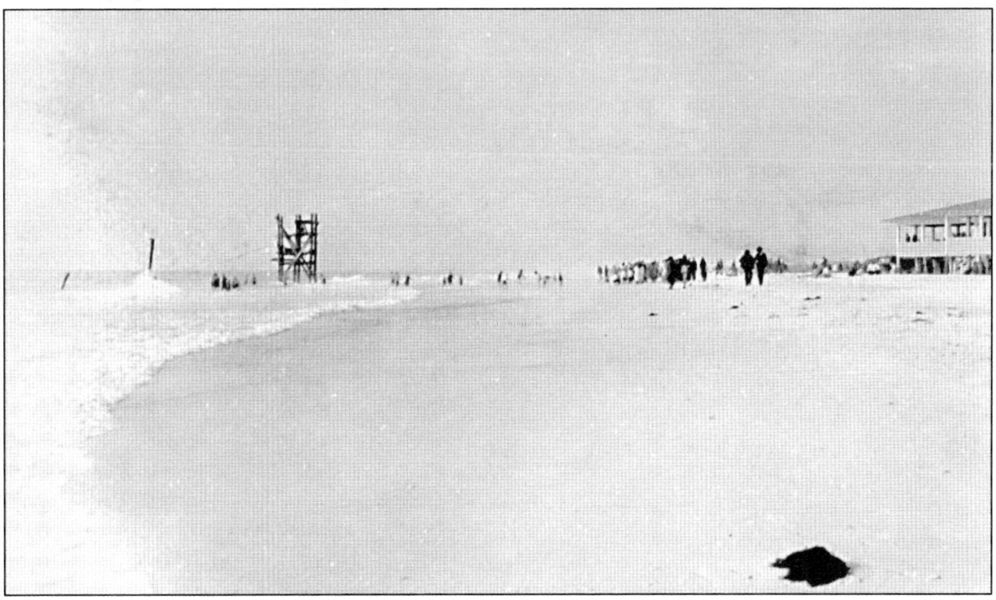

The pavilion was constructed in 1922 at a cost of about $30,000. Each side of the two-story main building had men's and women's facilities for changing into bathing suits, each with 100 lockers. It soon burned down and was rebuilt at a cost of $40,000. The new structure lasted throughout the 1920s, but it, too, burned in 1929. In the early 1900s, the south end of Anna Maria Island and the bathhouse's location became known as Cortez Beach.

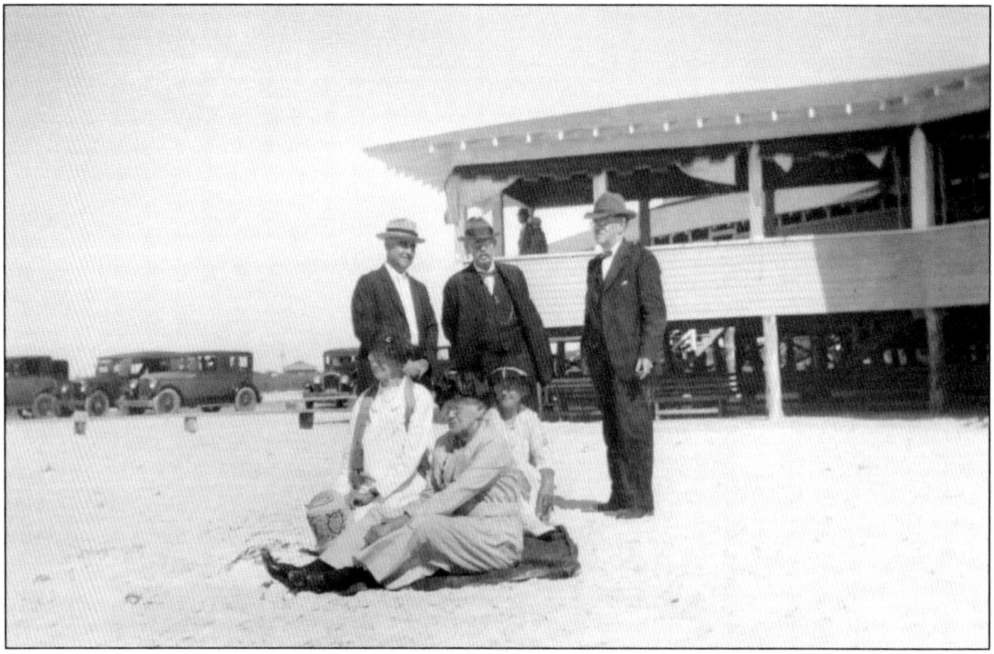

People were attracted to the shore and the facilities of the Bradenton Beach Pavilion in the 1920s. They came in droves, wearing their Sunday best, ready for a day at the beach. They came for the sun and lounging. They came to play and swim. With little amenities along the beach on the island and a long day planned, the beach pavilion was the primary destination. It included restrooms, picnic tables, a dining room, and a dance hall. It had changing rooms and lockers. It was the go-to place before people had any other place to go on the beach. And Bradenton Beach and Bridge Street evolved with the pavilion.

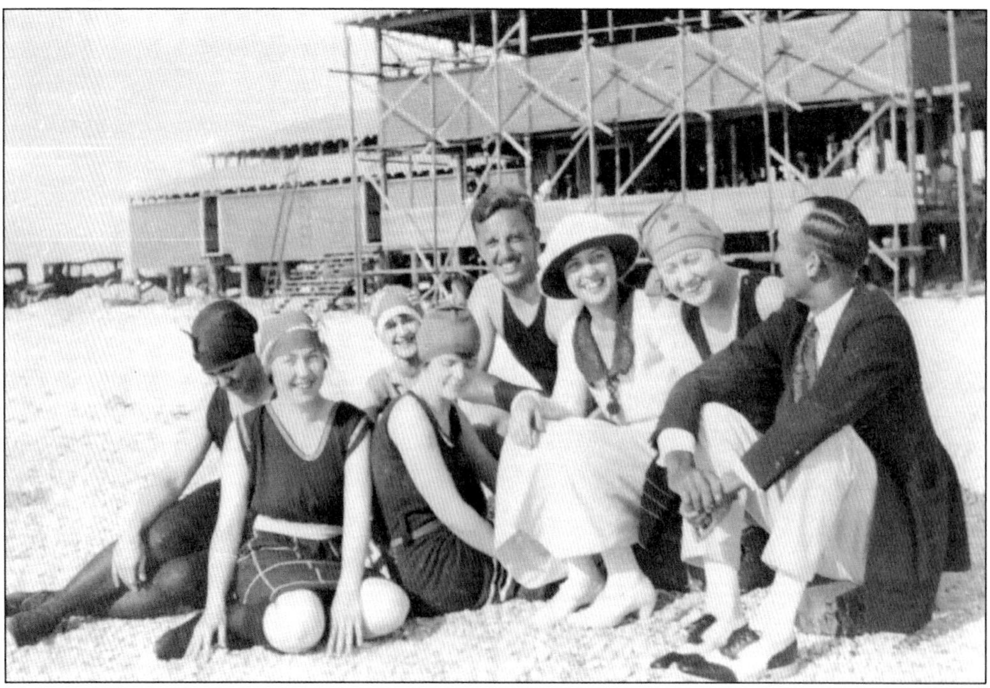

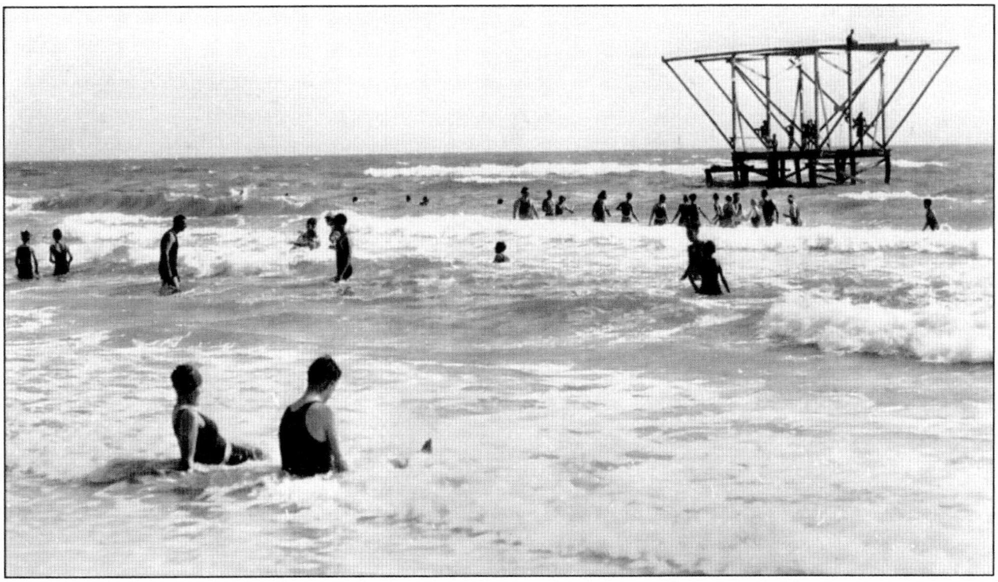

People enjoy relaxing in the mild surf near the shoreline in Bradenton Beach, some jumping in the surf and from the diving platform—a challenge for the better swimmers. The platform was built in the 1920s near the Bradenton Beach Pavilion to provide recreation for beachgoers.

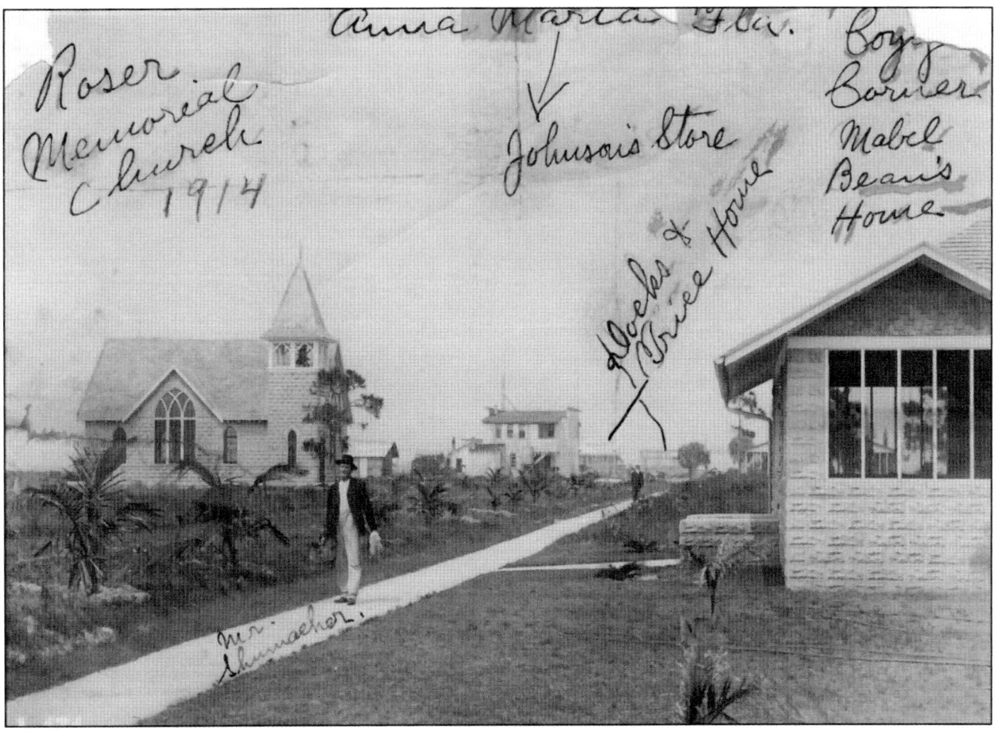

A Mr. Shumacher walks on Pine Avenue west from the bayfront end of the street toward the Gulf of Mexico in the 1920s. The street is now fully developed, with a variety of businesses, restaurants, and residences, including the Rosedale Cottage, on the right, now part of the Historic Green Village shops, and the Roser Chapel, now part of the larger Roser Memorial Community Church. The notes on the original photograph were made by Mabel Bean. (Courtesy of the *Islander*.)

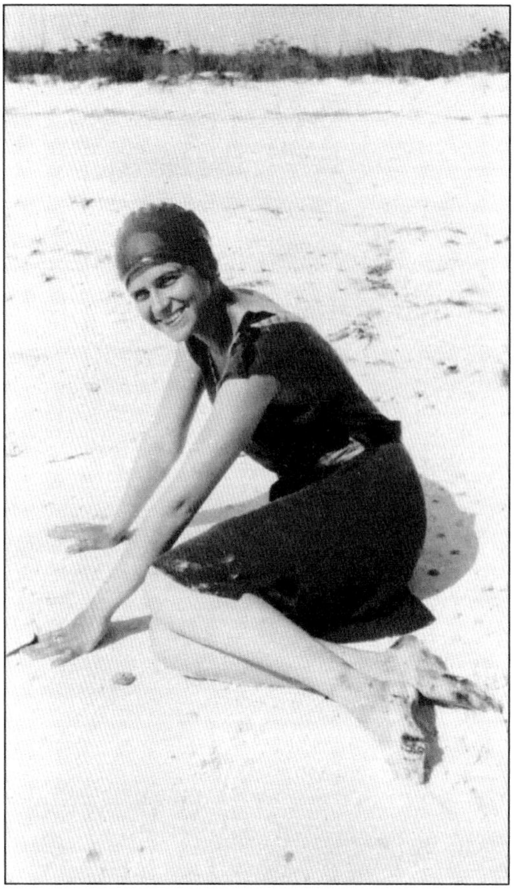

Sunbathers—in various forms of early 1900s beach attire—enjoy the beach and having their photographs taken on Anna Maria Island. One can imagine many a family or class reunion at the beach or gatherings of friends on the shore, where the sun and the Gulf of Mexico waters were considered healing and rejuvenating.

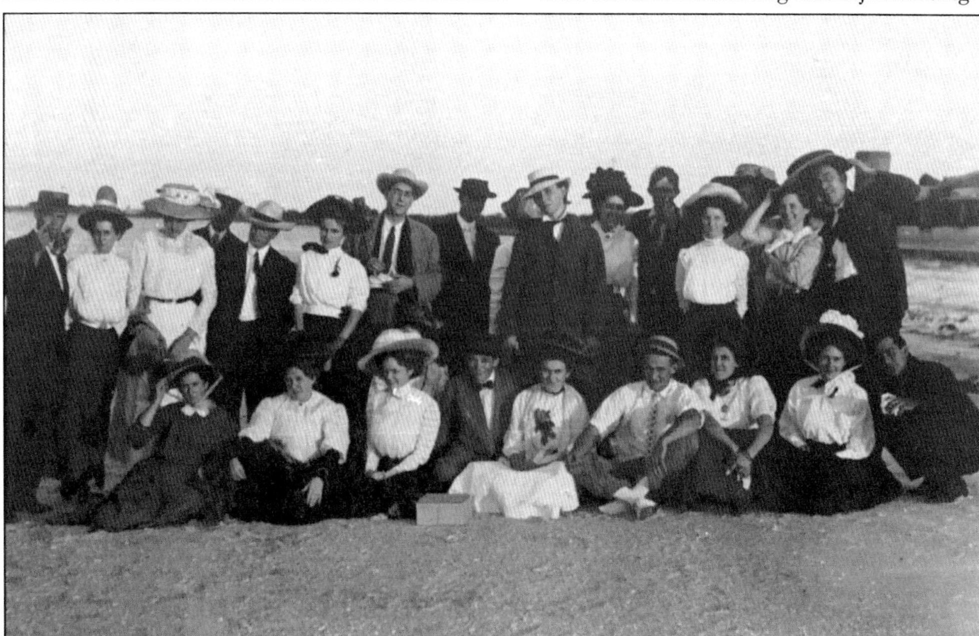

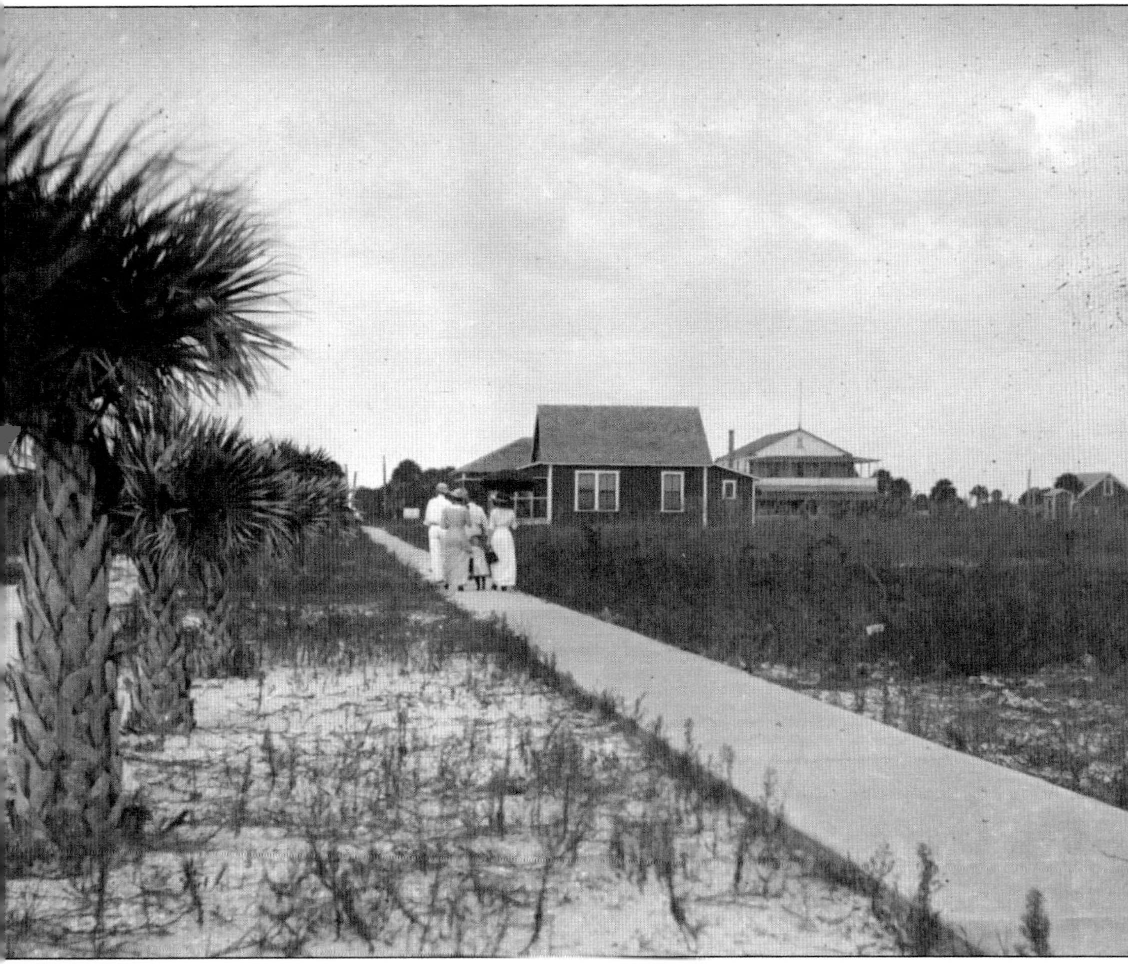

A group walks on Pine Avenue toward the Gulf of Mexico in the 1920s. Thanks to the pier and the steamers that docked there, the beach development company had great success attracting people from Tampa to buy cottages. Before bridges and airports, the people who lived and worked in Tampa found their place in the sun on Anna Maria Island.

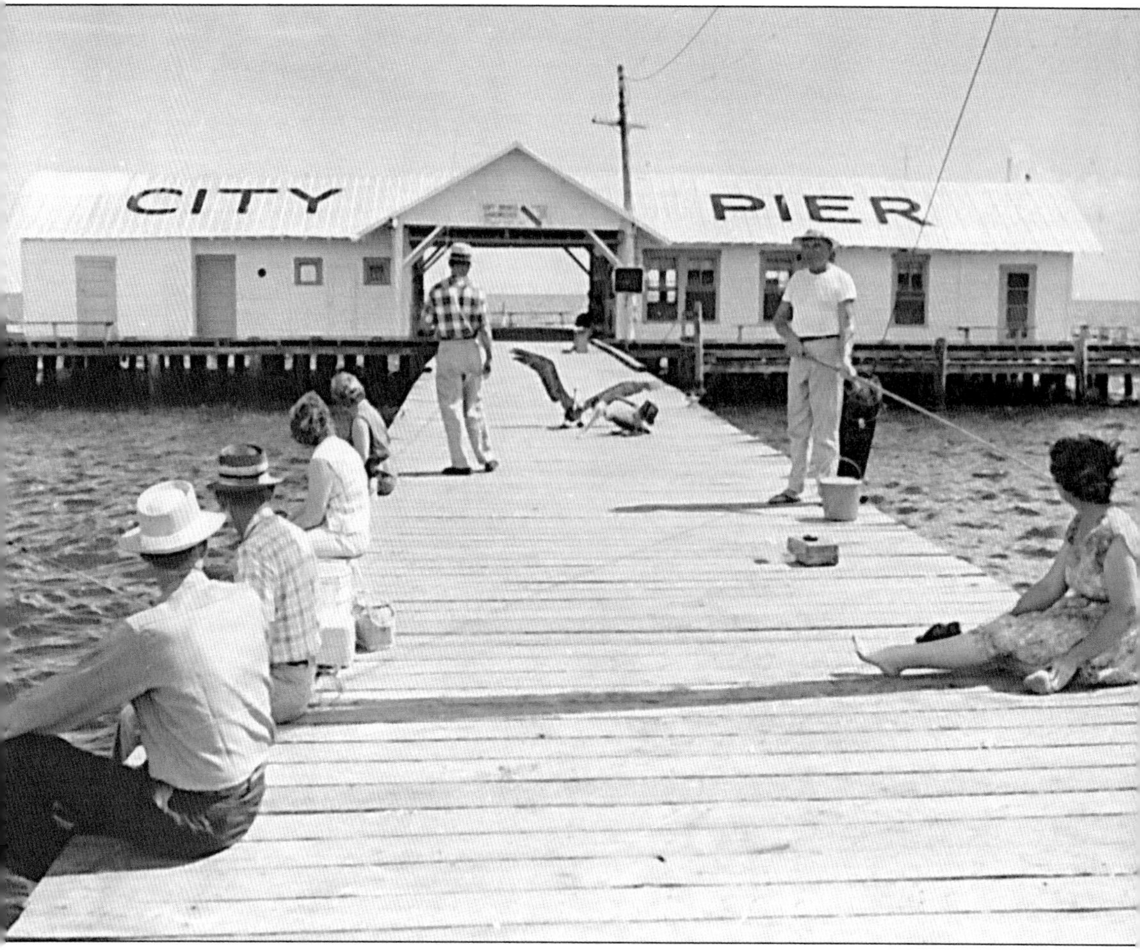

Anglers at the Anna Maria City Pier seated on the decking take a look as the fisher walking with his pole away from them toward the T-end has his bait stolen by one of two pelicans there looking for a handout. The scene is from the 1950s, with a billboard on the roof advertising the pier location to airplane passengers. The open-air buildings at the Tampa Bay end of the pier welcomed people arriving by ferry, and housed a bait shop and concession stand—long before a restaurant was added to attract people to the waterfront atmosphere. On a clear day, there was a view of the Sunshine Skyway Bridge, which opened on US Highway 19 in 1954 to connect Pinellas and Manatee Counties.

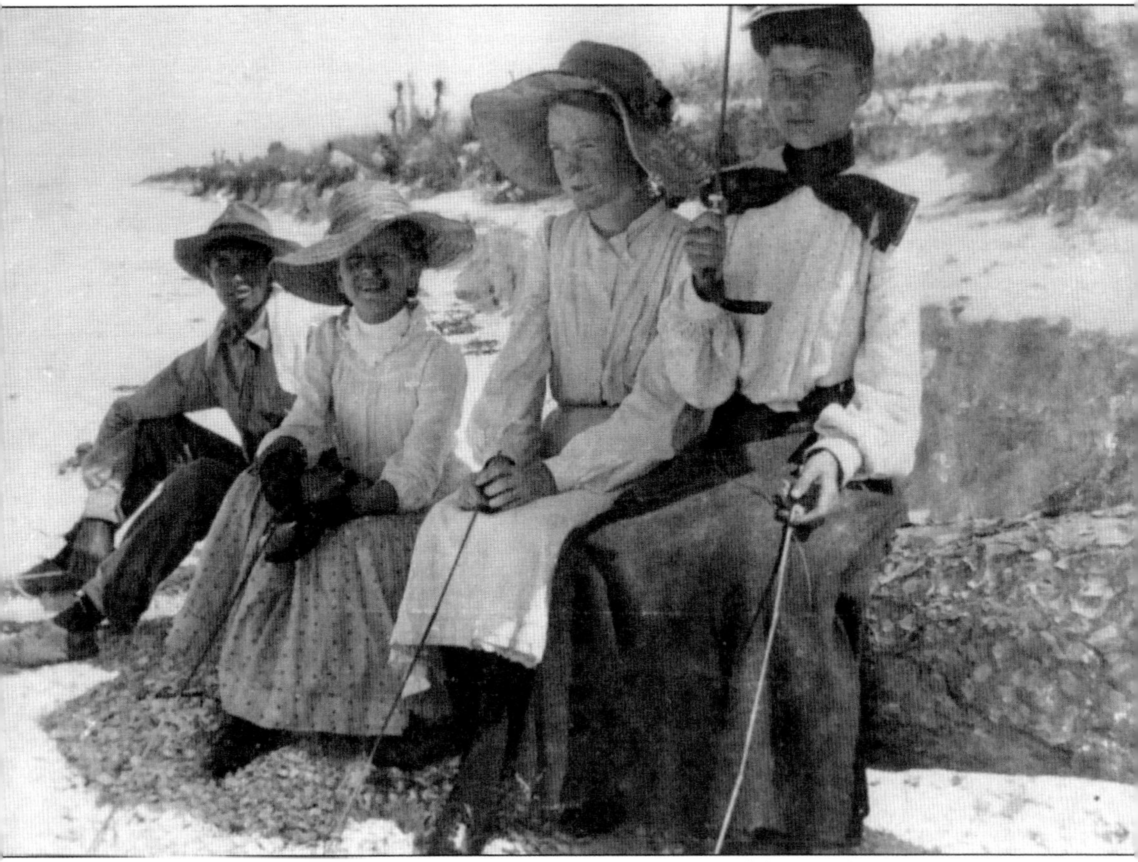

Four youths pose for a photograph at the beach in fashions typical of the time between 1910 and 1915, with protective hats and an umbrella and switches, possibly to search crab holes or swat at mosquitoes or diving birds.

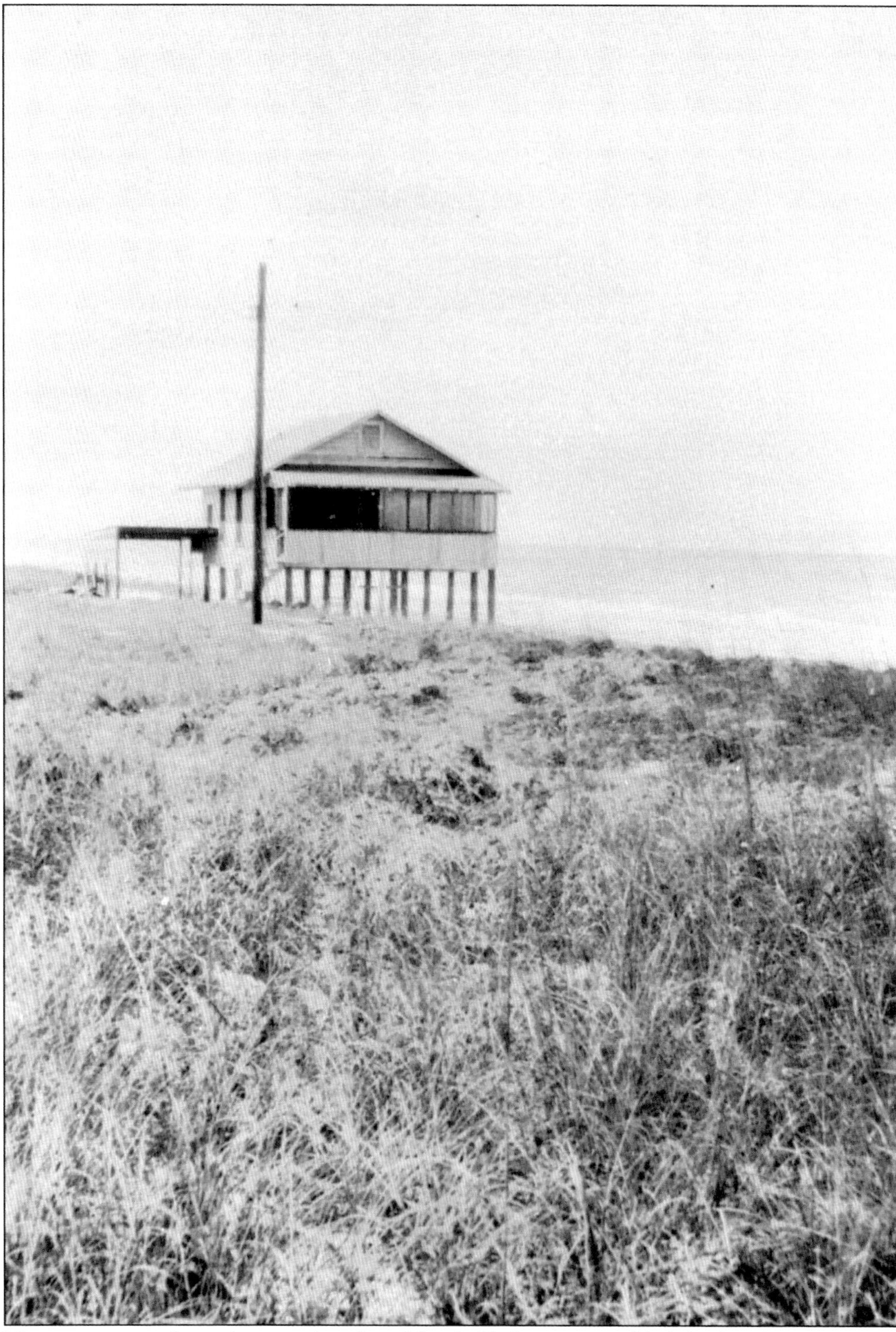

This cottage raised on pilings on the edge of the Gulf of Mexico was likely built to house weekend beachgoers or fishers, but few people lived year-round on Anna Maria Island in those years. The Anna Maria Beach Company sold cottages by encouraging weekend rentals for profit.

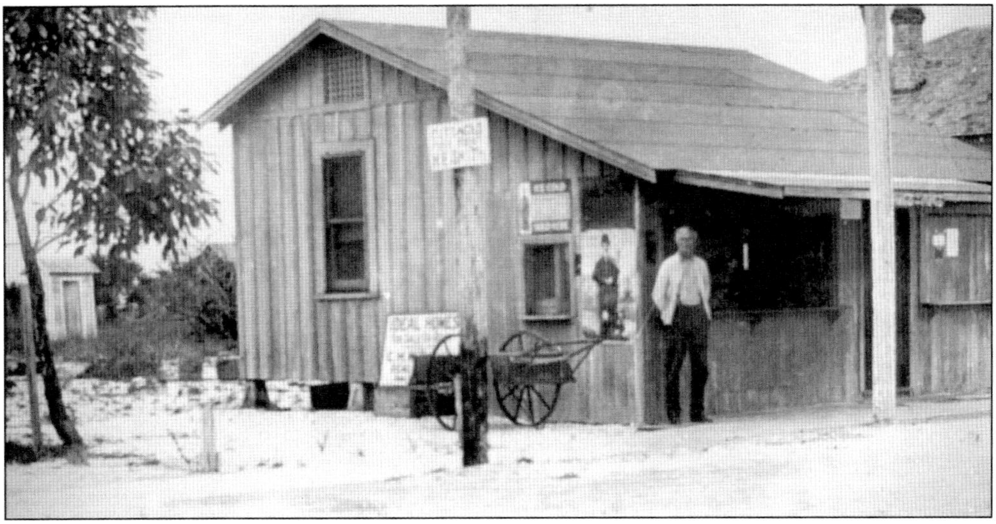

As noted on the photograph, taken in sometime in the 1920s, in typed text, the grocery store in Bradenton Beach was owned by C.H. McDonald. And K.E. Smith has a "cottage for rent" advertised on a post, while McDonald advertises "Ideal Homes" to passersby. A Coca-Cola sign hangs over the entry, and the outhouse is visible at the rear on the left.

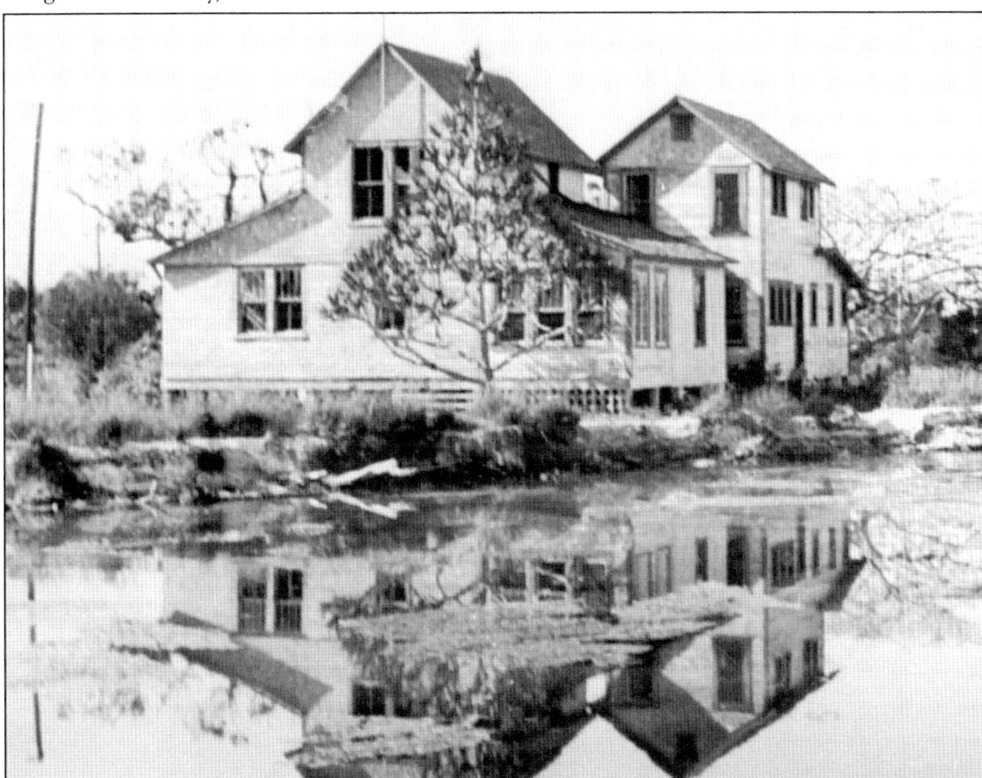

The home of Capt. Jonathan R. Jones on Pine Avenue in Anna Maria was built in 1905. Jones was justice of the peace on the island, and he built a large comfortable home for his family. The tree in the foreground is said to have been planted in 1906. Four decades later, the tree would grow to be more than twice as tall as the house.

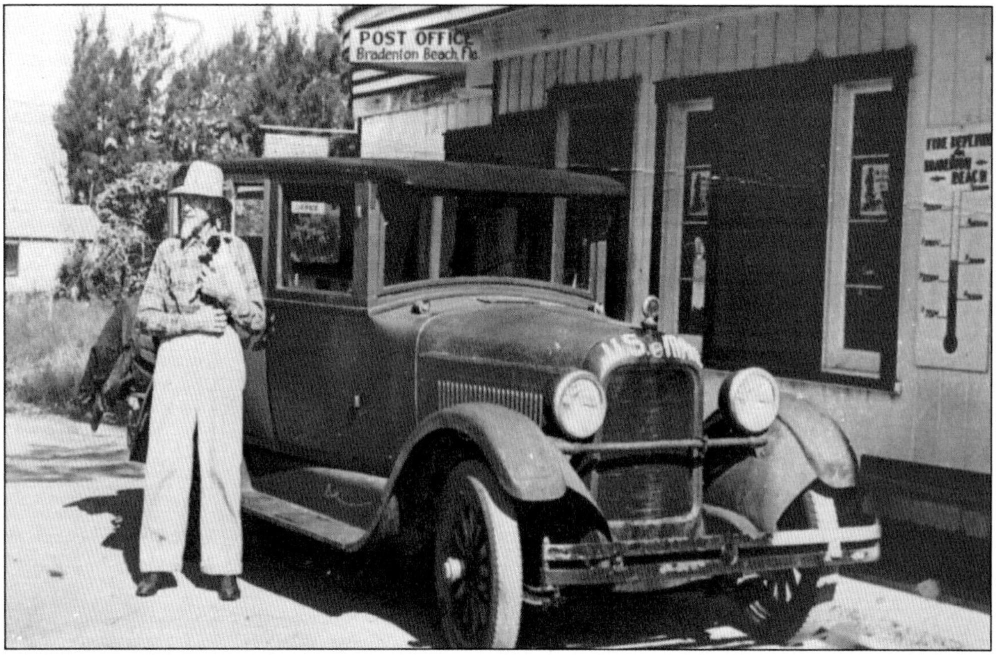

Harry Ditmus, known on Anna Maria Island and in Manatee County as Uncle Sam Ditmus, became Anna Maria's postmaster in 1922. He came to Florida in 1916 from Brooklyn, New York, having traveled as a minstrel and burlesque entertainer. With white hair and beard, he dressed often in the costume of Uncle Sam and began delivering mail in 1924 to Anna Maria and Bradenton Beach. He also served the growing village of Cortez. Ditmus sold advertising on his truck —until the Post Office Department ordered it removed. The enterprising mailman then had a mural scene of a Wells Fargo coach outrunning some Native Americans painted on the truck—an image familiar at the time as a Chesterfield cigarette advertisement. (Below, courtesy of the *Islander.*)

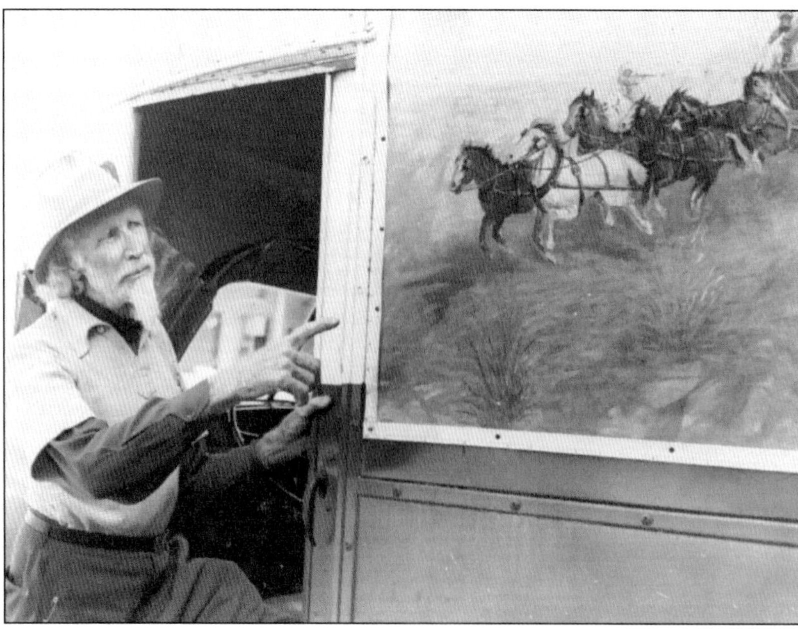

Two

A Sense of Place

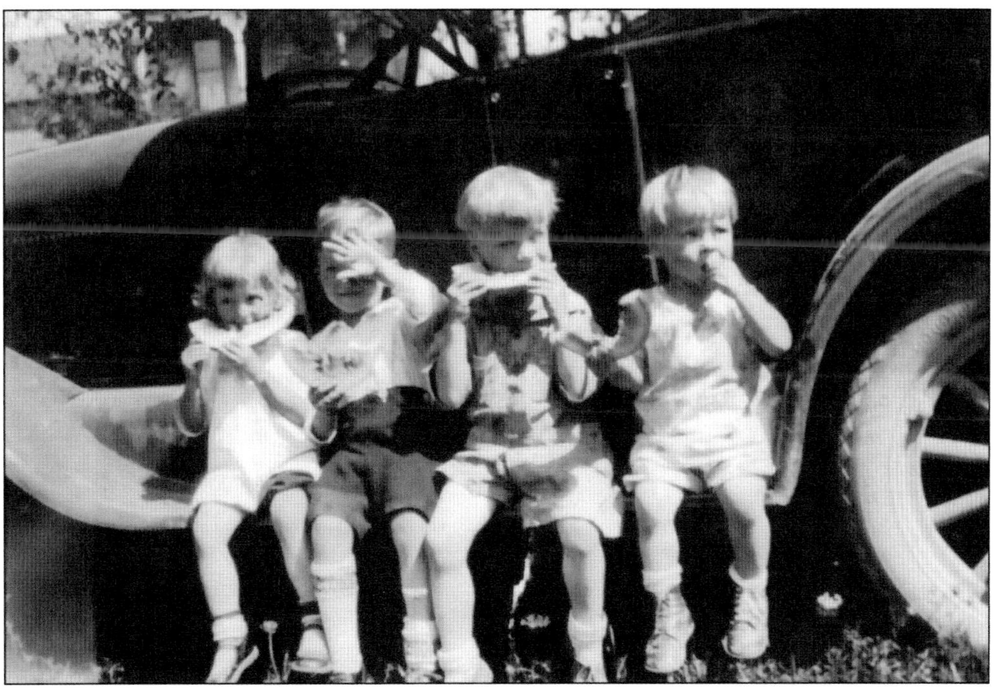

Watermelon is always better iced down in a tub, at a picnic with relatives on the beach, or seated on the running board of the family car. This snapshot is from a collection that belonged to the late Paul M. Roat, whose parents lived in Bradenton Beach and managed cottages there, including Whispering Pines, owned by Maynard Roat's grandmother. Maynard later worked for the Bradenton Beach Post Office. (Courtesy of the *Islander* and the Roat family collection.)

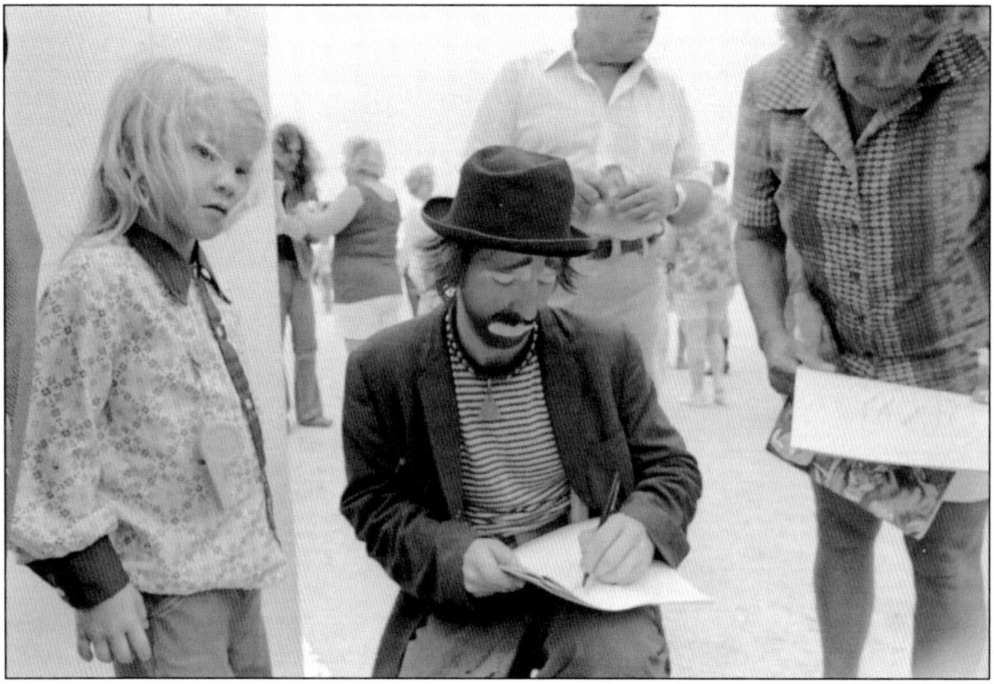

The circus comes to the beach. A Stebbing European Circus clown takes time to create signed drawings for kids of all ages. The circus troupe performed in a fundraiser at Coquina Beach for the Bradenton Beach Police Auxiliary in February 1976.

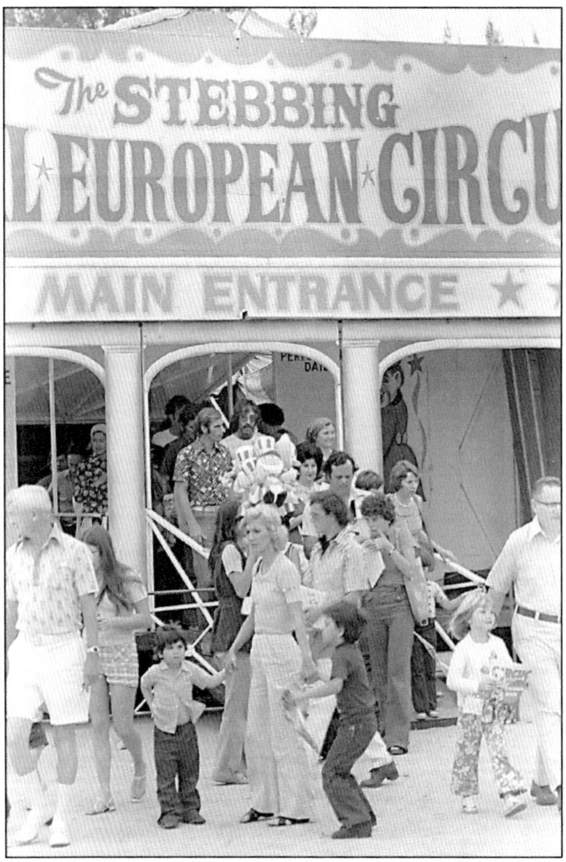

Children and adults of all ages exit the Stebbing European Circus on the beach in Bradenton Beach. The circus troupe set up and performed under its big tent in a fundraiser at Coquina Beach in February 1976.

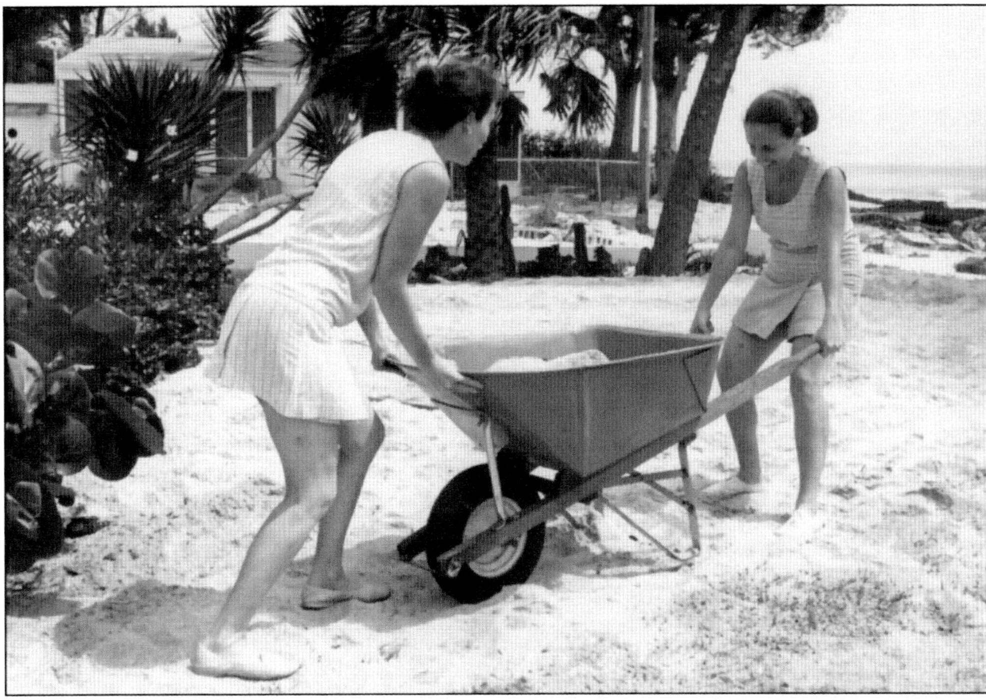

Two women use a wheelbarrow to move sand in front of a beachfront house. Sand washes up and washes away, and a beachfront home could easily find the door that faces the Gulf of Mexico blocked by a pile of sand after the surf comes ashore in a storm. (Courtesy of the *Islander*.)

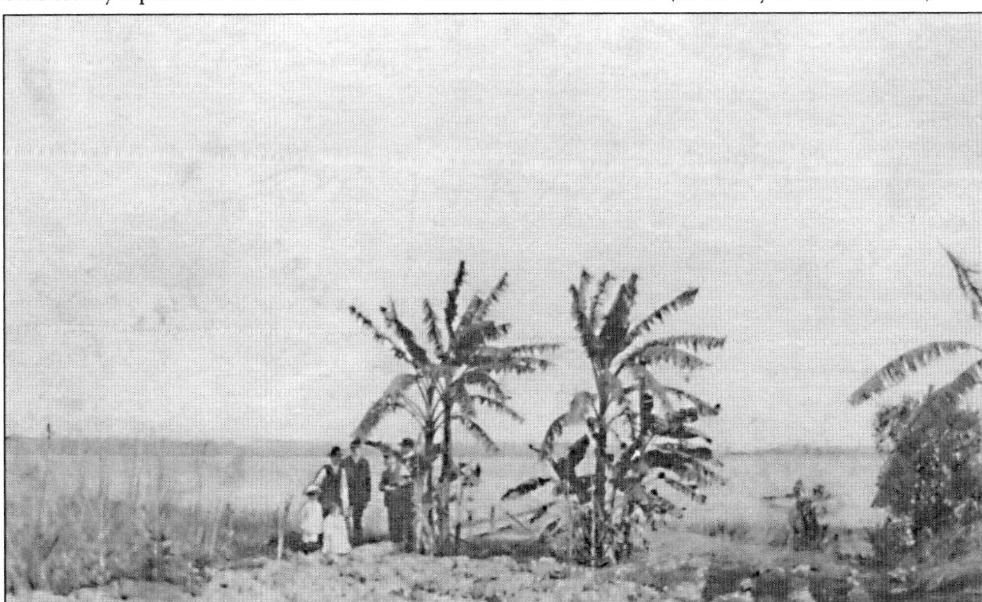

A group of four adults and two children looks over a garden on the bayfront on Anna Maria Island near the beach. It is thought to be Capt. Johnathan Jones's garden. Rows of cabbages, some type of beans, and several clusters of banana palms grow directly on the waterfront. Among the early settlers on the island, gardeners and farmers raised crops—and palm trees—for their tables and for sale. (Courtesy of the *Islander*.)

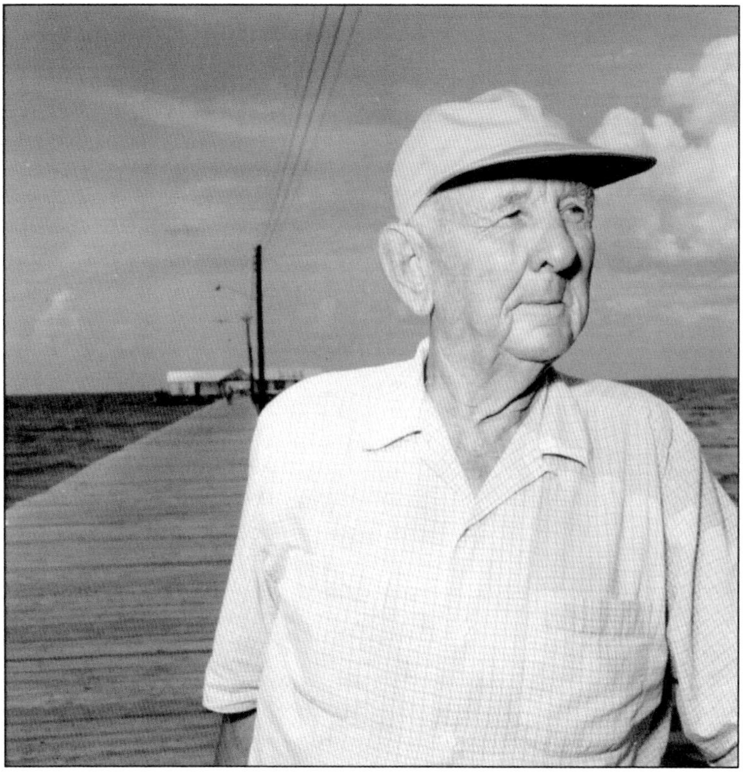

Capt. Mitch Davis, born on December 17, 1883, in Lowndes County, Alabama, was a pioneer on Anna Maria Island, having moved to the island in 1908 from Palmetto, Florida. He became the first mayor of Anna Maria in 1925 on its incorporation and served the city five years. As a developer, he built the new Roser Memorial Community Church, the old Anna Maria city jail (now a photo opportunity for visitors to the historical society on Pine Avenue), and a number of homes across the island.

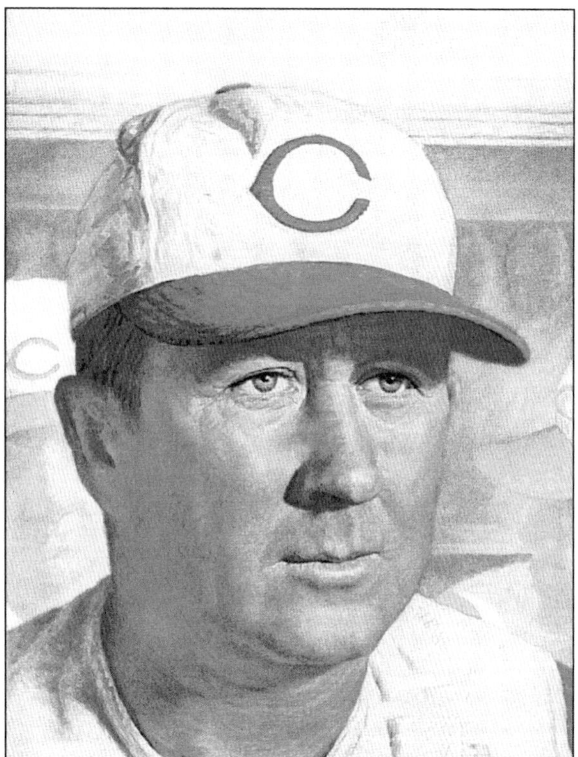

This photograph of an original oil painting that hung in the Anna Maria home of baseball great Birdie Tebbetts is featured on a 1957 *Time* magazine cover. Tebbetts died in 1999 at age 86, leaving the legacy of a lifetime spent in baseball, memorabilia, five World Series rings, and endless stories for his three daughters and son, all raised on Anna Maria Island. (Courtesy of the *Islander*.)

In 1930, Birdie Tebbetts was manager of the Chicago Cubs. He had a legendary career in baseball up to the 1990s as a catcher, manager, scout, and executive. In 1957, Birdie had the Cincinnati Reds in first place by mid-season, earning him the cover of *Time* magazine. He moved to Anna Maria Island in the late 1950s, following his good friend Fred Hutchinson. Birdie's wife, Mary, served as Anna Maria city clerk. Along with the Hutchinsons, they helped open a youth center and baseball field in Anna Maria. Birdie was among the most respected scouts in baseball, and rumors often circulated at center ball games that a major-league scout was watching. He also was a legendary storyteller, one of the original fraternity of baseball, and a great friend. (Courtesy of the *Islander*.)

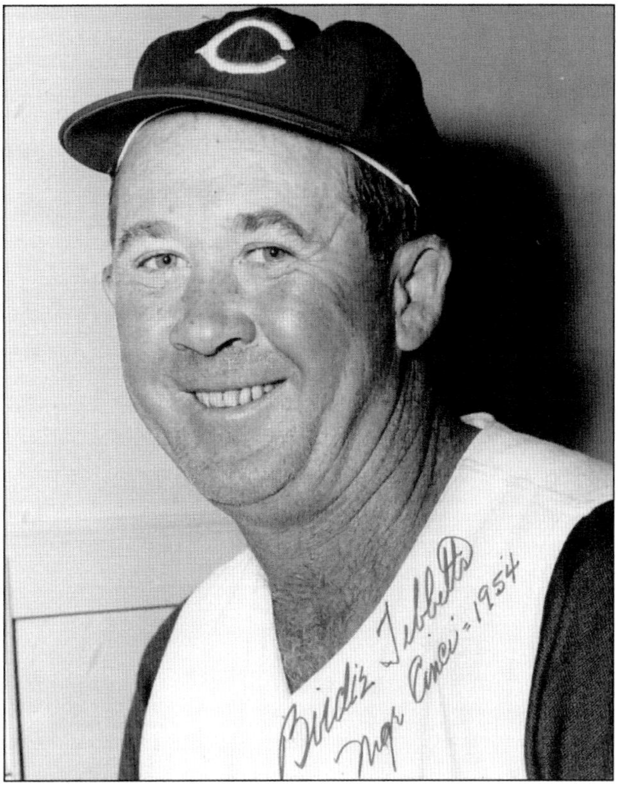

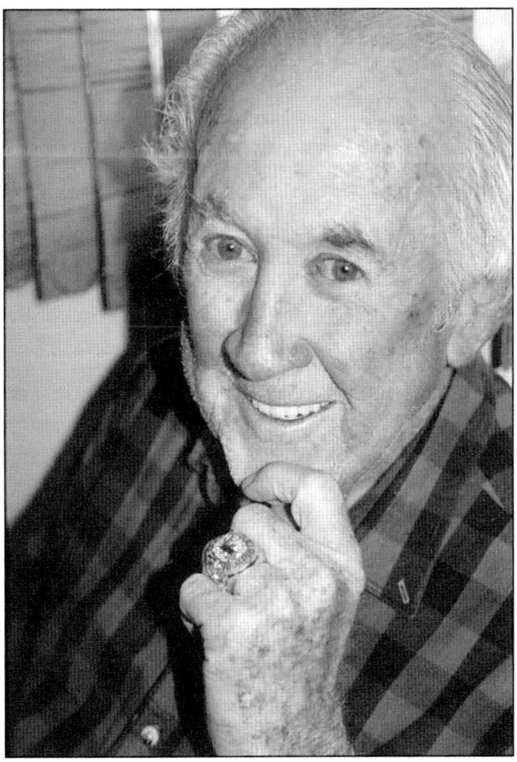

Baseball great Birdie Tebbetts models his 1997 Florida Marlins World Series ring. As master scout, he established the new team's scouting program. Tebbetts asked to be remembered as "Baseball Man." He spoke daily with baseball legend Ted Williams and was immortalized as the catcher in the famous photograph of Joe DiMaggio's home run at Yankee Stadium. Tebbetts loved to talk baseball, and his stories were welcome wherever he went on Anna Maria Island. (Photograph by the author, courtesy of the *Islander*.)

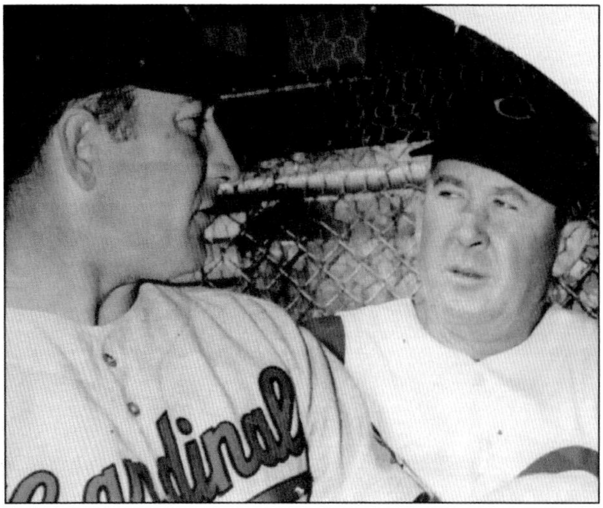

Pictured here are Fred Hutchinson (left) and Birdie Tebbetts. Hutchinson started his baseball career in 1938 in Seattle and soon was signed as a pitcher for the Detroit Tigers. He was manager for three major-league baseball teams before losing his battle to cancer at age 45 in 1964. "Hutch," as he was known, had a great a postseason. It was in 1961 that the Reds took the National League championship with a 93-61 record, winning their first pennant since 1940 and heading for a World Series with the New York Yankees. (Courtesy of the *Islander.*)

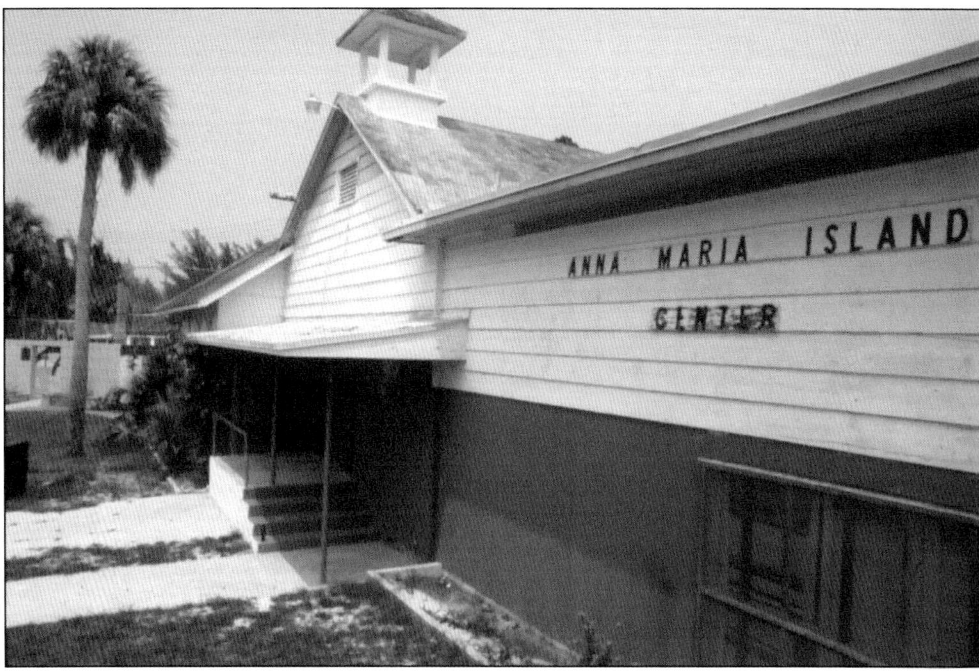

The Anna Maria Island Youth Center was built in the 1960s, starting with a new baseball stadium and the old schoolhouse. The schoolhouse later expanded with a half-court gym, a stage, and a few classrooms. The field was sized for youth games. The small tower on the top of the building is the bell tower from the one-room schoolhouse that originally occupied the site. The property was deeded to the City of Anna Maria and dedicated as a community center. It now hosts a new center with a full-court gym, fitness center, classrooms, and offices, as well as baseball and soccer fields and tennis courts.

Author Wyatt Blassingame, aka W.B. Rainey, moved to the city of Anna Maria in 1936 when it was little more than a jungle with scourges of bird-sized mosquitos and gazes of raccoons. He and his wife, Gertrude, raised two daughters. Wyatt died in 1985 and Gertie in 1976. He authored more than 600 short stories and articles for magazines, four adult novels, and dozens of young-reader nature-related nonfiction books. He penned a story, "Anna Maria, I Love you," in 1956 for *Ford Times*, a travel magazine published by Ford Motor Co. In that story, he recounts a phrase that earned him acclaim that continues to this day: "If you unscrew a screwball anywhere in the United States, blindfold him, turn him around twice and turn him loose, he'll wind up in Anna Maria."

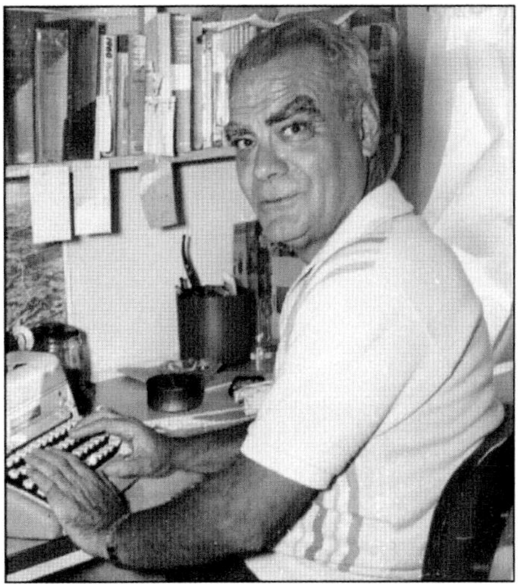

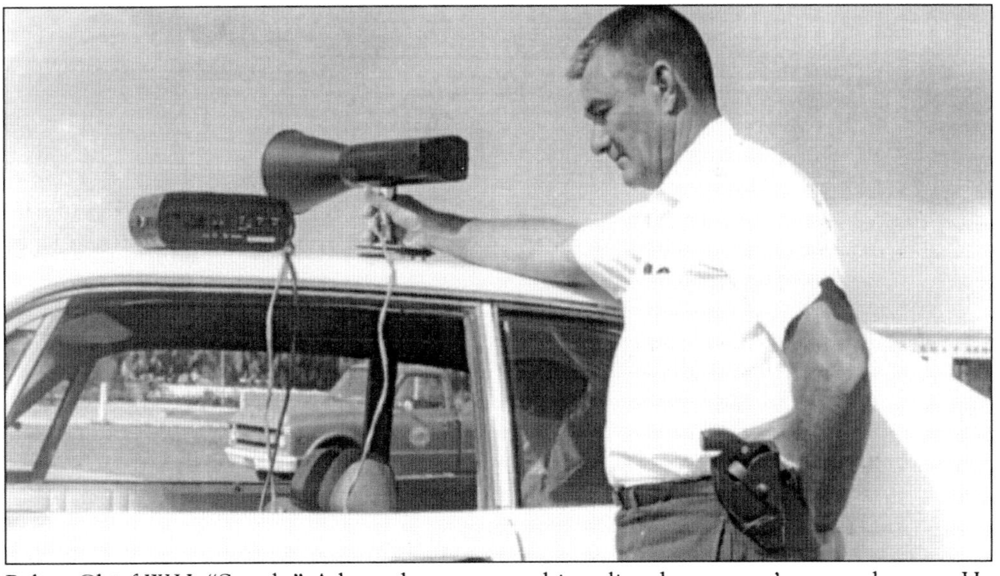

Police Chief W.H. "Snooks" Adams demonstrates his police department's new radar gun. He was born in Cortez and spent much of his life in Cortez and on Anna Maria Island—except for a stint in the US Navy during World War II—as a law enforcement officer who used common sense as his guide. He served as an island law enforcement officer from 1952 until retiring as chief from the Holmes Beach Police Department in 1978. He started Snooks Adams Kids Day in 1954, an end-of-school tradition that was later taken over by the Anna Maria Island Privateers and continues to this day in August. (Courtesy of the *Islander*.)

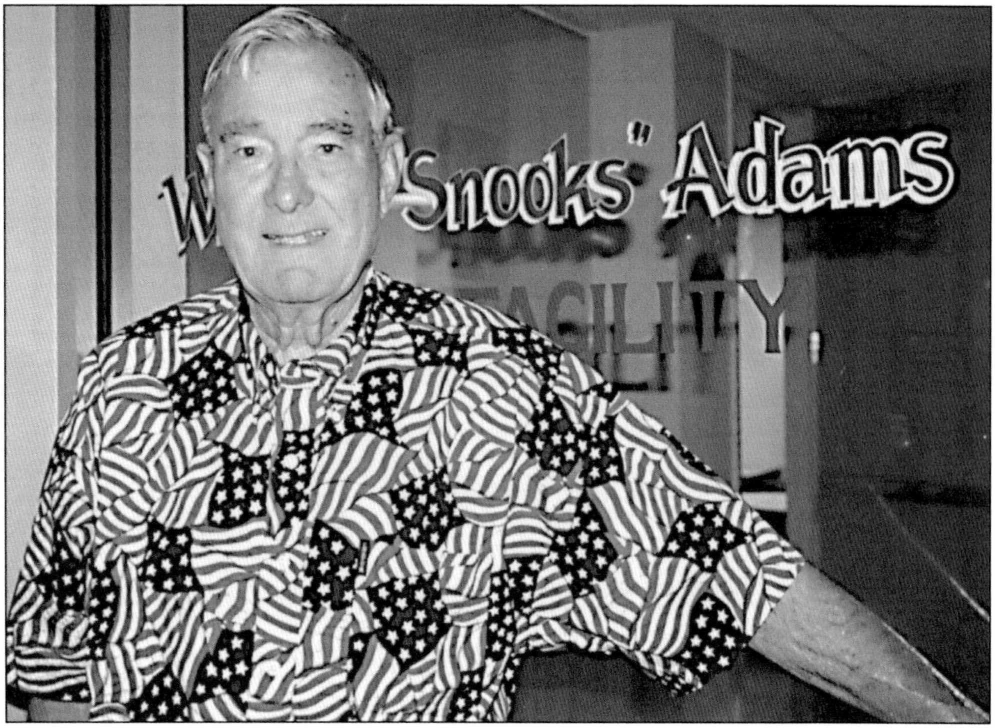

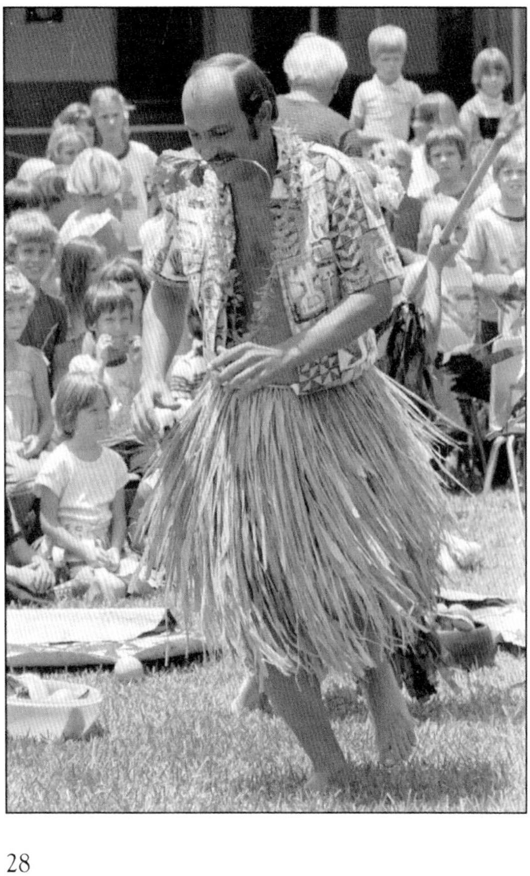

Former Holmes Beach police chief W.H. Snooks Adams poses at the door to the police department at the new city hall, dedicated in his honor. He served as chief in Holmes Beach for 25 years until retirement in 1975. Before that, he patrolled the island for the Manatee County Sheriff's Office. Adams was named 1996 Islander of the Year by the *Islander* newspaper. (Courtesy of the *Islander*.)

Anna Maria Elementary school principal Jim Kronus gets into the island spirit in 1979 for a school luau party. Kronus was much loved by his students and families on the island. He retired from 25 years as Anna Maria Elementary principal in 1998 and was named as 1998 Islander of the Year by the newspaper.

The Anna Maria Island Lodge 2188 of the Loyal Order of Moose formed in August 1935. As of this writing, the lodge that opened on Gulf Drive in Bradenton Beach is undergoing major renovations expected to be finalized in October 2015. Meanwhile, the bar and food service and the fun continue for one of the largest member rosters—some 4,000 members and Women of the Moose—of any Moose lodge.

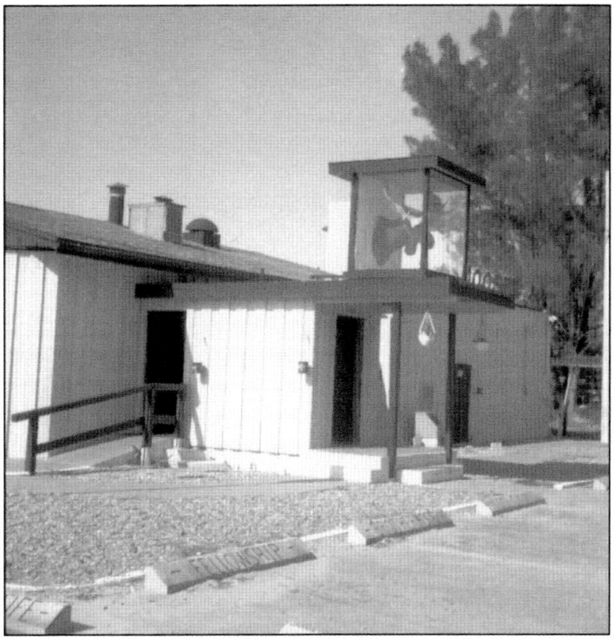

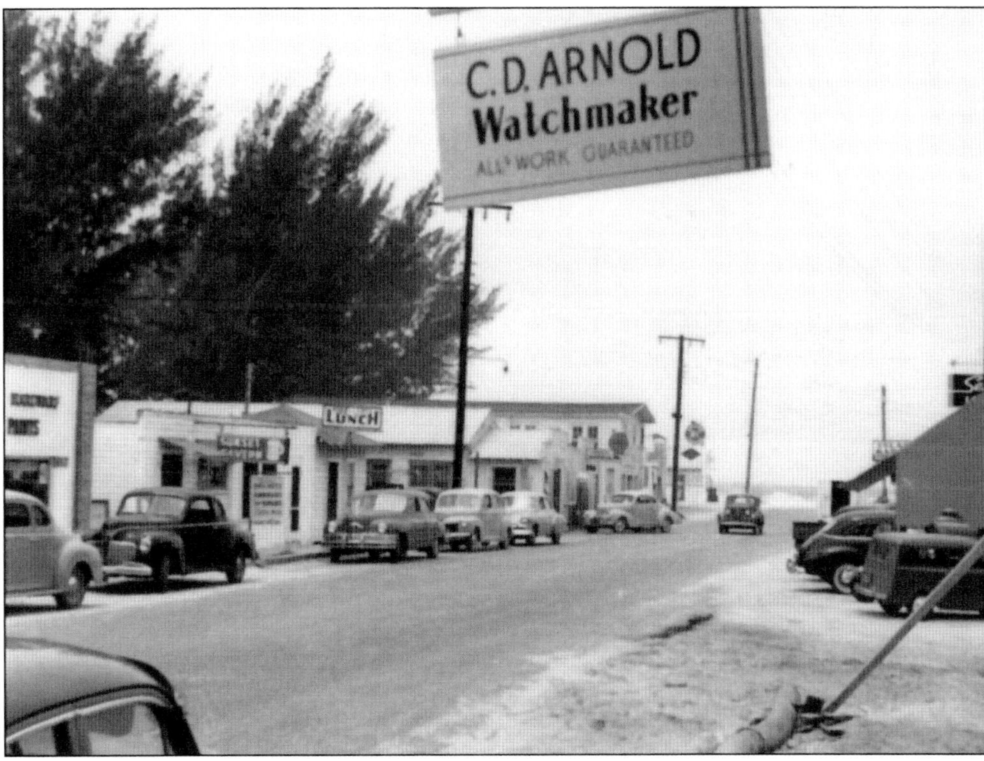

With the first bridge linking the mainland to Bradenton Beach built in 1927, the southernmost city on Anna Maria Island quickly became the hub of business and the destination for mainland day-trippers. In this photograph from 1947, the hardware store is on the far left, followed by the Sunset Tavern, a few other spots, and, at the far end opposite the beach, a Shell gas station. C.D. Arnold, watchmaker, was well known in the community. (Courtesy of the *Islander*.)

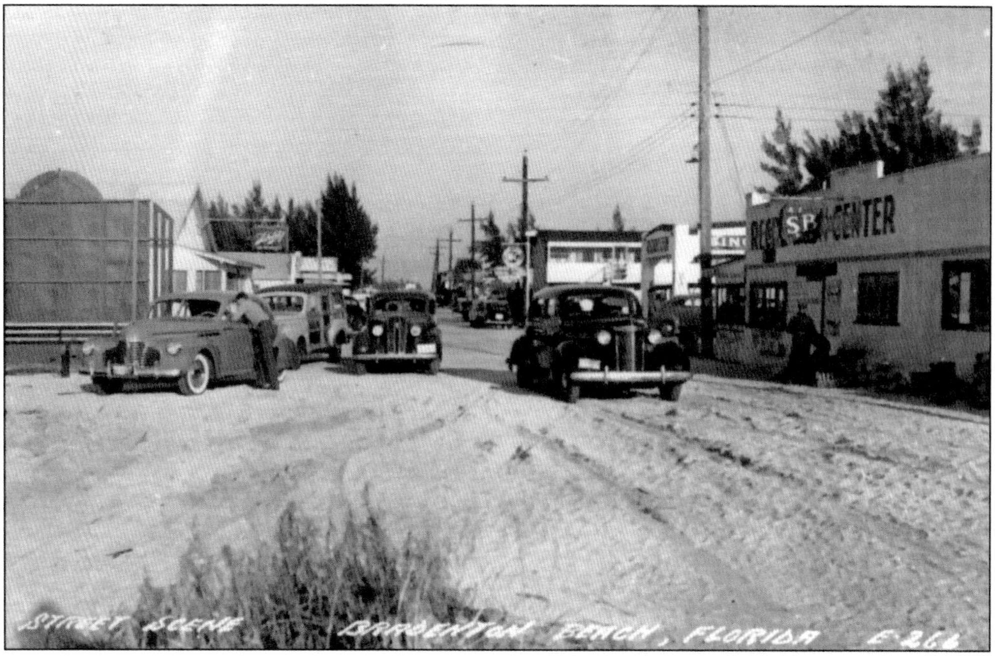

Another street scene in 1947 in Bradenton Beach on Gulf Drive depicts ruts in the sand road, a recreation center, and a Sinclair gas station at the end of the thoroughfare, which leads to the Cortez Bridge. With the only bridge to the island, Bradenton Beach had become a hub of business and social activity. (Courtesy of the *Islander*.)

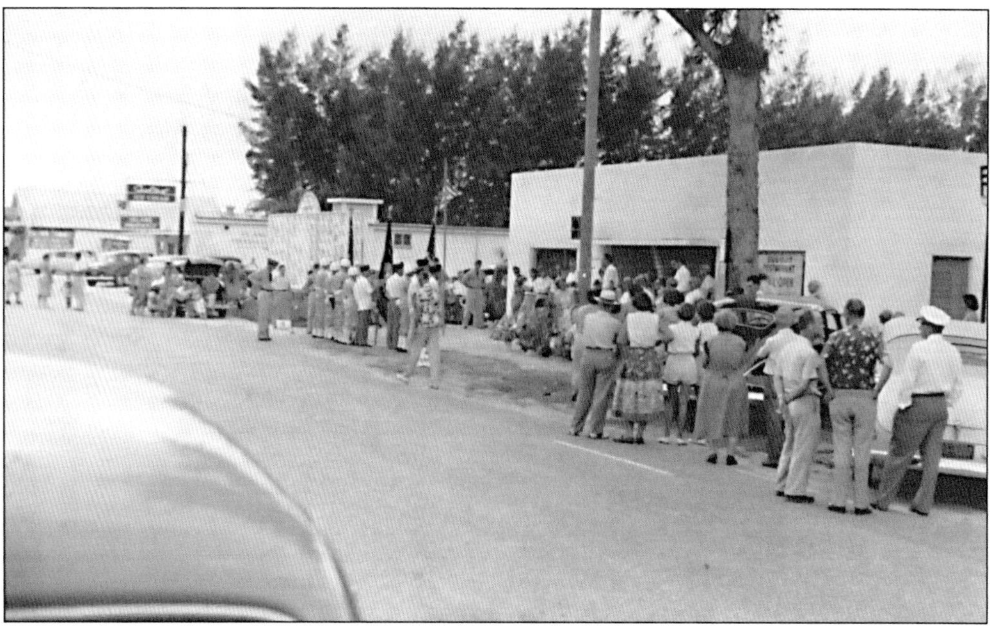

The 1952 opening of the new US post office on Bridge Street in Bradenton Beach drew a crowd of dignitaries, elected officials, post office officials, and honor guard and island residents. The wooden bridge was still serving the island from the east end of Bridge Street, and all mail arrived to the southernmost postal center for distribution. The event was marked with speeches and a dedication. (Courtesy of the *Islander* and the Roat family collection.)

Everyone is welcome but the dog in July 1949. Todd's Bar at the corner of Gulf Drive and Bridge Street facing the Gulf of Mexico was well known far and wide. This structure was eventually home to the Wreck restaurant and its Silver Dollar Bar, Key West Willy's, and now, Island Time bar and the Bridge Street Bistro. (Courtesy of the *Islander*.)

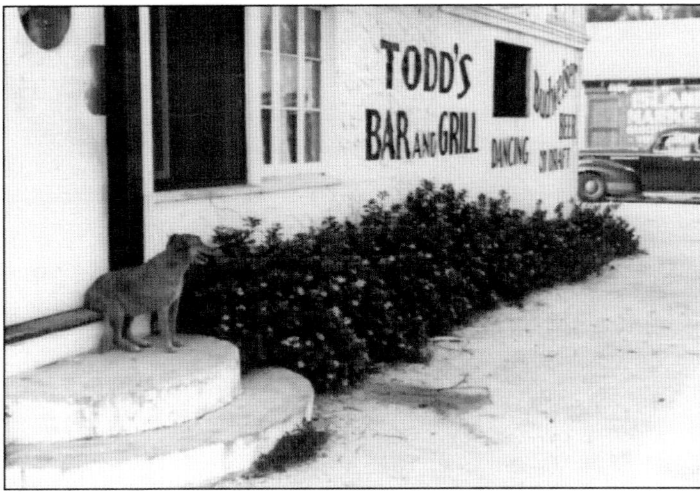

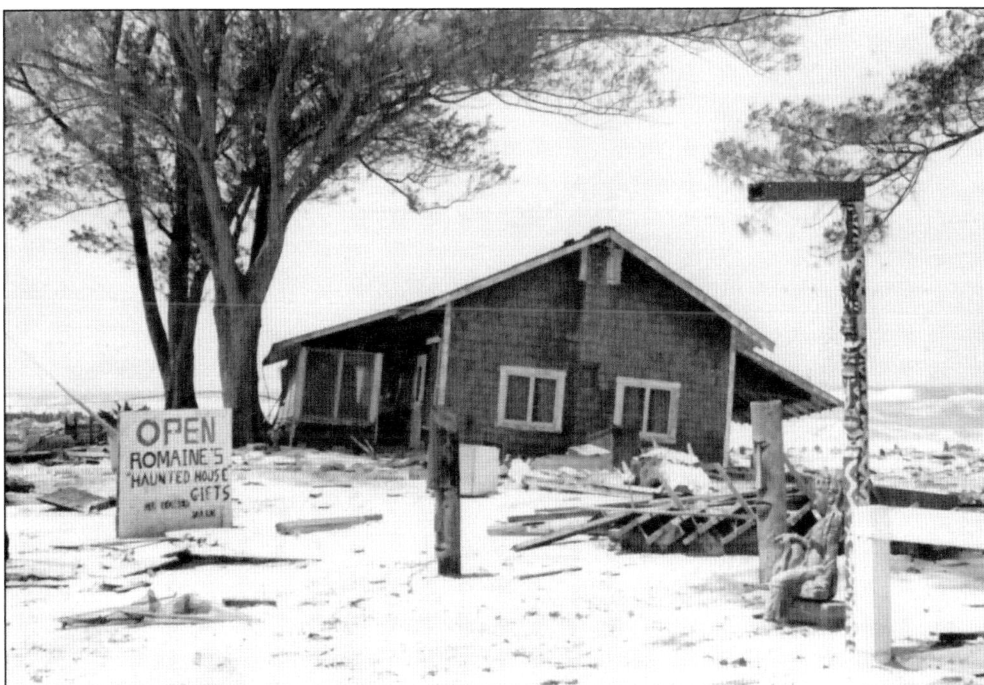

Pictured here are the house next door and the sign for what was once Romaine's Gift Shop. The Bradenton Beach house came with a 1940s ghost tale of a young wife who searched after her death for her husband, long ago lost at sea. The occupants in the 1970s perpetuated the legend by frightening young and old at Halloween with tales of invisible barking dogs at their house of horrors—hopefully barking from a recording. They sent many a kid running on his heels. But others frequented the ground-level gift shop during the year. Note the statue and totems near the entryway. (Courtesy of the *Islander*.)

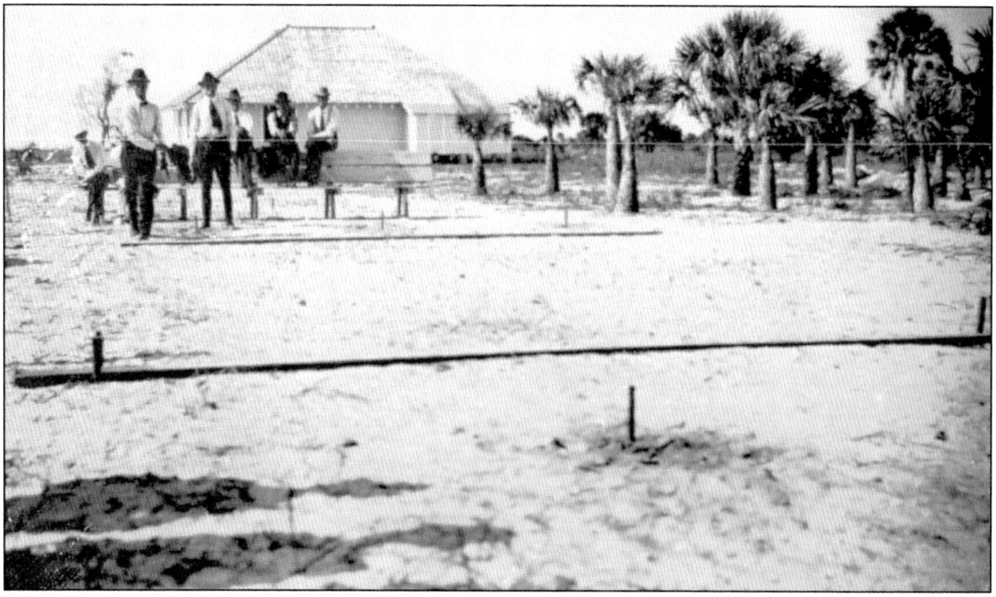

Men play horseshoes in 1915 in front of the Anna Maria Community Hall, which now serves as the playhouse for Island Players, at the corner of Pine Avenue and Gulf Drive. The community hall also served as a sales office for the first developers in Anna Maria, the Anna Maria Beach Company, and as a USO facility to entertain troops after World War II. City hall would later be built adjacent to the community hall, and today there are horseshoe pits kept busy by regular players on Wednesdays and Sundays.

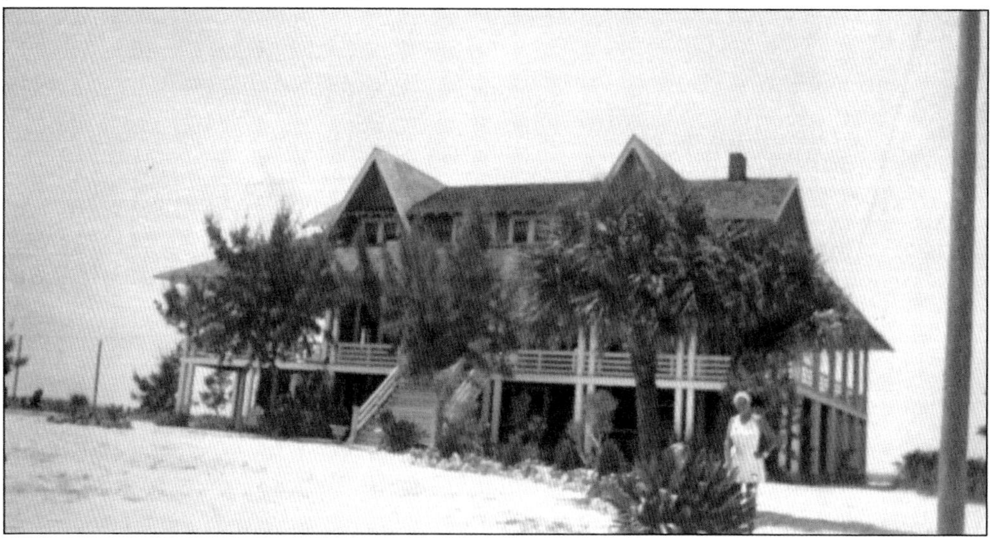

The Gulf Park Hotel of the 1920s, one of the earliest businesses on the island, was built across from what became the Sandpiper Resort/mobile home park. It was a hotel, restaurant, and bar —and legend has it at one time it operated as a brothel. While the upstairs was condemned, the ground-level bar reopened as the Oar House in the 1970s, operated by two young entrepreneurs, David Reid and Warren Jerrems. It was frequented by Gregg Allman—an island resident at the time—which spawned a reunion of the Allman Brothers Band after a concert there with Dickey Betts and his band, Great Southern. The Oar House also hosted a one-night performance by Tom Waits.

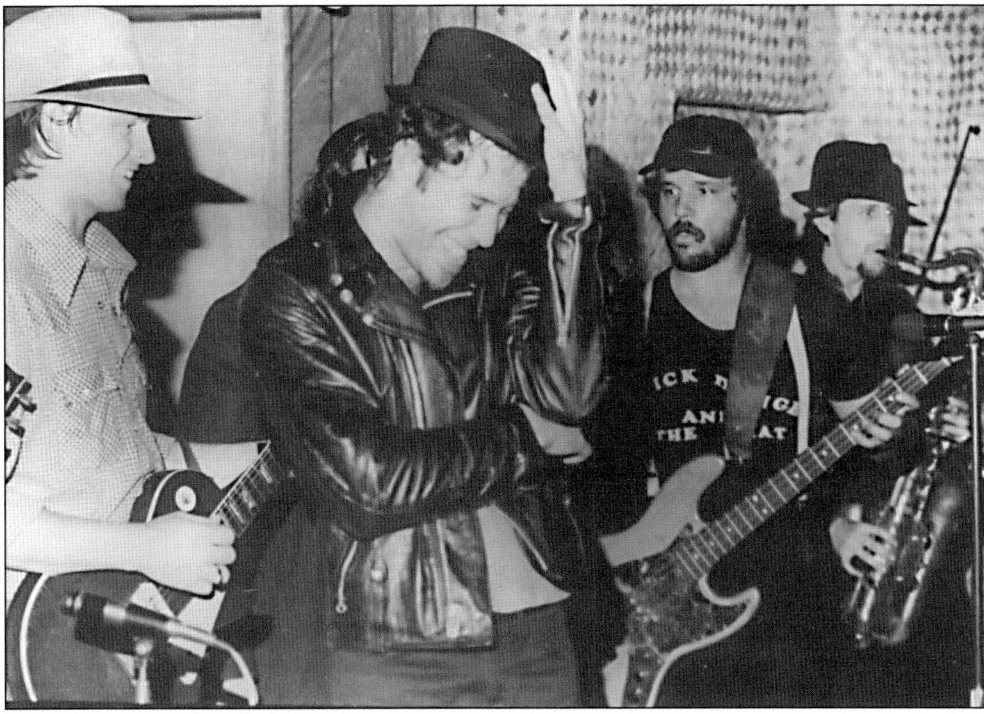

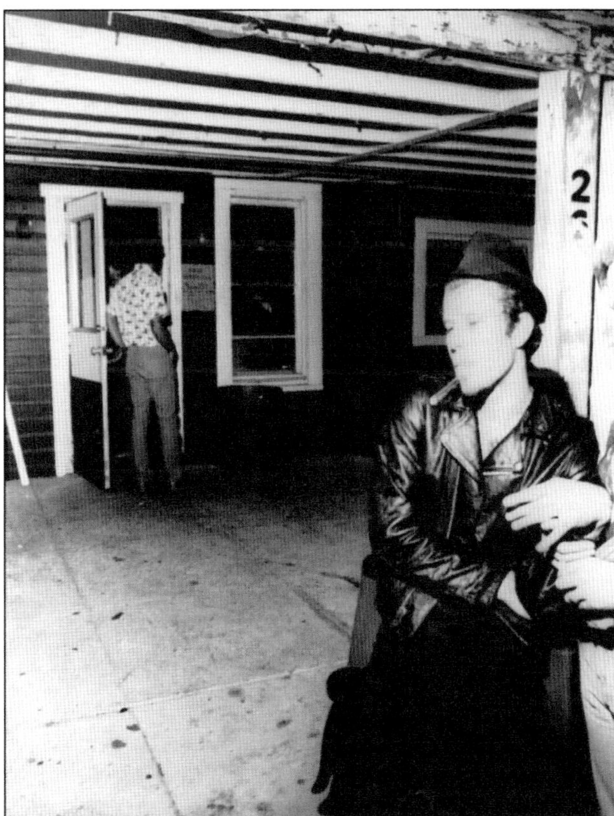

Tom Waits is pictured here at the Oar House in 1978, where he performed his popular hits "Closing Time," "Small Change," and "The Piano Has Been Drinking." The Oar House band for the night, Nick Danger and the Heat, were happy to oblige. (Photographs by Paul Roat, courtesy of the *Islander*.)

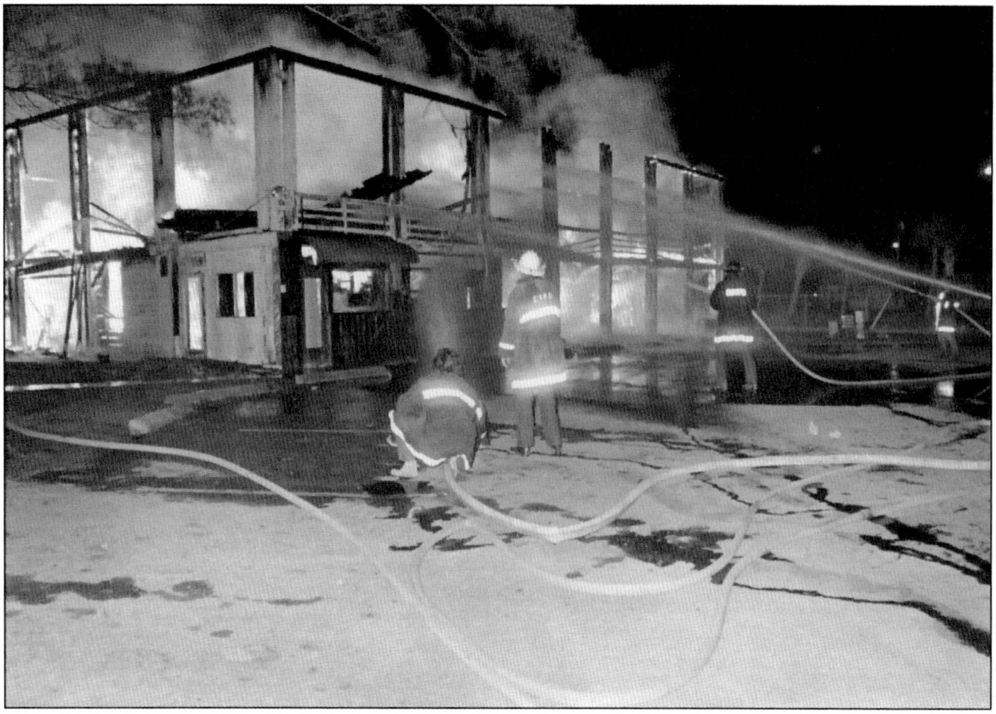

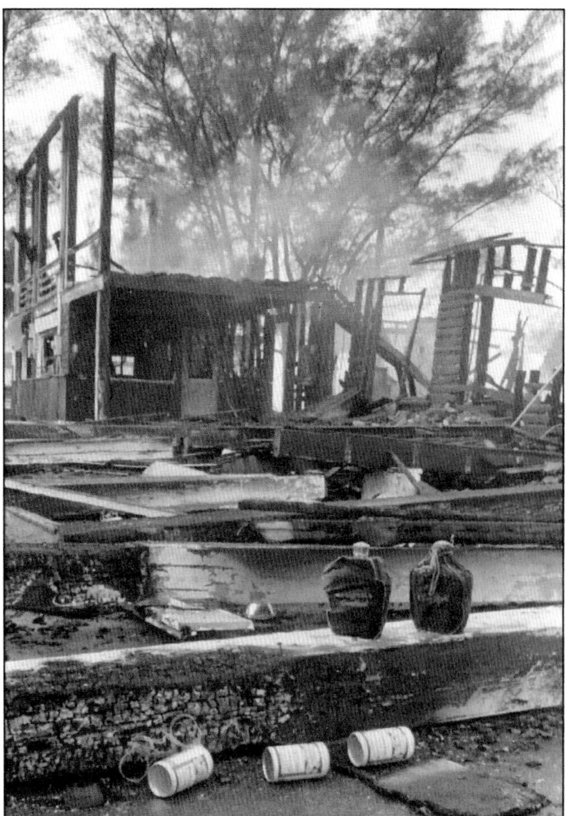

The Oar House burned to the ground on February 21, 1979. After the fire, the Anna Maria Island Club condominiums were constructed on the site. (Photograph by Gene Page, courtesy of the *Islander.*)

Co-owner David Reid of the Oar House bar at the Gulf Park Hotel salvaged two bottles of Crown Royal from the building in the moments before the fire spread throughout the wooden two-story structure. He shared some other items, including a Heineken bottle or two and some cans of Budweiser, and still has his Crown Royal displayed at his home in Hollywood, California. (Courtesy of the *Islander.*)

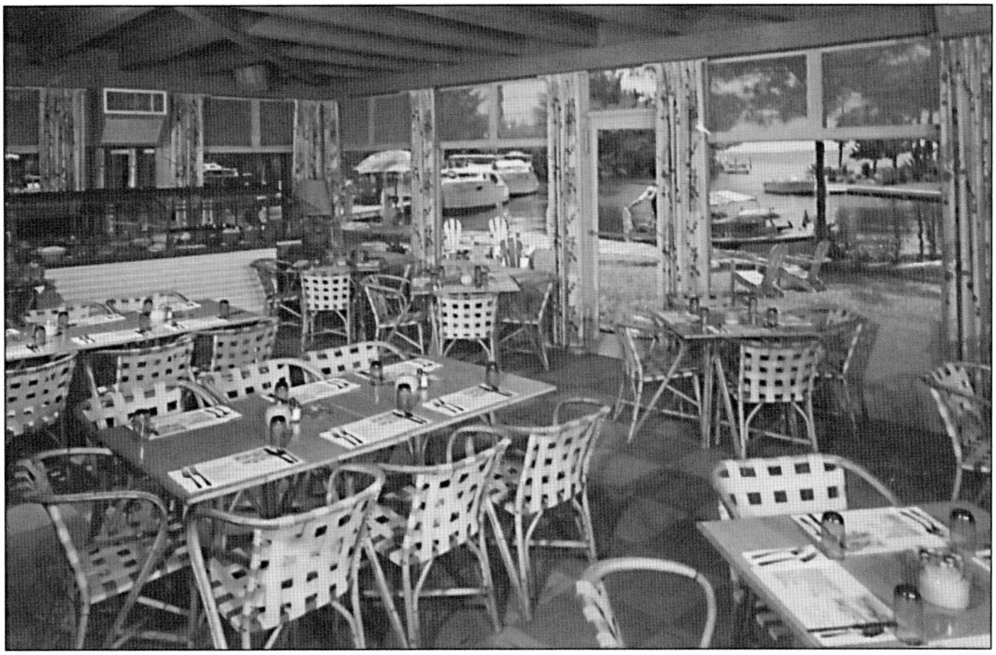

Pete Reynard's Yacht Club Restaurant is pictured here sometime before 1965, prior to a devastating fire. The dining rooms featured views of the boat docks in the basin and a waterway leading to the open waters of Anna Maria Sound and Tampa Bay to the north.

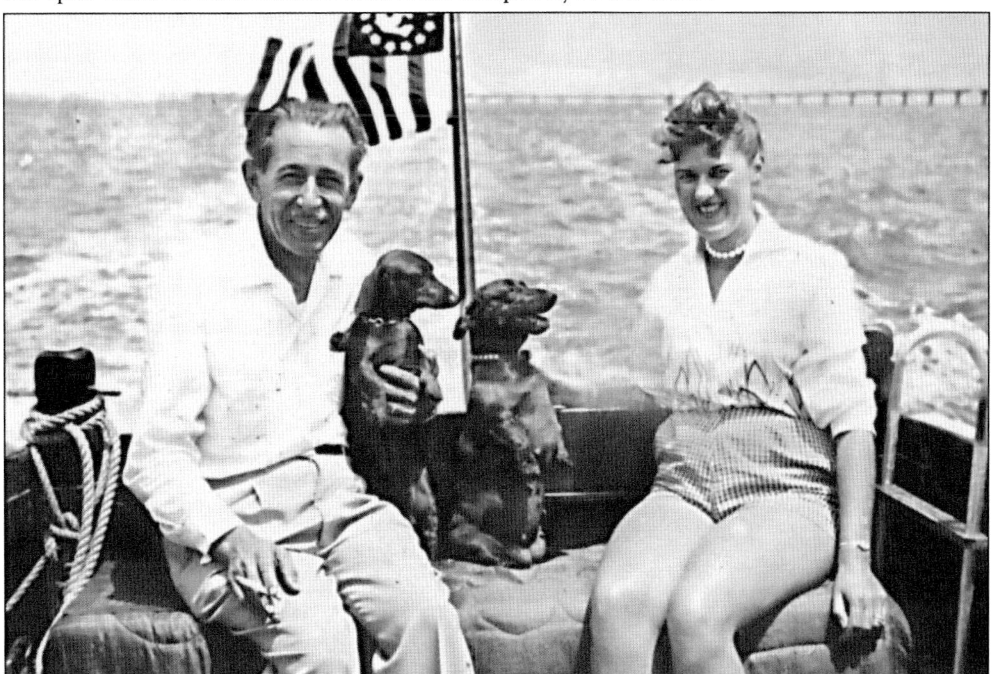

Pete and Eleanor Reynard enjoy time on the waters surrounding Anna Maria Island with their pet dachshunds. The couple enjoyed a busy social life on the island, and special events, anniversaries, and birthdays brought baseball's elite and other celebrities to enjoy their restaurant. (Courtesy of the Anna Maria Island Historical Society.)

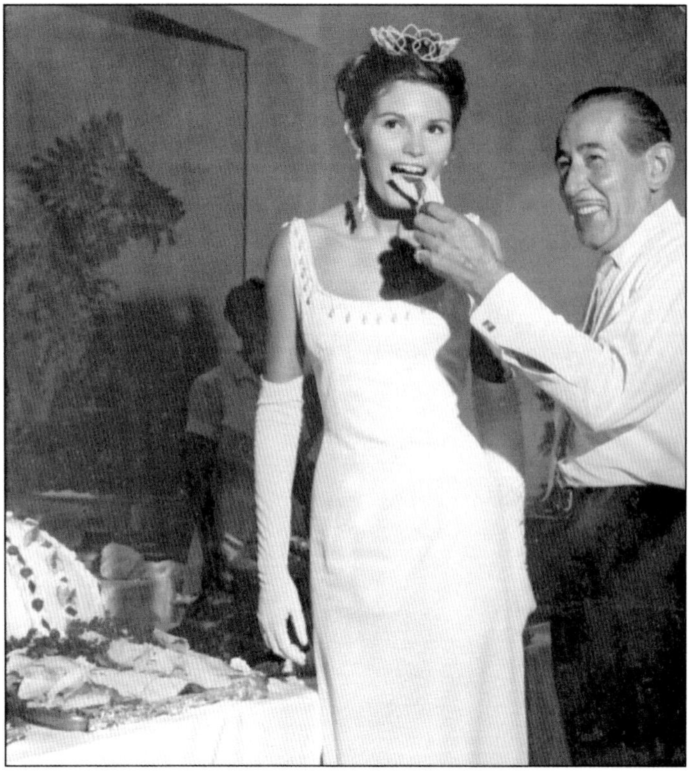

Christine Torgenson of Anna Maria, newly crowned Miss Florida for 1966, visits Pete Reynard's Yacht Club Restaurant in Holmes Beach for a celebration of her new title, where the illustrious host, Reynard, serves her a sample from his buffet. (Courtesy of the Anna Maria Island Historical Society.)

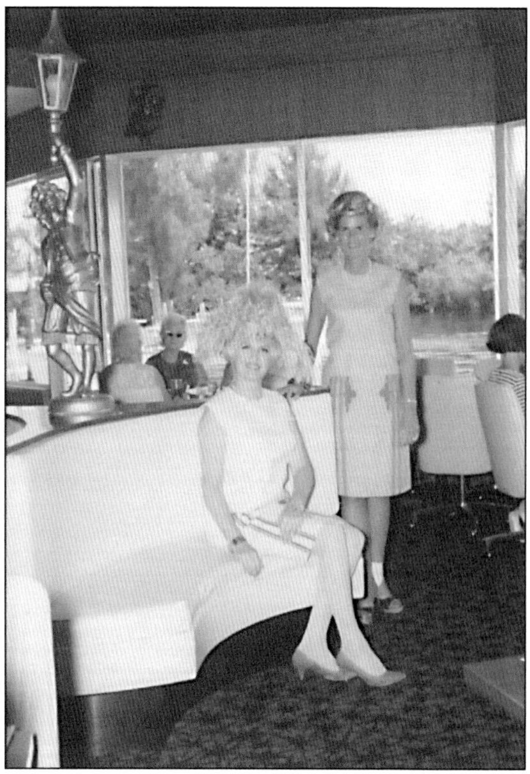

Eleanor Reynard (right) poses with a fashion model in the center of the Compass Room at Pete Reynard's Yacht Club Restaurant in Holmes Beach. After a fire in 1965, the Reynards spared no expense in redesigning their dining attraction, adding a room with numerous tables and booth seating that slowly rotated 360 degrees. Upscale boutiques often offered fashion modeling for the lunch clientele. The restaurant also featured "Florida's largest lazy Susan," a motorized circular salad bar, and a mermaid room, with a large movie projection behind the bar of mermaids swimming in an aquarium. (Photograph by Paul Bartley, courtesy of the *Islander.*)

Three

SUNNY BEACH

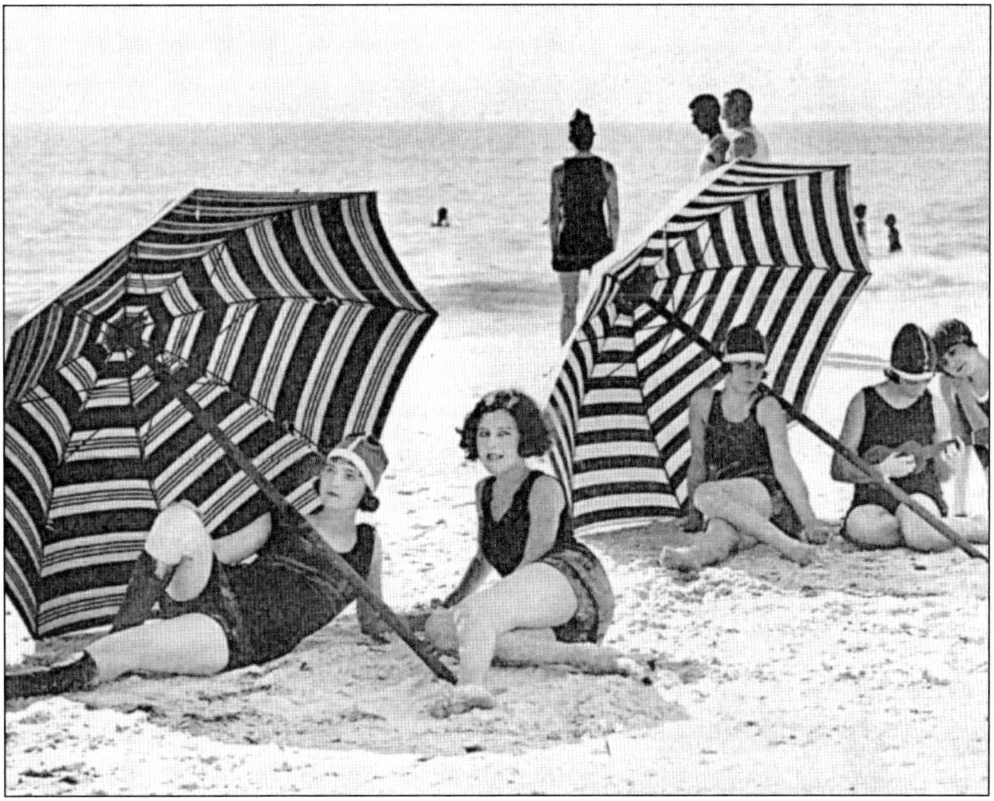

These women look to be daydreamers on the beach—with little concern for other people or swimming. But what could be better than a day on the sandy shore of the Gulf of Mexico with gentle waves lapping and a friend playing ukulele in the shade of a striped beach umbrella?

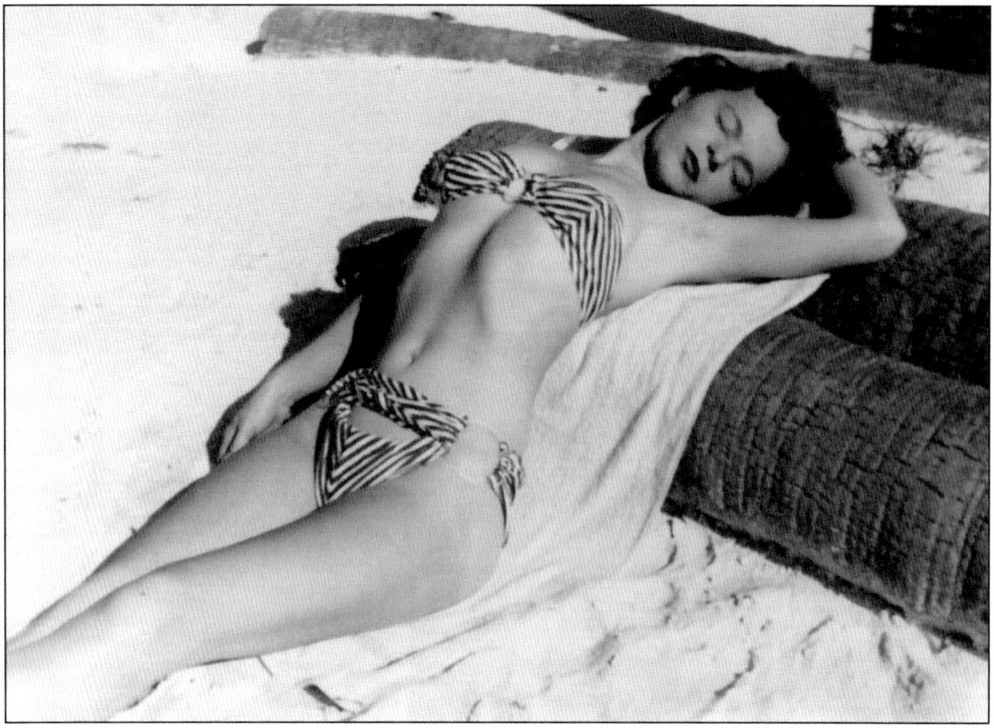

This image fast-forwards from the beauties under the umbrellas to this bathing beauty, Jeanne Roat of Bradenton Beach, who makes good use of some downed palm trees for her sunbathing. Jeanne's husband, Maynard, took many photographs of his wife and their pet dog Kipper. Many in their scrapbook are dated and indicate the f-stop used in capturing the image. This one is from 1951. (Courtesy of the *Islander* and the Roat family collection.)

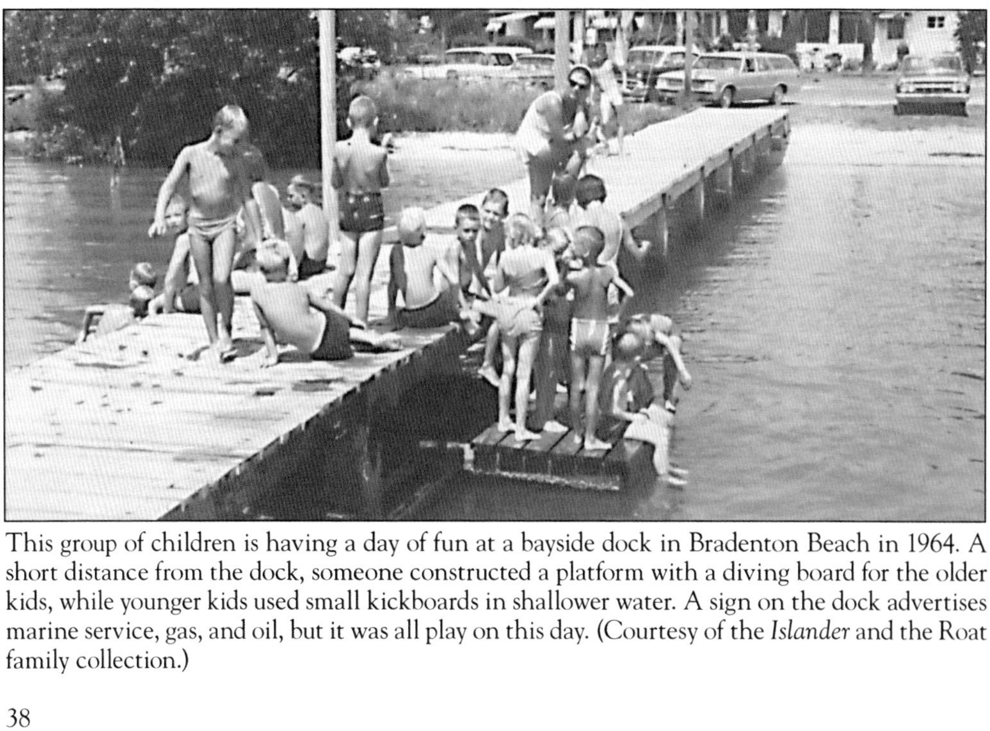

This group of children is having a day of fun at a bayside dock in Bradenton Beach in 1964. A short distance from the dock, someone constructed a platform with a diving board for the older kids, while younger kids used small kickboards in shallower water. A sign on the dock advertises marine service, gas, and oil, but it was all play on this day. (Courtesy of the *Islander* and the Roat family collection.)

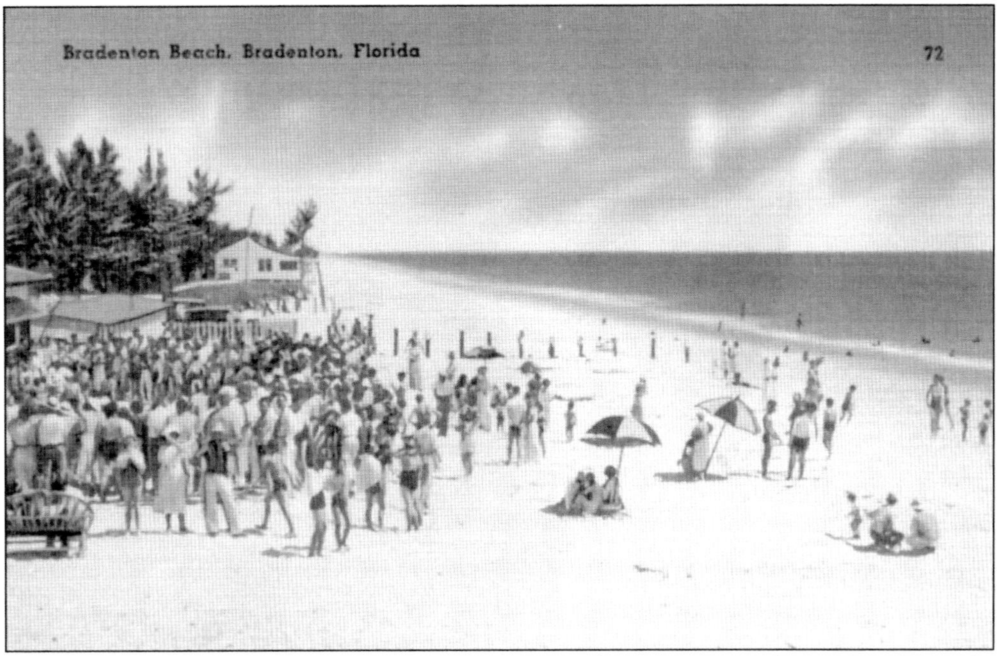

This crowd on the beach in front of a building near Bridge Street in Bradenton Beach may be gathered for a picnic, an announcement, an entertainer, or a political speech, as some are in business suits and others in swimsuits. Some hold umbrellas, and others wear sun hats. There were plenty of activities on the beach to enjoy after the wooden bridge opened to bring crowds from the mainland.

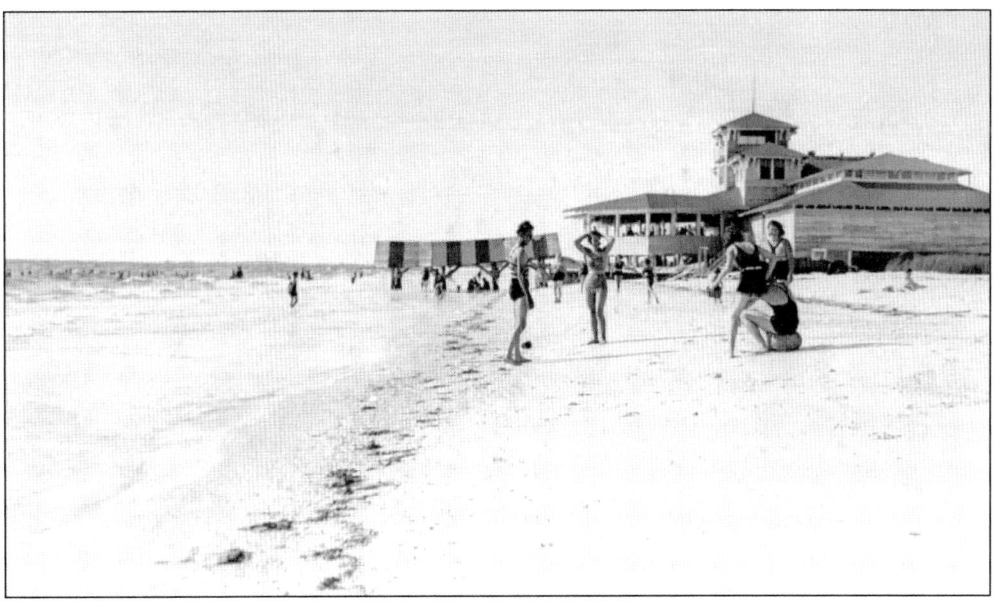

In this view from the shoreline of the Bradenton Beach Pavilion and Bathhouse at the beach end of Bridge Street, a group of women appears to have been playing with a beach ball when a playful someone arrived to steal it and use it for a seat. The pavilion was a focal point for recreation on the island.

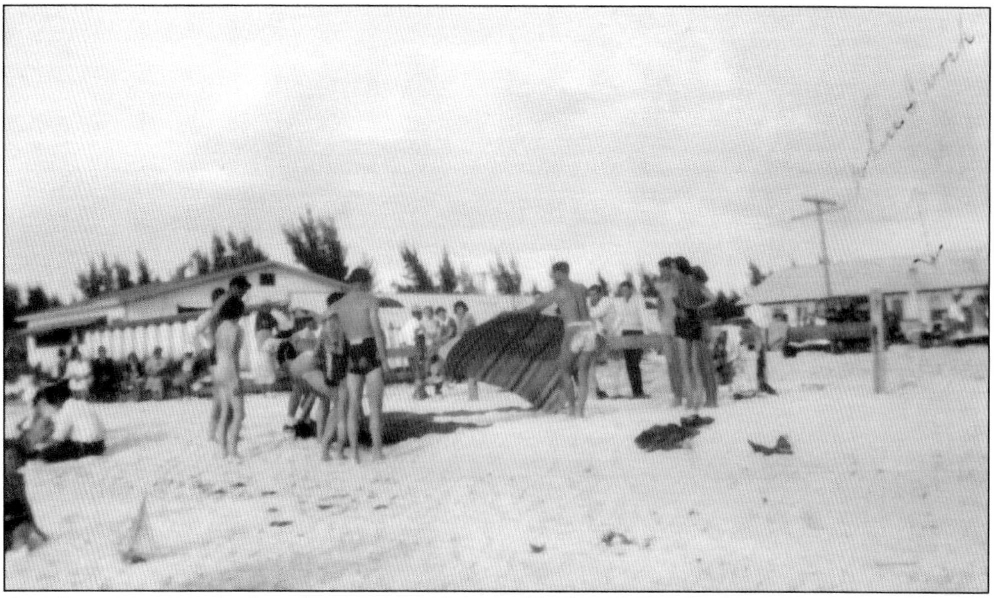

Another group on the beach is putting down a blanket for sunbathing in 1938 adjacent to the Bradenton Beach Moose Lodge (left) and Todd's Bar and Grill (right). Someone wrote on the photograph, "Where I work," with an arrow pointing to the building. (Courtesy of the *Islander*.)

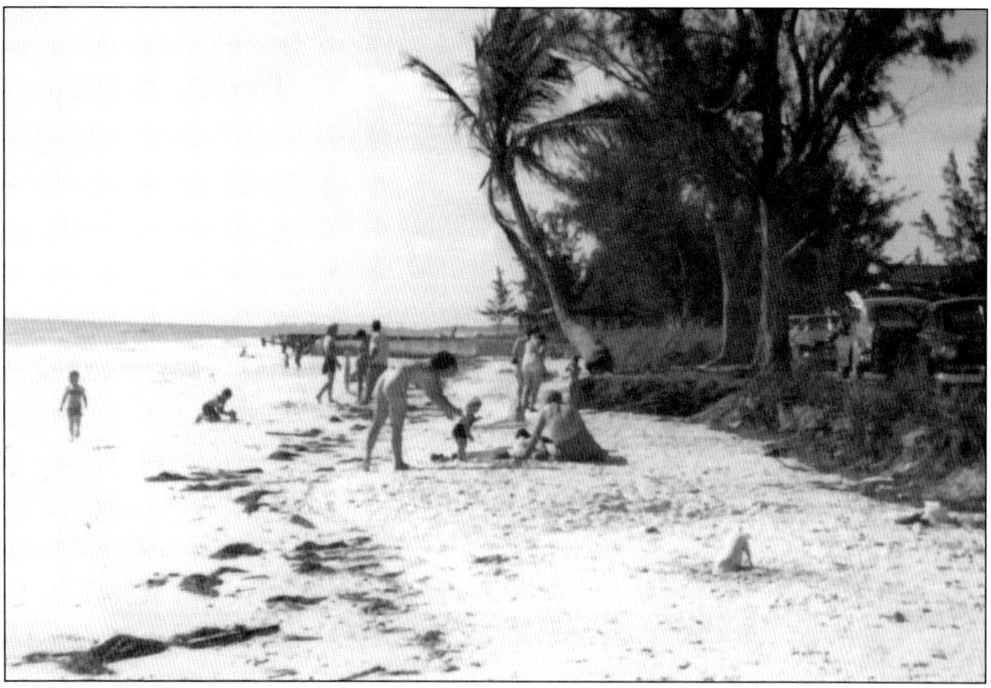

In this photograph from July 1949, a woman steadies a youngster in the sand as others search for shells, build a sandcastle, or check out the surf. A coconut tree curves skyward on the edge of the sand, while Australian pine trees provide shade for the cars parked on the right. And a dog, a small white terrier, possibly the Roats' Kipper, digs into a crab hole in the foreground. (Courtesy of the *Islander* and the Roat family collection.)

Four

Where the Fishing Is Great

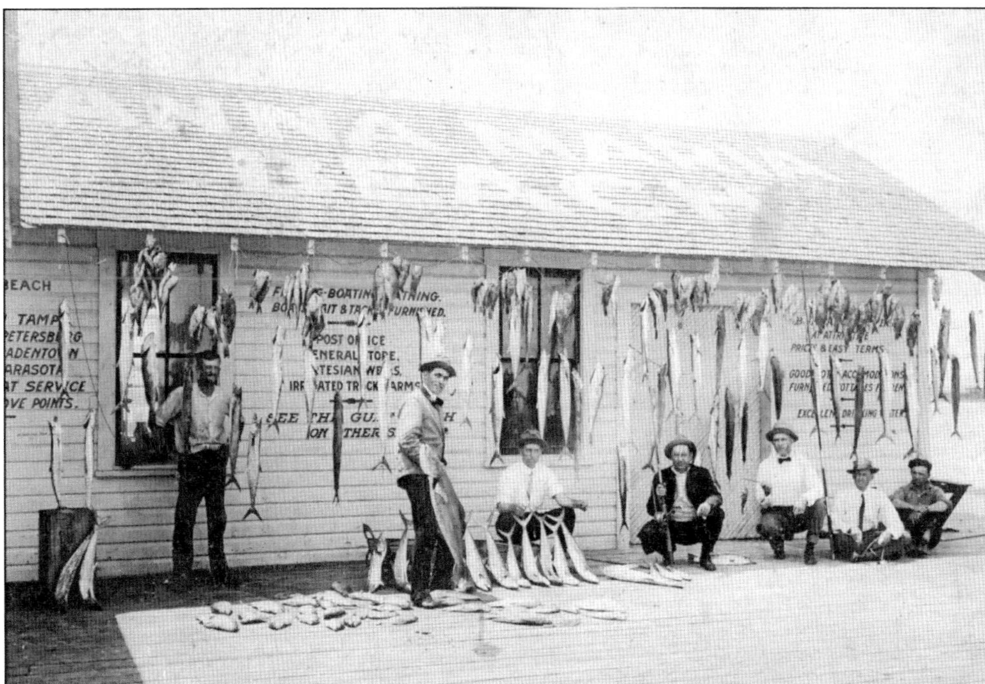

The catch of the day for these well-dressed anglers appears to be mackerel, but a report of the day claims 14 species in only three hours of fishing. A rooftop message proclaims to aviators that they are passing over Anna Maria Beach. Advertising on the roof is complemented by more sales pitches on the side of the building, touting the distance to Anna Maria from Tampa, St. Petersburg, Bradenton, and Sarasota and inviting visitors to see the Gulf beaches on the other side of the island.

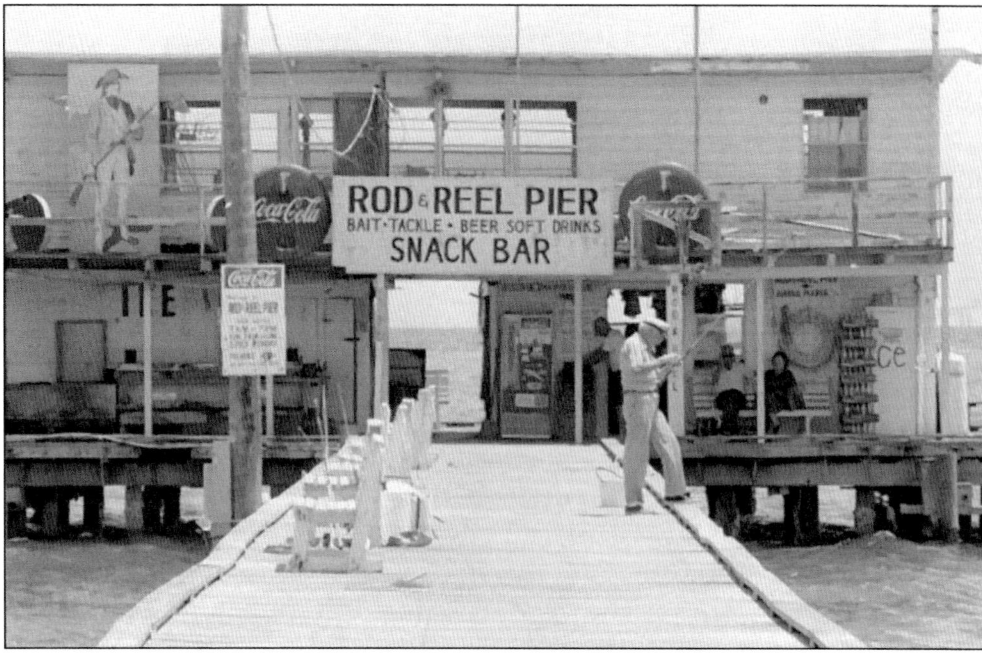

The Rod & Reel Pier in Anna Maria, built in the 1950s over Tampa Bay and with a panoramic view of the Sunshine Skyway Bridge that links Manatee and Pinellas Counties and the wildlife refuge Passage Key, remains popular with island residents. The downstairs includes a dining counter and kitchen as well as a bait shop, while upstairs, it originally housed an office for longtime owner Frank Cavendish, who was rumored to host nightly card games where men gathered to tell fish tales. It is now a dining room. (Courtesy of the Anna Maria Island Historical Society.)

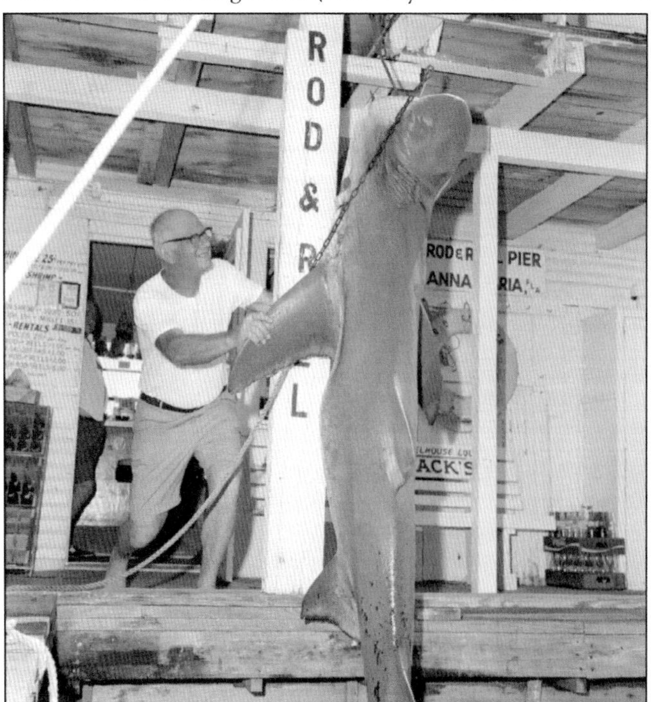

Rod & Reel Pier owner Frank Cavendish is pictured here with a shark he caught in the early 1970s off the pier. Longtime Anna Maria fishers say anglers have been shark-fishing from the pier since it was built in the early 1950s, although the city pier opened in 1911. Cavendish was said to have a tire mounted with chains to one of the pier pilings—to which he attached a large hook baited with meat to attract his prey. (Courtesy of the Anna Maria Island Historical Society.)

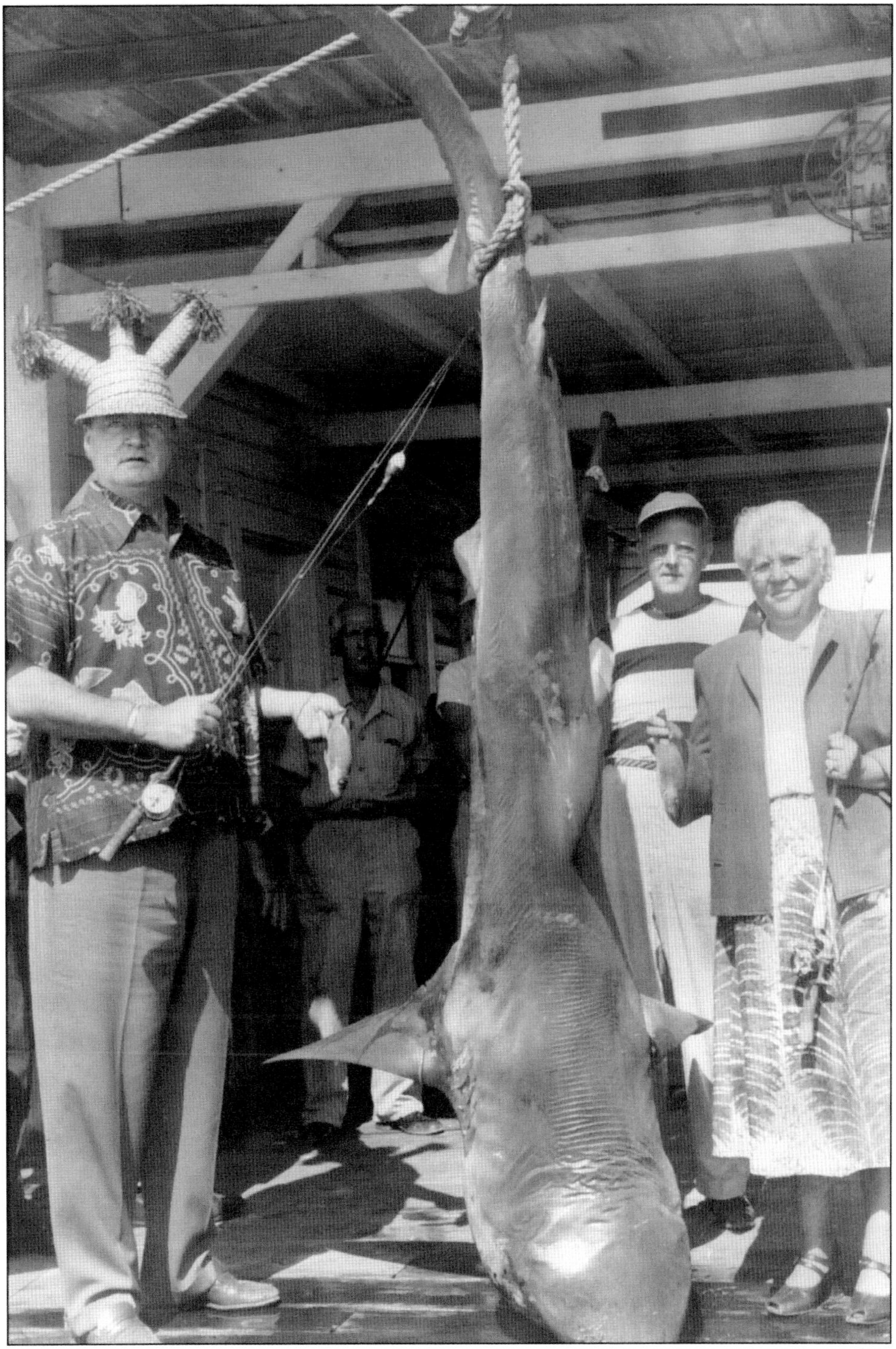

Larl (left) and Francis Karel (right) each show off their light tackle and a small catch, while the crew at the pier hangs its biggest catch of the day at the Anna Maria Pier. The 10-plus-foot-long bull shark likely weighed more than 800 pounds—and also put up a great fight. (Courtesy of the *Islander*.)

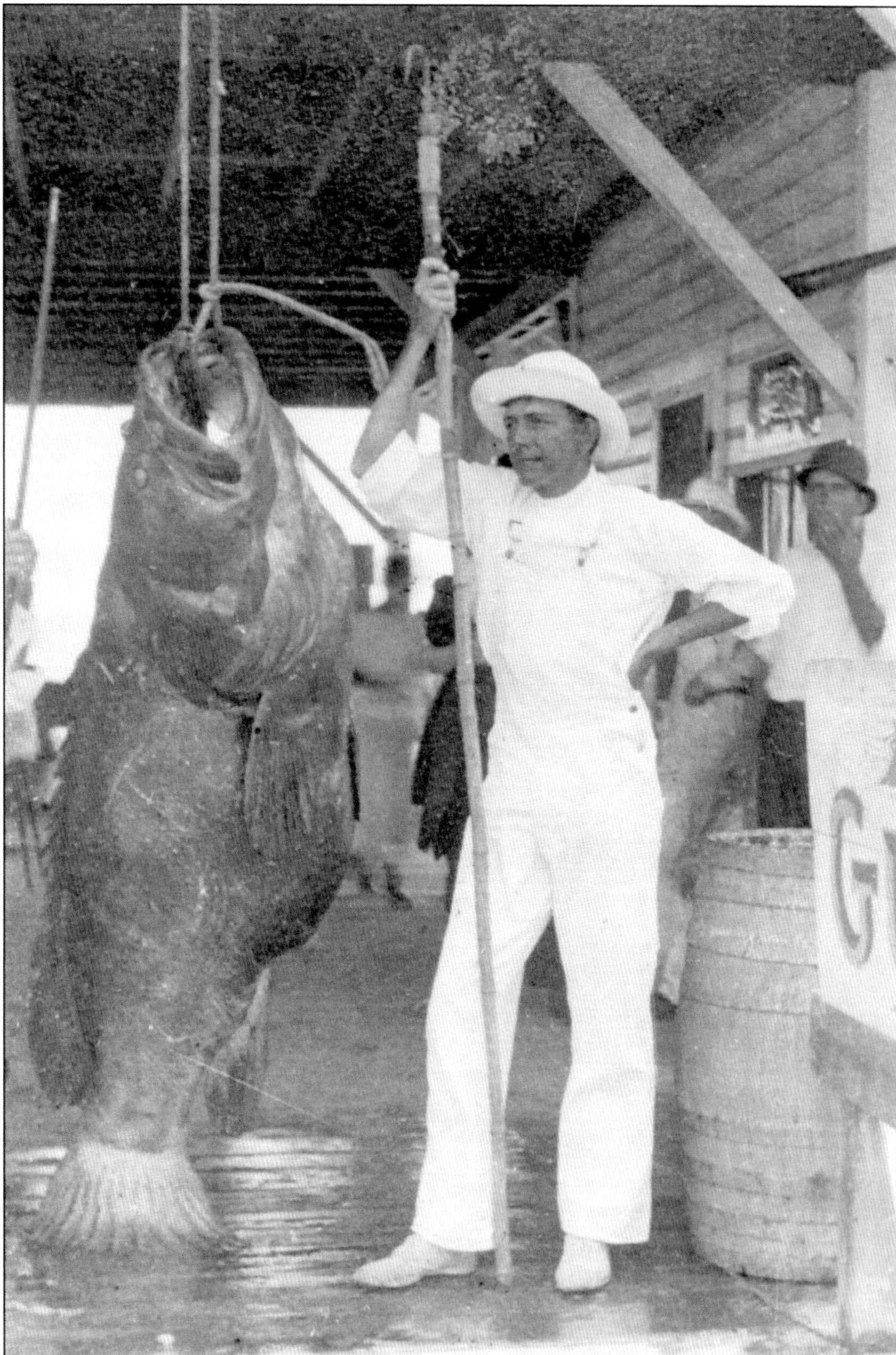

John Vanderipe shows off his catch made in 1913 at the Anna Maria Pier—a large jewfish, part of the grouper family. It is illegal to keep the fish, now known as the goliath grouper, and due to its size, some fishers jump in the water for a photograph with their catch.

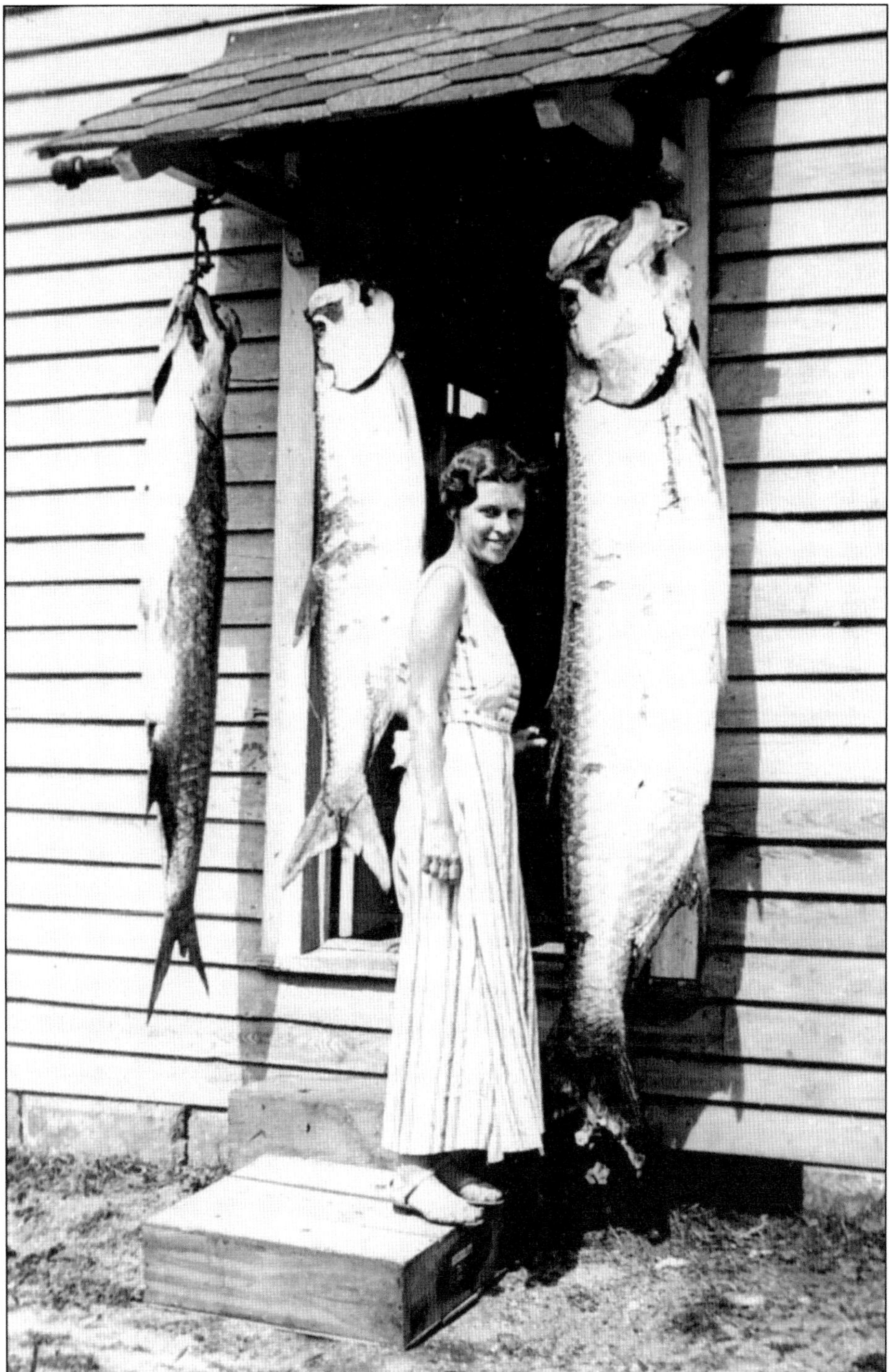

Proud angler Dorothea Zoller Vanderipe stands beside her catch—a very large tarpon and a couple of average silver kings. She and her husband, John F. Vanderipe Jr., a banker, were avid anglers who owned a large home in the city of Anna Maria.

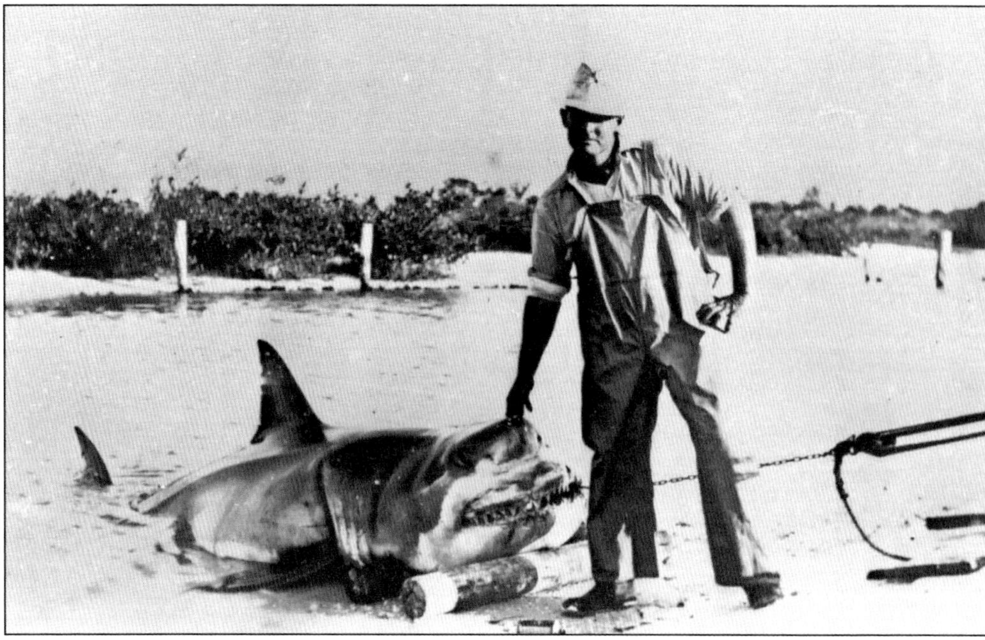

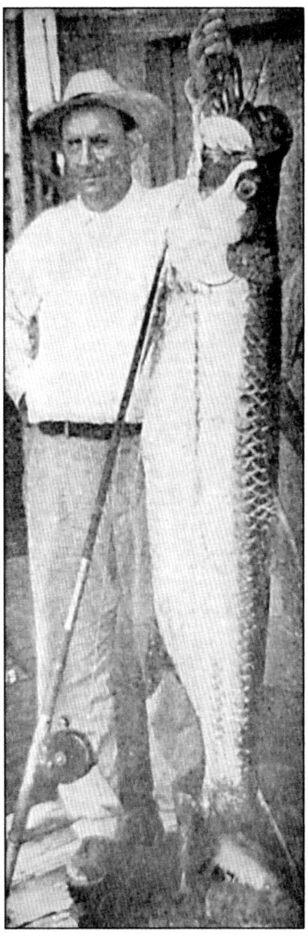

Edgar J. Green of Cortez caught what most believe to have been a record-size catch—20 feet long, 8 feet in girth, and 2,536 pounds. It was either a great white or a nurse shark, caught in the Gulf of Mexico about six miles from Longboat Pass. It was towed to the Longboat Key beach for a photograph and processing and rendered a liver that filled three wash tubs; and after cooking, the liver oil filled a 50-gallon drum. Green was fishing alone and used a flipper from a 30-pound skate for bait. The previous record for a shark catch was a 15-foot, 1-inch shark caught in Australia.

George W. Bean, son of the island's first permanent settler, George Bean of Anna Maria, poses in 1913 for a rare photograph with his catch—a large tarpon, also known as the king of sport fish and a silver king.

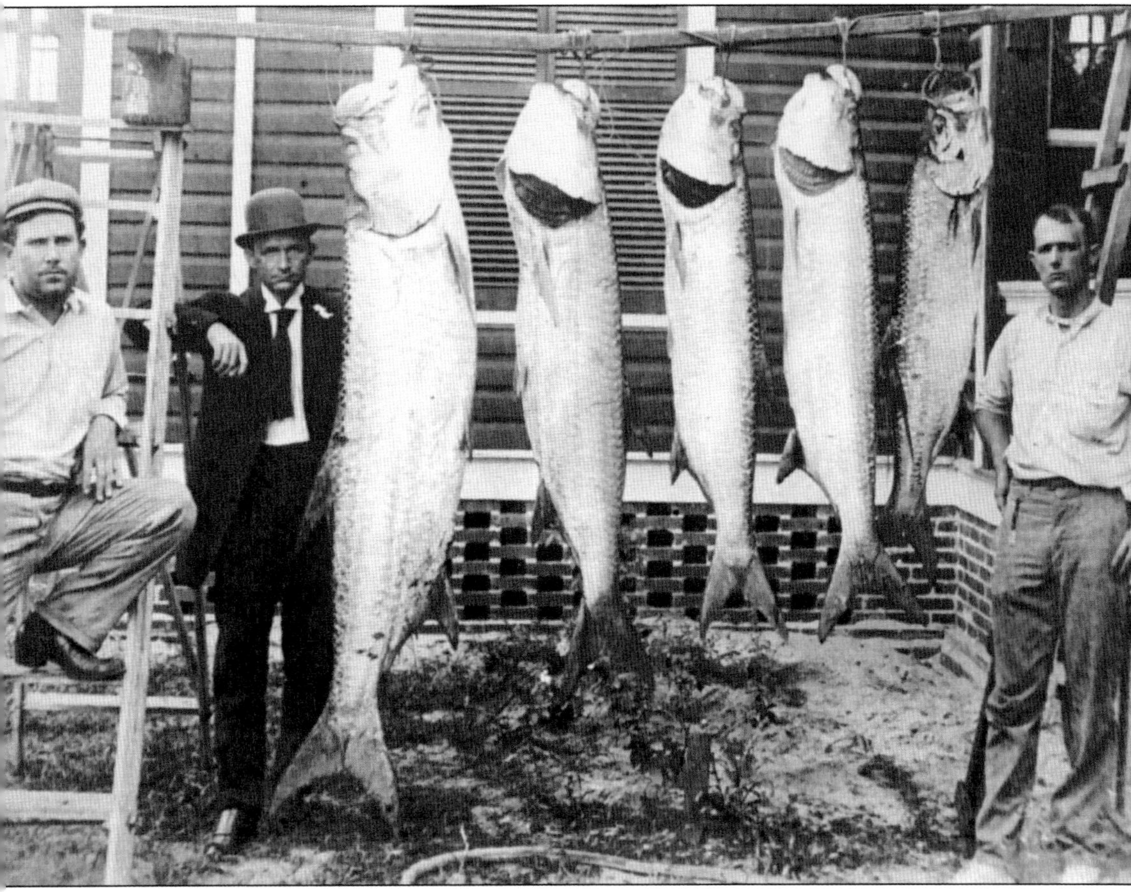

These men pose with their day's catch on returning home from a fishing trip in Tampa Bay around 1915–1920 with a fine showing of tarpon, but the silver king is not known to be tasty enough to eat. The biggest fish likely weighed more than either of the anglers—150 to 200 pounds—but it would have made for a nice trophy mount.

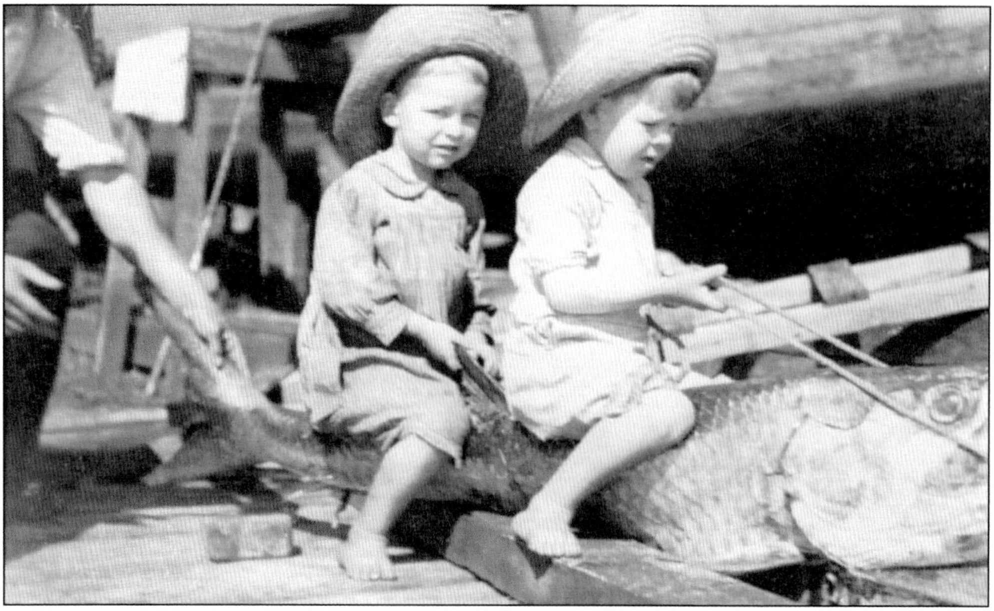

Young Lynn Willis (left) and Hubbard Fogarty may not have reeled up this nice-sized tarpon in 1915, but the kids got a chance to take it for a ride on the dock at the Anna Maria Pier. The pier was prime grounds for fishing in its spot looking out over the waters of Tampa Bay.

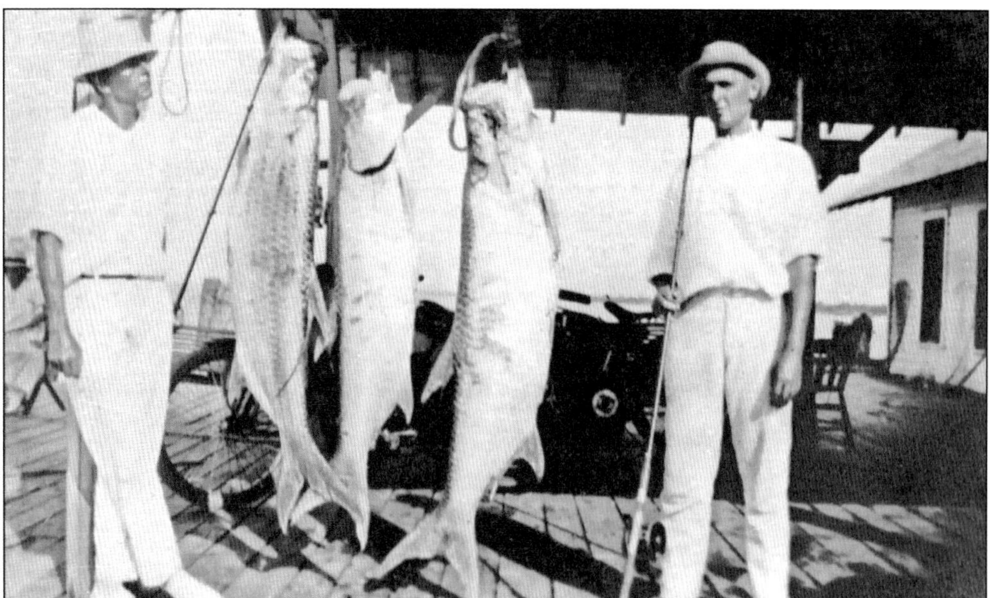

John Vanderipe (left) and Henry Curry pose with their day's catch from a nice run on a school of tarpon at the Anna Maria Pier in 1915. They went to a great deal of trouble to hang their catch for the photograph, possibly with help from the unidentified man to the left, who may have been their fishing guide.

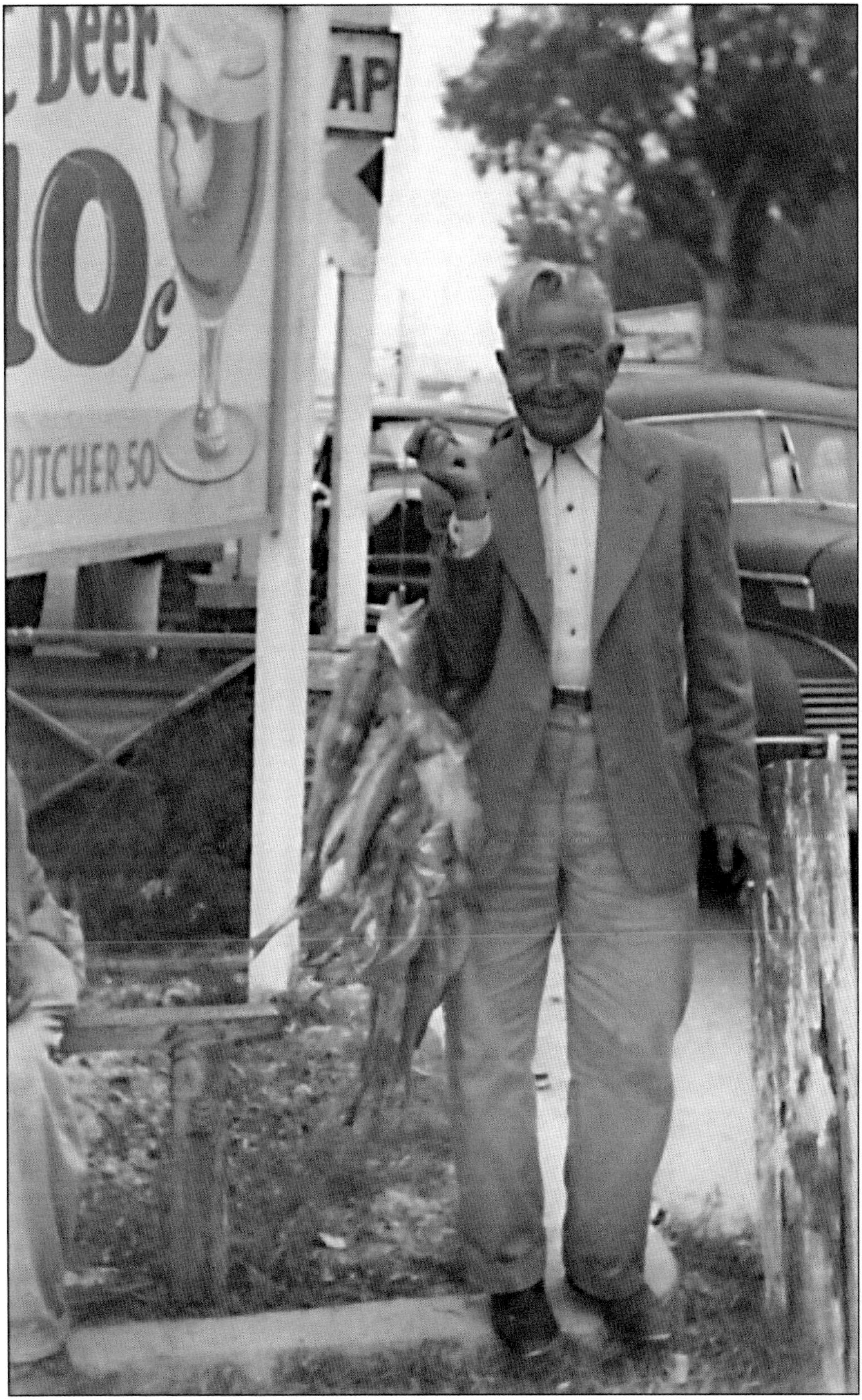

A man known in 1951 to folks in Bradenton Beach as "Soda Bar Jim" walks with his catch on a stringer—enough fish for a nice fry up—past a bar that offers 50¢ pitchers of beer. Jim would carry his catch from the beach to a location where they could be cleaned before heading home with dinner. (Courtesy of the *Islander*.)

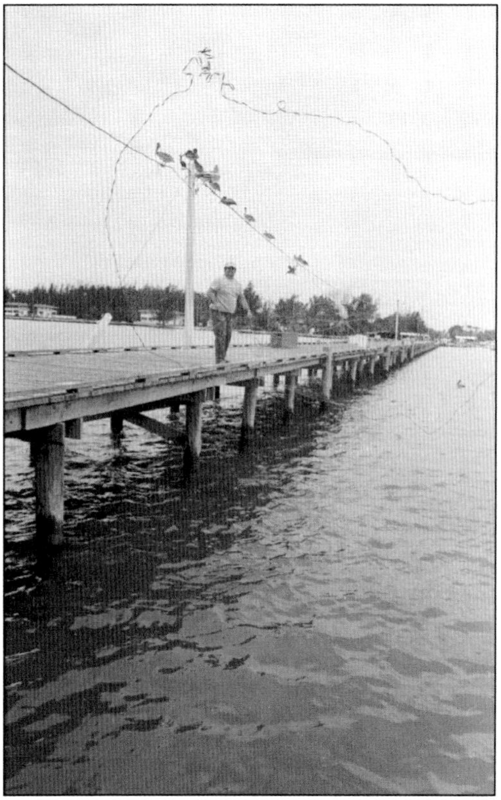

A fisher tosses his cast net into the waters at the Anna Maria City Pier in 1979 in the hopes of pulling up a mess of bait for himself and the pelicans awaiting the bait landing on the pier planks. The pier allows bait-netting from the landing up to a mark on the planks labeled "Cast Line." Beyond the cast line to the T-end, no netting is allowed.

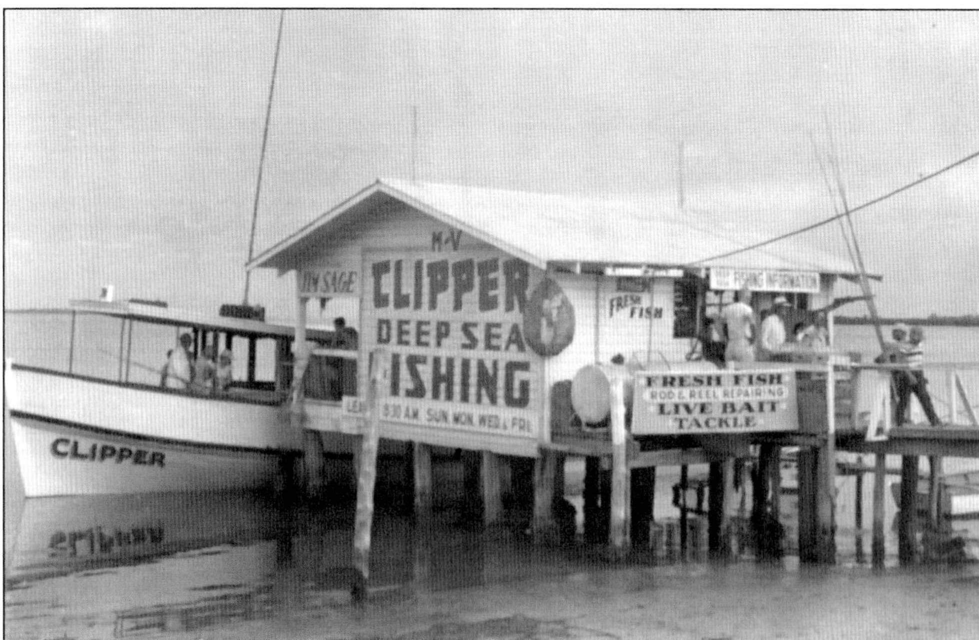

Capt. Jim Sage docks the *Clipper* in Bradenton Beach after a day's deep-sea fishing in the Gulf of Mexico offshore Anna Maria Island. Sage also sold fresh fish, bait, and tackle, and he repaired rods and reels for customers—who likely had some tall fish stories to tell. (Courtesy of the *Islander*.)

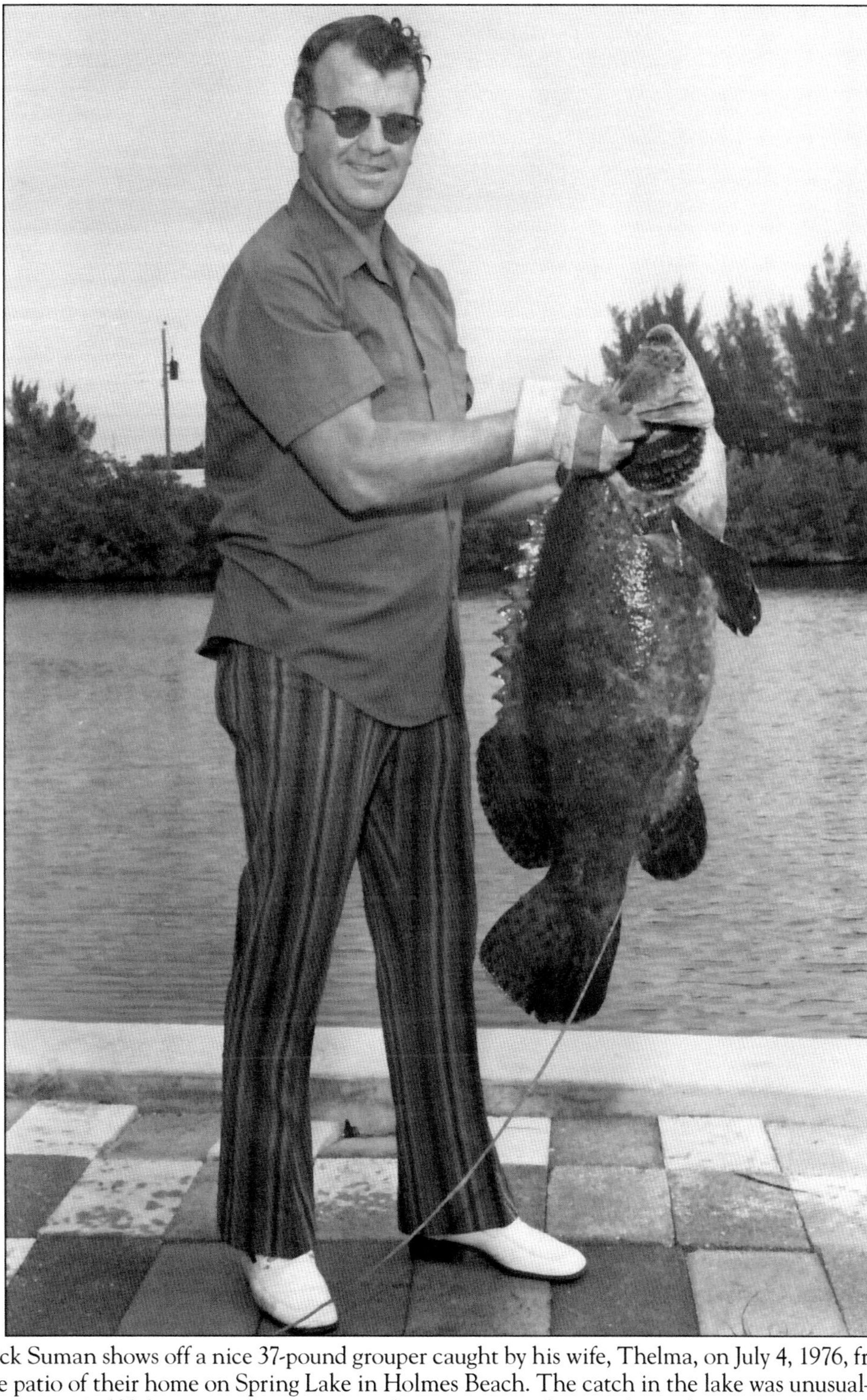

Dick Suman shows off a nice 37-pound grouper caught by his wife, Thelma, on July 4, 1976, from the patio of their home on Spring Lake in Holmes Beach. The catch in the lake was unusual—a deepwater Gulf fish. It caused quite a stir in the newspaper, where Dick ran the presses and Thelma was a bookkeeper. (Courtesy of the *Islander*.)

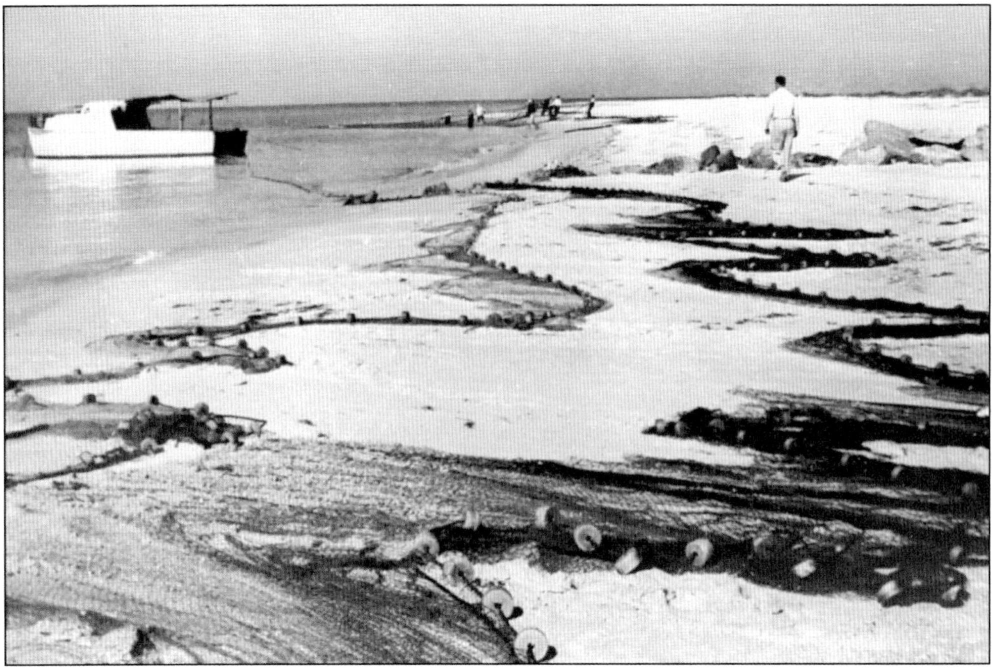

Commercial fishers work their nets in 1950 on the shoreline in Anna Maria. The long net was designed for the fishers to run out from the boat, trailing the net from the shoreline in a large sweep of the water, taking in fish along the way. As the net ran out, the boat would head back to the shore and run the end of the net onto the beach. After waiting a few hours, the fish net would be hauled ashore to reveal the catch left behind. It was backbreaking labor, but it paid off, especially when schools of mullet were running along the beaches.

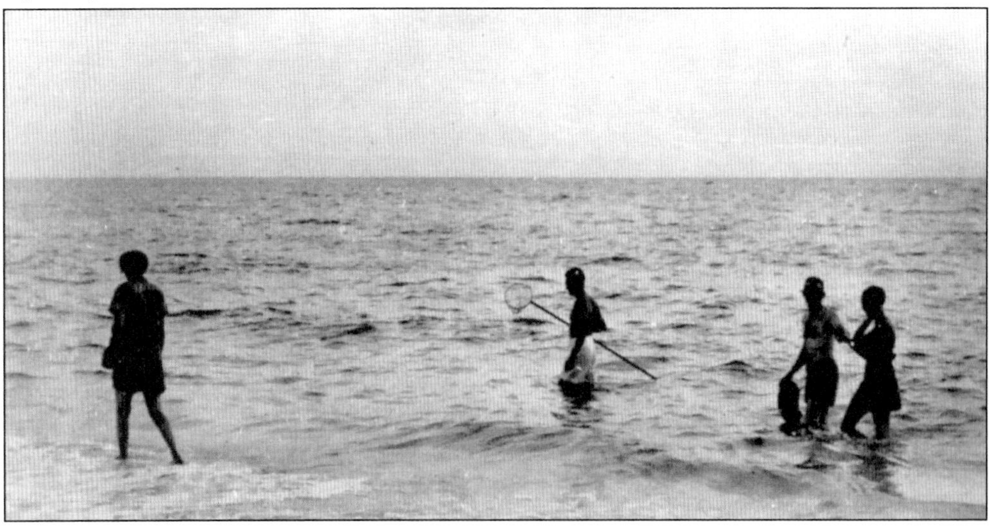

A group of people walks in silhouette along the water's edge in the Gulf of Mexico on Anna Maria Island as one of the four holds a net—the better to scoop up a blue crab lurking in the shallow water where the waves break. Blue crabs are abundant in the gulf and bay waters surrounding Anna Maria Island, but the fishery is now closed part of the year to protect the area from overfishing. Stone crabs are prominent, but must only be harvested from October to May. Scallops also used to be prevalent, but are all but extinct in local waters and strictly prohibited from harvest.

Five

Hollywood Comes Calling

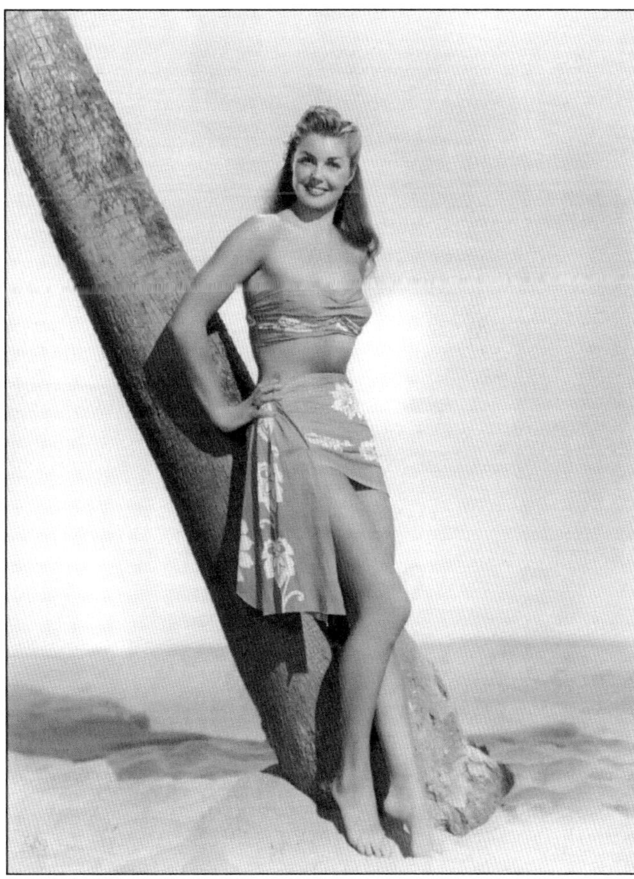

Imagine the excitement on the sparsely populated Anna Maria Island of the 1940s on learning a Hollywood movie would be filmed there. As the story goes, an MGM executive discovered the airport in Holmes Beach, surrounded by mangrove jungle and palm trees, and believed it to be the perfect location for a film starring Esther Williams. Like all of her films, *On an Island with You* was a moneymaker for MGM, reportedly earning over $3 million in the United States and Canada. (Courtesy of the Anna Maria Island Historical Society.)

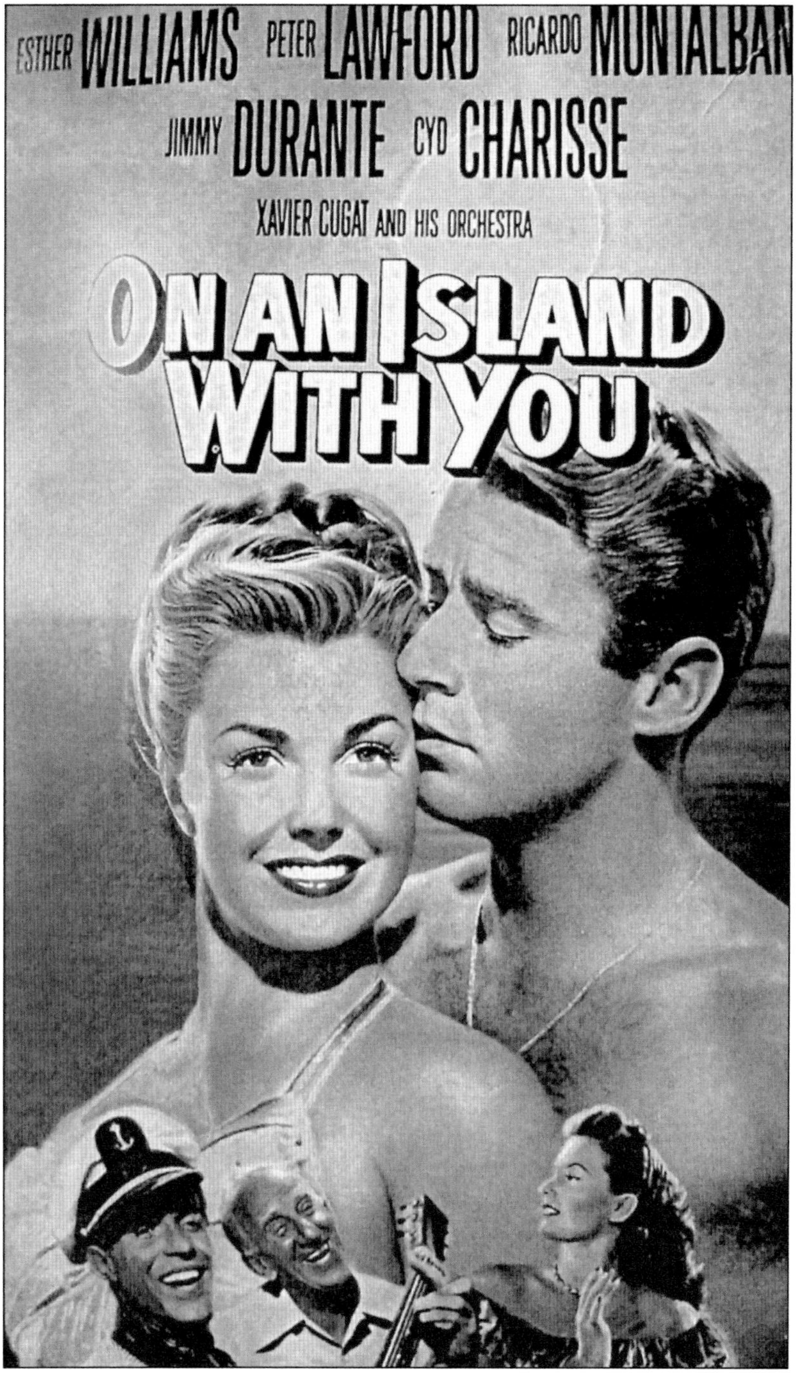

Esther Williams, Peter Lawford, and Ricardo Montalban share top billing in the MGM movie *On an Island with You*, filmed on MGM lots and on Anna Maria Island between June and September 1947. Williams appears as Rosalind Reynolds, a swimming star who goes to Hawaii to film on a tropical island and brings along her fiancé, Ricardo Montez, played by Montalban. A military advisor in the movie, Navy lieutenant Lawrence Y. Kinsglee, played by Lawford, falls in love with Rosalind. Meanwhile, Cyd Charisse, as Yvonne Torro, sets out to steal Ricardo for herself.

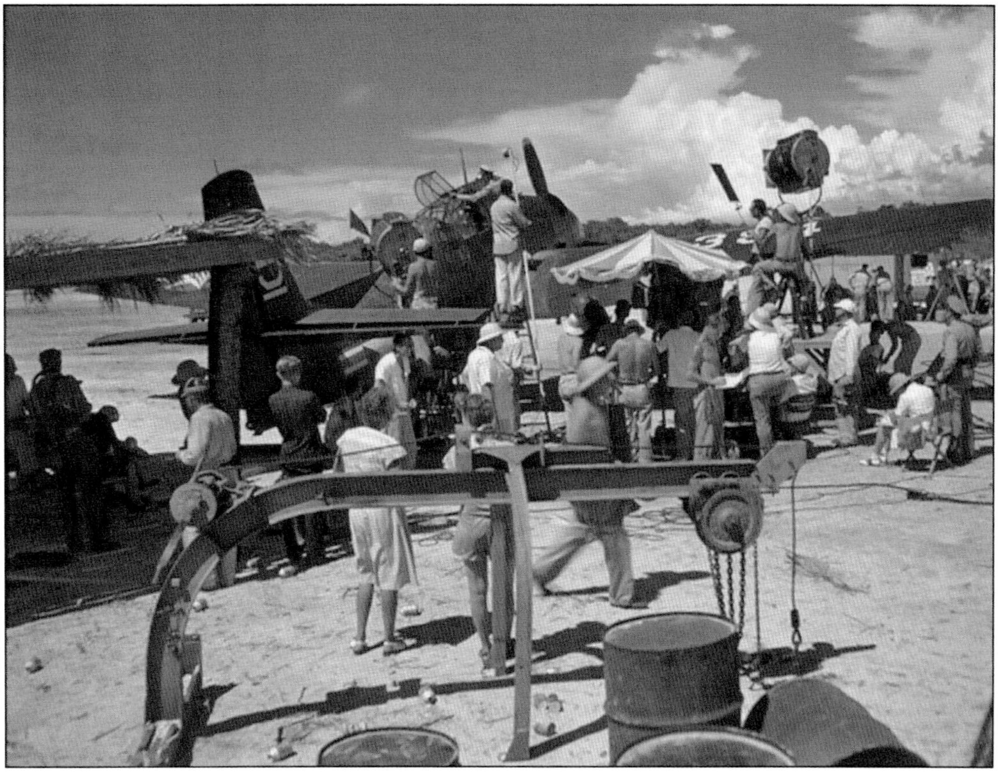

On the set of *On an Island with You* at the Holmes Beach Airport on Anna Maria Island, lots of the "natives," the real islanders, were allowed to work on the crew and mingle during shooting. The aircraft used in the film included a US Navy Grumman TBF Avenger torpedo bomber that played a pivotal role in the plot and a Grumman JRF-5 Goose flying boat. The large drums in the foreground hold fuel for the planes. (Courtesy of the *Islander.*)

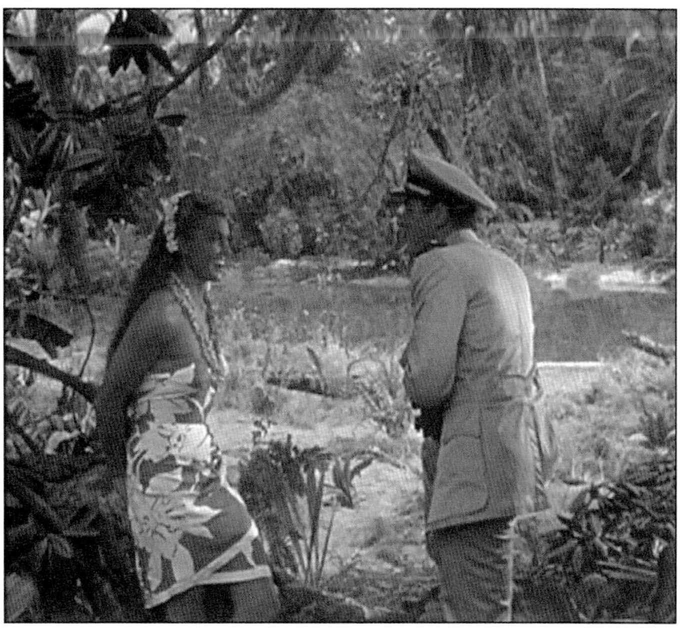

The filming of *On an Island with You* took advantage of natural scenery—a mangrove forest and a mixture of tropical plants that grew in thickets along the bayfront on Anna Maria Island. It also made use of tidal lagoons. In the plot, Larry (Lawford), who met Rosalind (Williams) three years before during a USO show at his Pacific base, makes it obvious that he is smitten with her. He then makes plans to spirit her away on his aircraft.

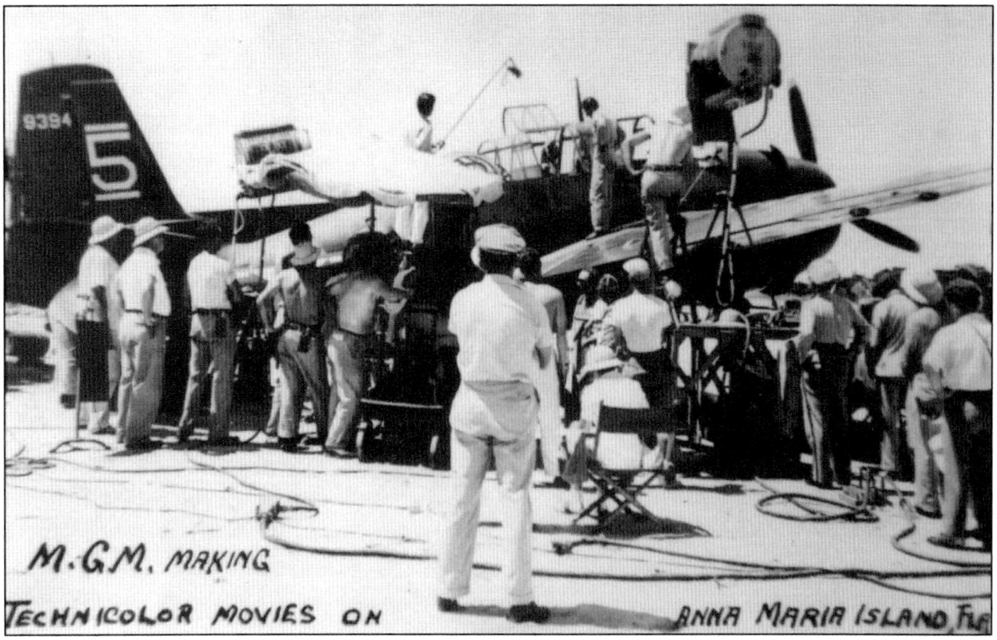

On an Island with You brought Technicolor artistry and plenty of equipment to the movie sets at the airport in Holmes Beach. The year was 1947, and filming took place from June to September, which any islander will confirm are the hottest months. They also had only boats and the old wooden 1921 bridge for transportation. The Hollywood crew relied on islanders for most of their needs. (Courtesy of the Anna Maria Island Historical Society.)

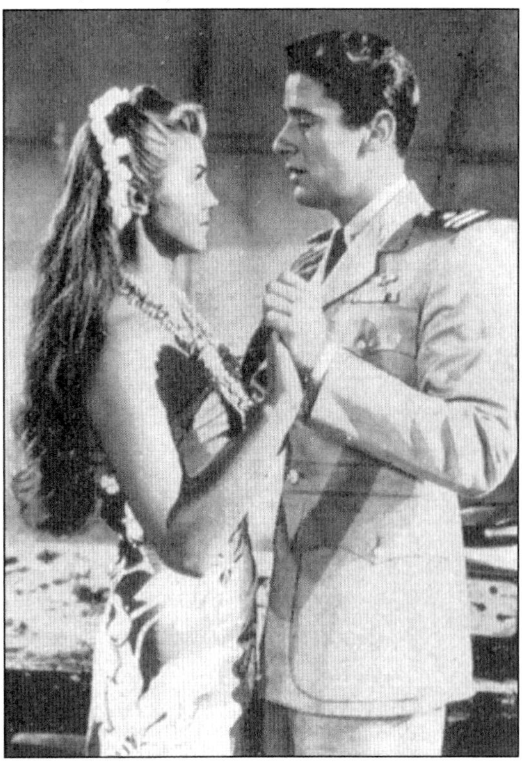

Esther Williams and Peter Lawford star in *On an Island with You*, filmed in part on Anna Maria Island. The movie is screened on the island from time to time, and most of the audience spends time looking for recognizable scenery, although few settings remain the same. Portions of the movie were filmed on the MGM lot, and near the end, the plot has Larry facing a court-martial. Rosalind tries to help by accepting blame for an unauthorized flight to the island. Eventually, viewers learn Yvonne is romantically involved with Ricardo, and Larry and Rosalind are in love.

Six

VIEWS FROM THE SKY

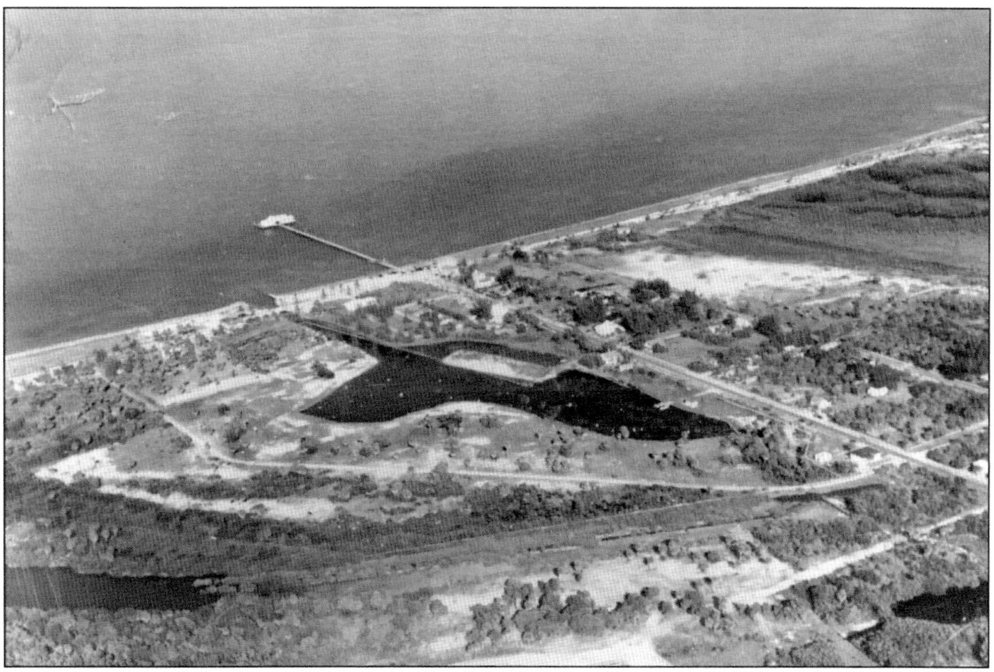

This 1944 aerial photograph of the north end of Anna Maria Island and the Anna Maria Pier shows limited development and progress. Pine Avenue, bisecting the photograph left to right, has some homes. A road is taking shape, South Bay Boulevard, reaching south from the pier, and there is a link on North Shore Boulevard for a bridge over the inlet. Land around Lake LaVista has been cleared, and a path leading north and back to the bay is visible, allowing for more homesites. (Courtesy of the *Islander*.)

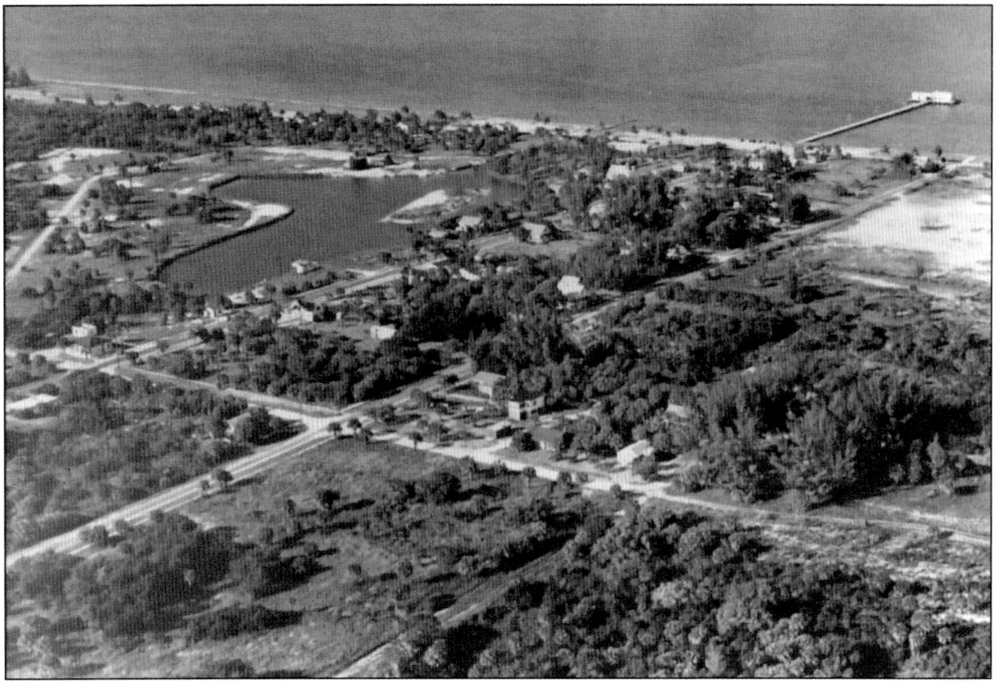

Looking north, this view of the north end of Anna Maria Island in 1948 shows more homes, roads and paths, and clearing. The steeple of Roser Church is barely visible to the left of the pier landing, and homes now have sprung up on Spring Avenue. (Courtesy of the *Islander*.)

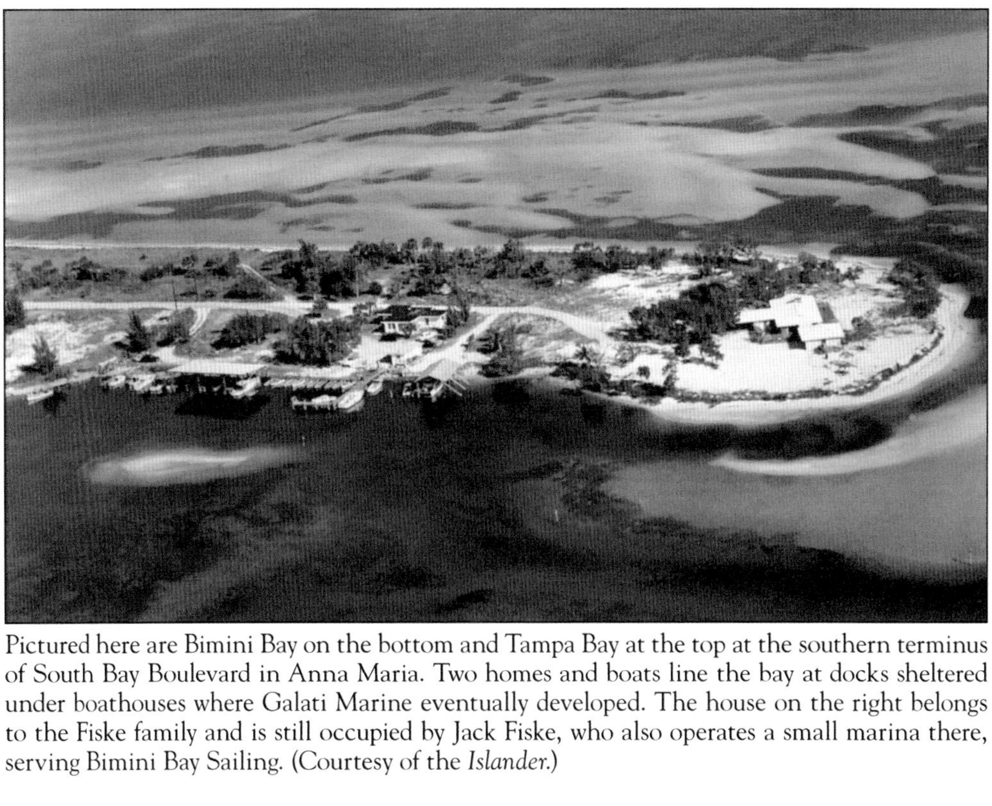

Pictured here are Bimini Bay on the bottom and Tampa Bay at the top at the southern terminus of South Bay Boulevard in Anna Maria. Two homes and boats line the bay at docks sheltered under boathouses where Galati Marine eventually developed. The house on the right belongs to the Fiske family and is still occupied by Jack Fiske, who also operates a small marina there, serving Bimini Bay Sailing. (Courtesy of the *Islander*.)

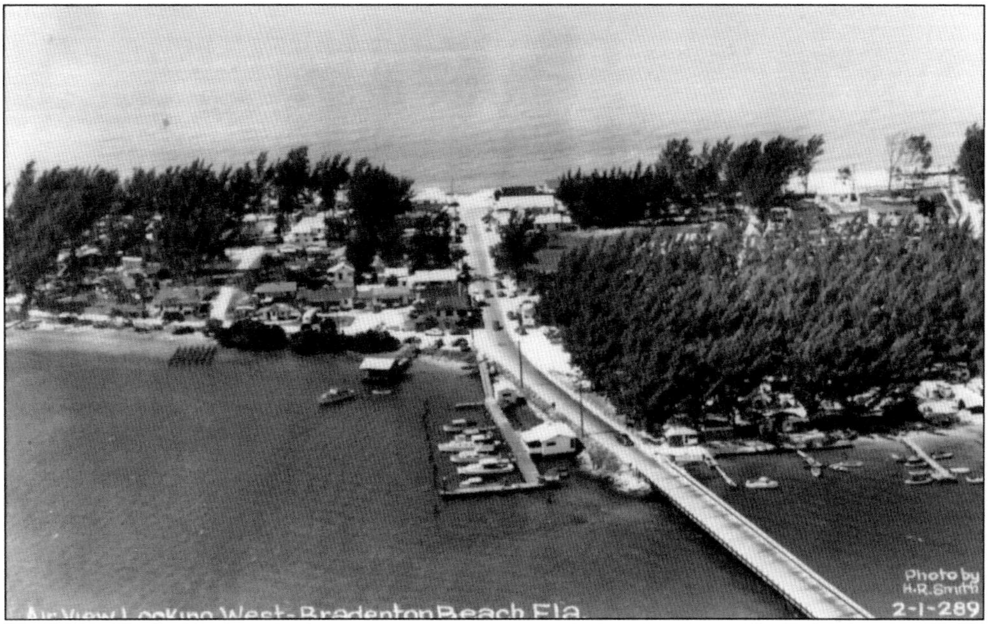

In this view looking from Sarasota Bay to the Gulf of Mexico, the wooden bridge landing in the 1940s leads past fishing boats for hire and homes shaded by Australian pine trees and businesses on Bridge Street. The stand of pines to the right is the site of the Pines Trailer Park. (Courtesy of the *Islander*.)

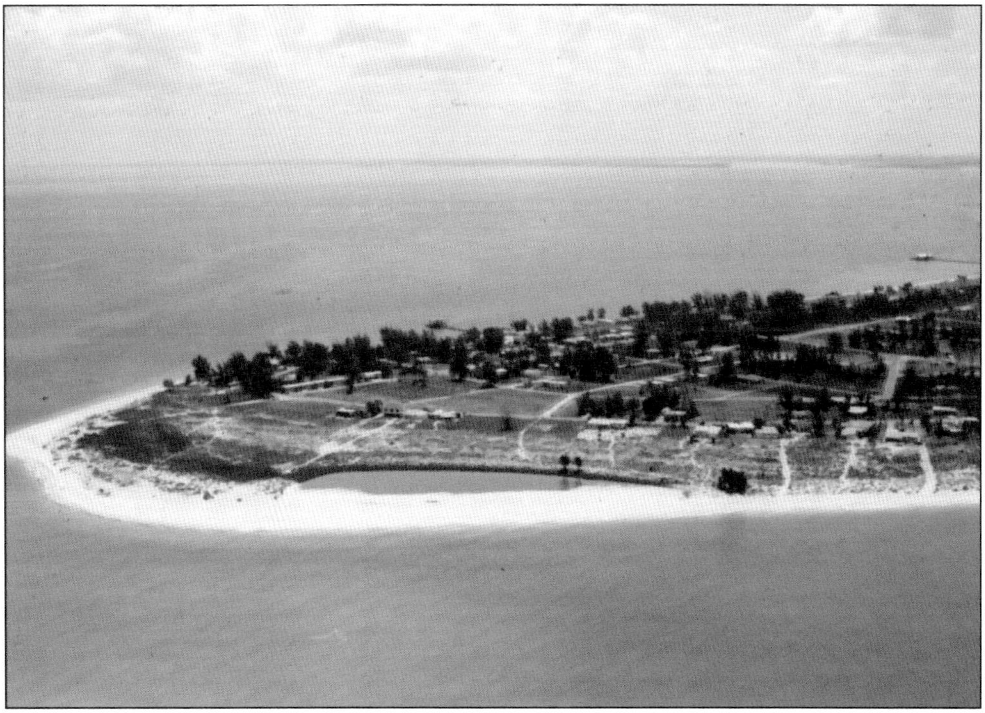

By 1964, North Shore Drive and other roads leading northward, as well as the Rod & Reel Pier and a number of bayfront and beachfront homes, have been built, and there are roads to serve them. (Courtesy of the *Islander*.)

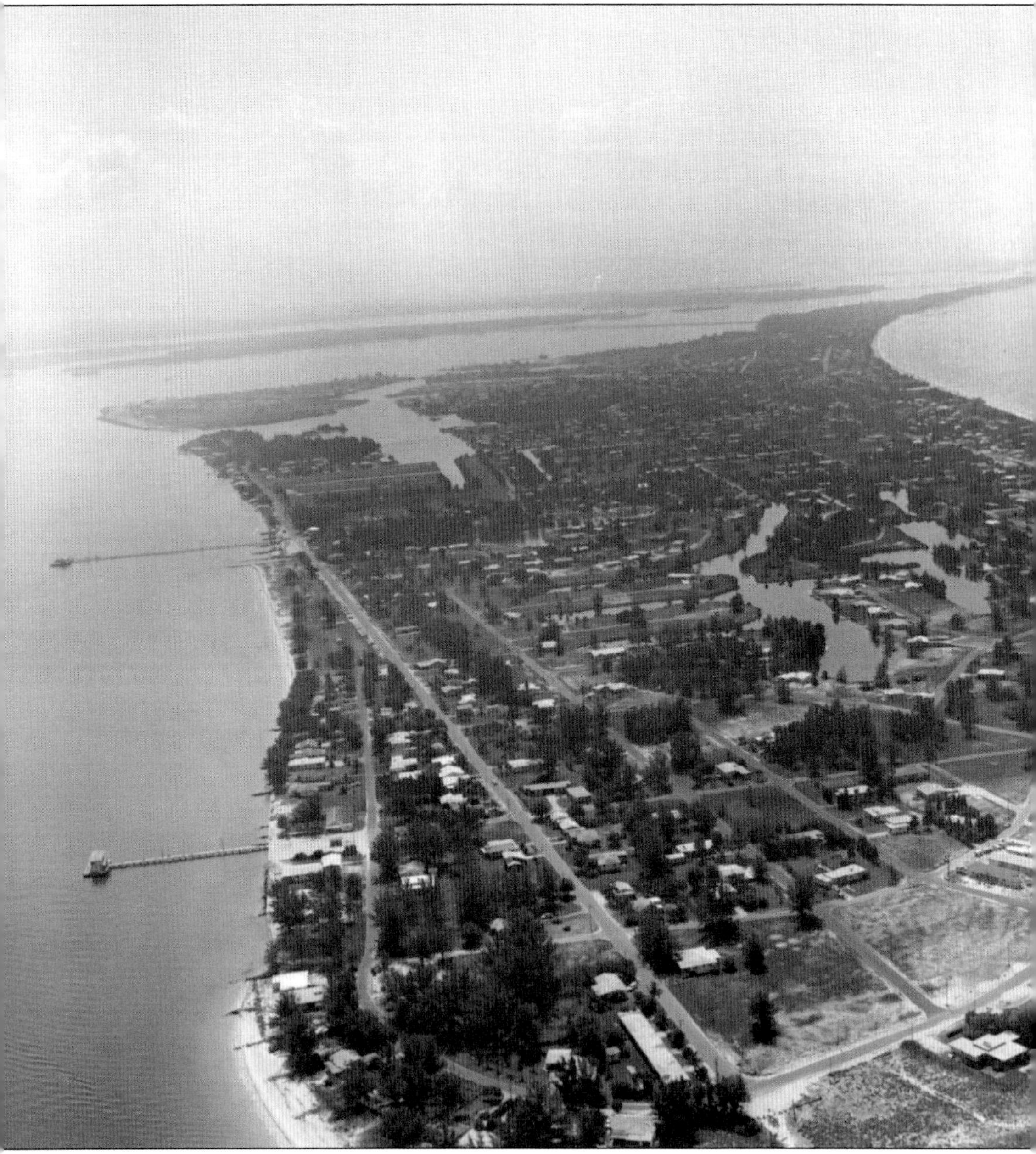

In the late 1960s and early 1970s, the two piers in Anna Maria were surrounded by development reaching to the Gulf of Mexico and southward to Holmes Beach. School Key—now being developed with high-end homes and renamed Key Royale—is at the top left of the photograph.

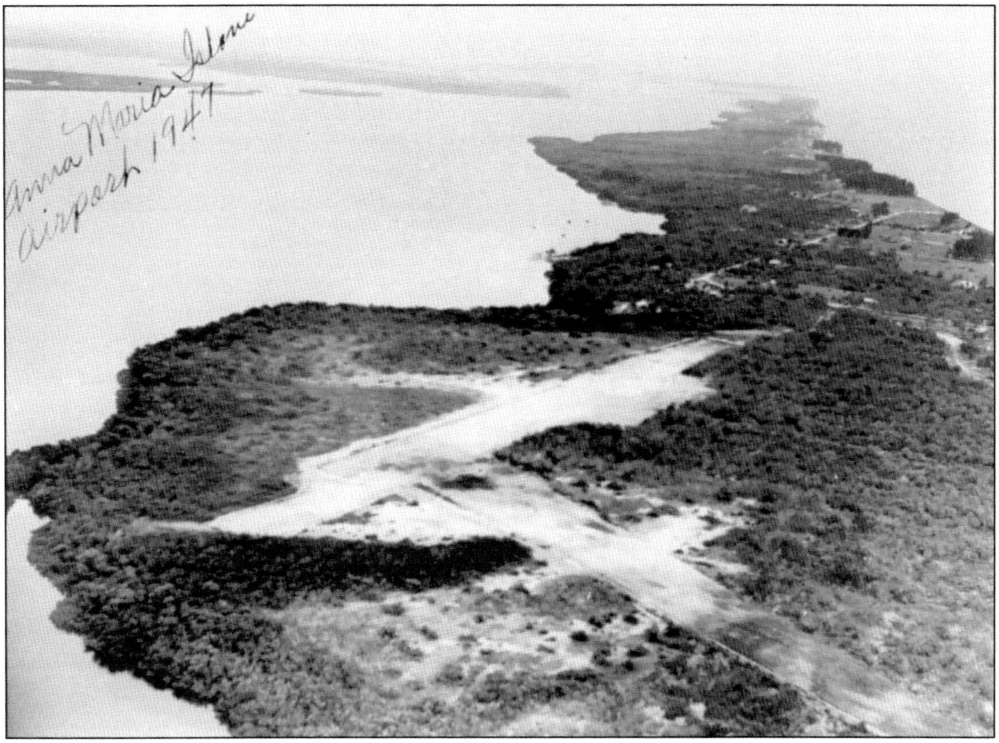

In this view looking south in 1947 from the land cleared in Holmes Beach for an airport, it is easy to see development of the central city on Anna Maria Island was slower than the north end, where the 1910 pier served visitors and brought homebuyers.

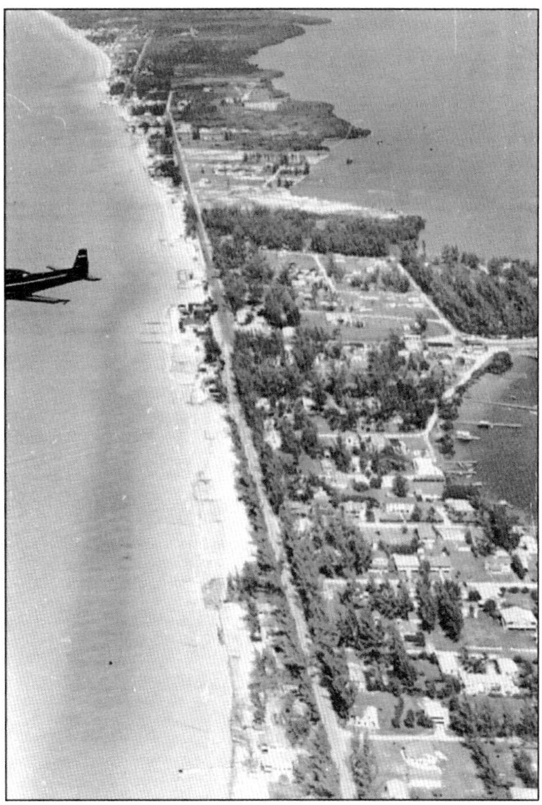

Pictured here is the central portion of the island in 1947, in a view looking northward from Bradenton Beach. Gulf Drive, the main road leading north on the left, is but a sliver; and few homes exist except on the Gulf of Mexico as one looks farther north. The new Cortez Bridge and the bridge connecting Holmes Beach to Perico Island and the mainland have yet to be built.

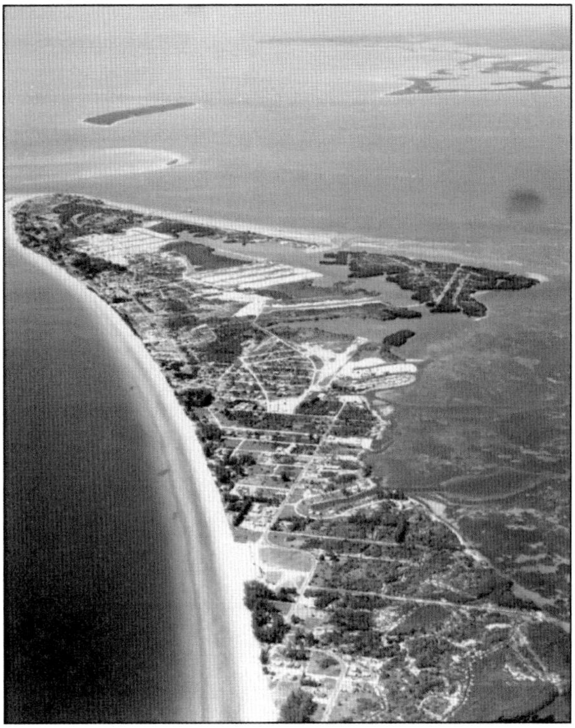

In this 1960 aerial photograph, Holmes Beach development has skyrocketed thanks to a new bridge to the city from the mainland. An elite development on Key Royale was being platted for homes. The airport was serving visitors in small private planes. The rows of vacant white land in the center became the Bimini Bay development—a dredge-and-fill project that produced rows of canal-front homes. At the northern tip of the island, Passage Key, a federal wildlife preserve, is visible, as are Egmont Key, a former US artillery base that still houses a lighthouse and pilot station in Tampa Bay.

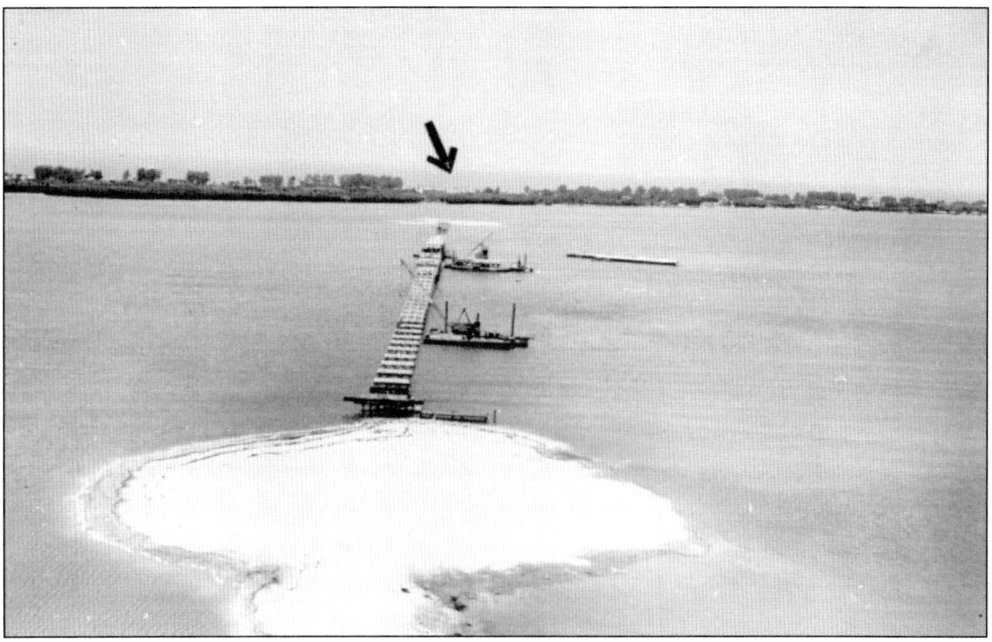

In this view looking westward from Perico Island, the Anna Maria Island Bridge got underway in May 1956. Dredged sand was used to form the landing, and barges were employed to extend the construction over Anna Maria Sound. The Florida Department of Transportation undertook three bridges in 1956— this one linking Holmes Beach to the mainland on Manatee Avenue, as well as a new Cortez Bridge linking to Bradenton Beach and a bridge over Longboat Pass, linking Bradenton Beach to Longboat Key and Sarasota County beyond.

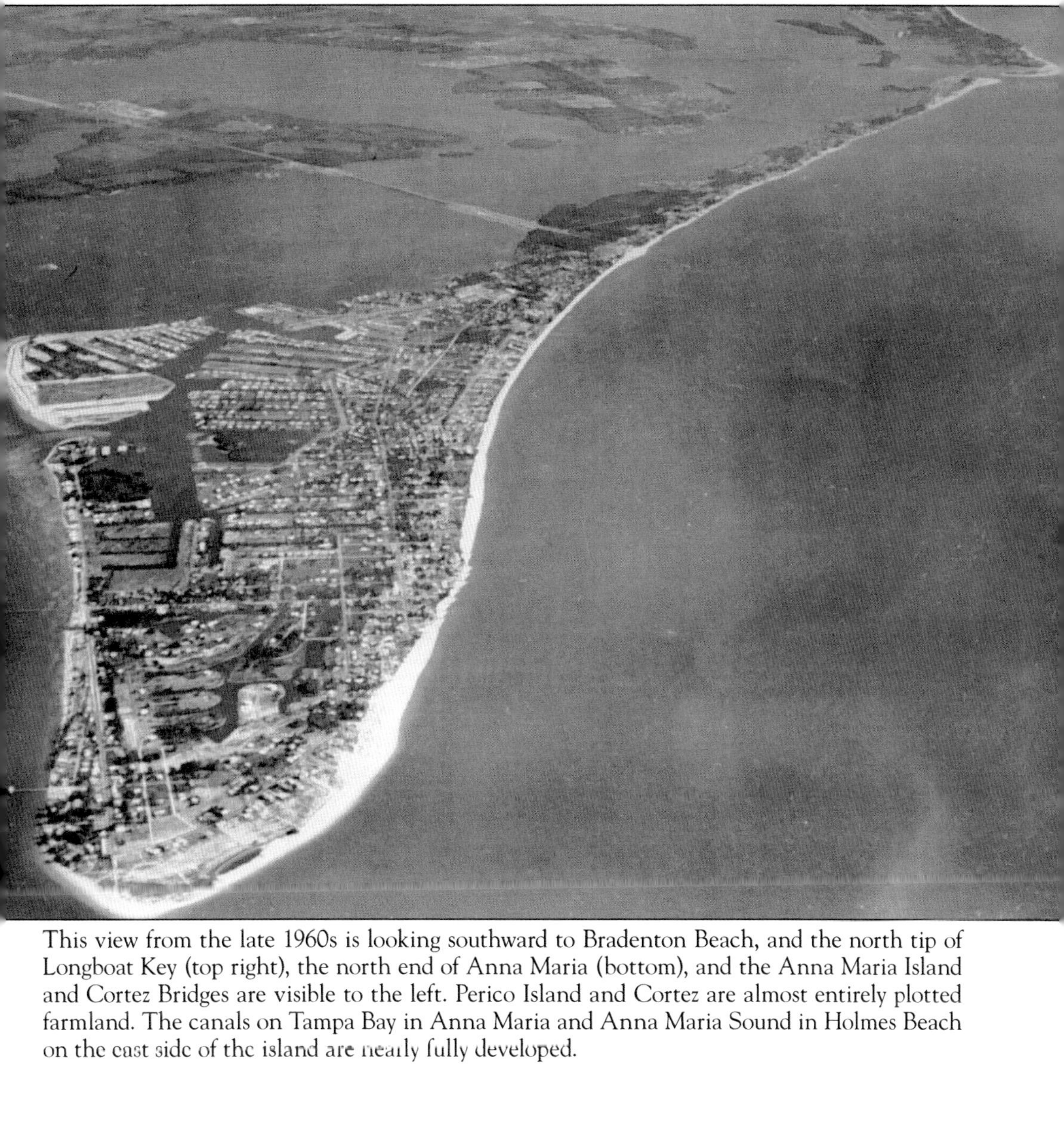

This view from the late 1960s is looking southward to Bradenton Beach, and the north tip of Longboat Key (top right), the north end of Anna Maria (bottom), and the Anna Maria Island and Cortez Bridges are visible to the left. Perico Island and Cortez are almost entirely plotted farmland. The canals on Tampa Bay in Anna Maria and Anna Maria Sound in Holmes Beach on the east side of the island are nearly fully developed.

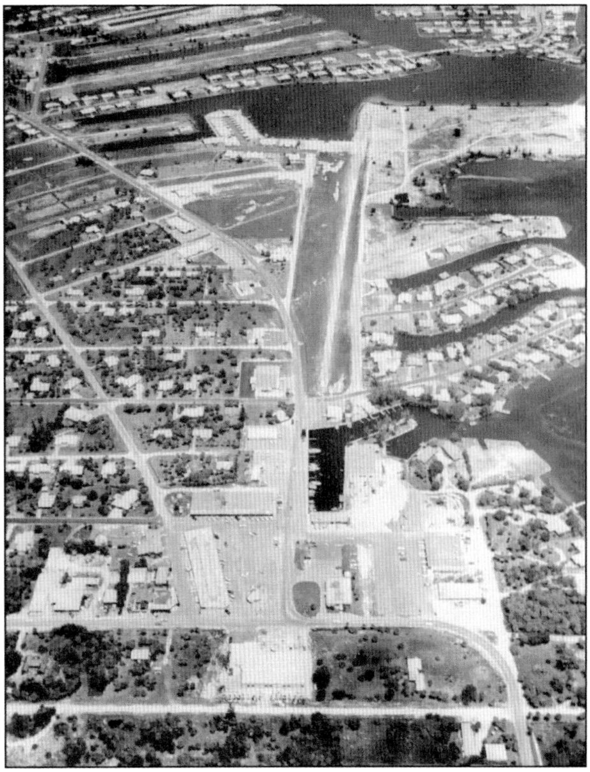

The S&S Plaza is pictured here in 1970–1971. Directly across Gulf Drive on the curve northward on Marina Drive is the Island Bank (right). Behind the bank, toward the east is a small strip of shops and Island Foodway. Opposite the bank on Marina Drive on the left is the Island Shopping Center. Farther northward on the east side of Marina Drive are Pete Reynard's Yacht Club Restaurant, a canal and basin of boat docks, and a marina. Stretching past the boat docks are the Holmes Beach Airport, a small sand-and-shell landing strip, and Holmes Beach City Hall.

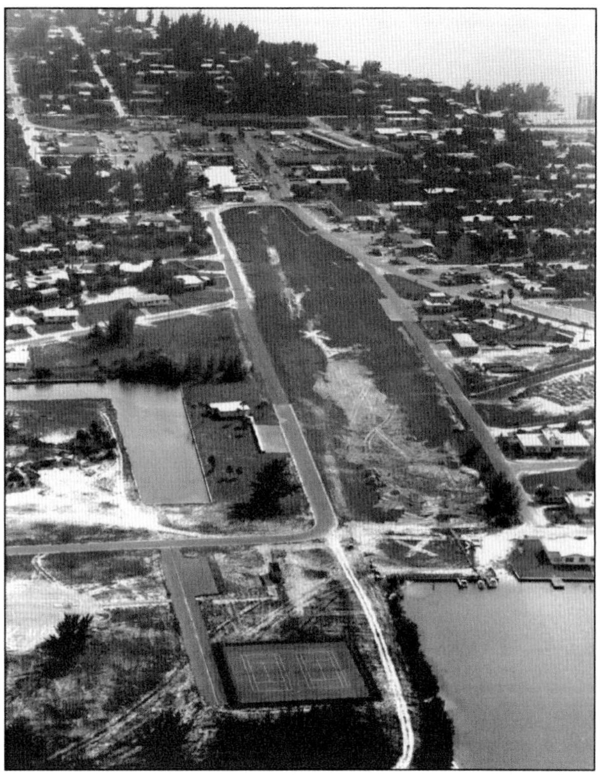

By 1973, this view looking south at the airstrip would soon change. Westbay Point and Moorings and Shell Point condominiums would be built at the bottom left, and Seaside Gardens would be developed on dredge-and-fill canals at the bottom right; the business district was growing at the south end of the airport.

In the late 1950s—the bridge pictured at the top of this photograph over Longboat Pass was completed in 1957—the long stretch of Coquina Beach was nearly barren. It now hosts a concession stand, trolley turnaround, picnic pavilions, Australian pine trees, and plenty of parking. The rock jetties on the Gulf of Mexico were installed to prevent sand from drifting into the pass. At the left is Leffis Key, and situated in the pass to the right of the bridge is Beer Can Island.

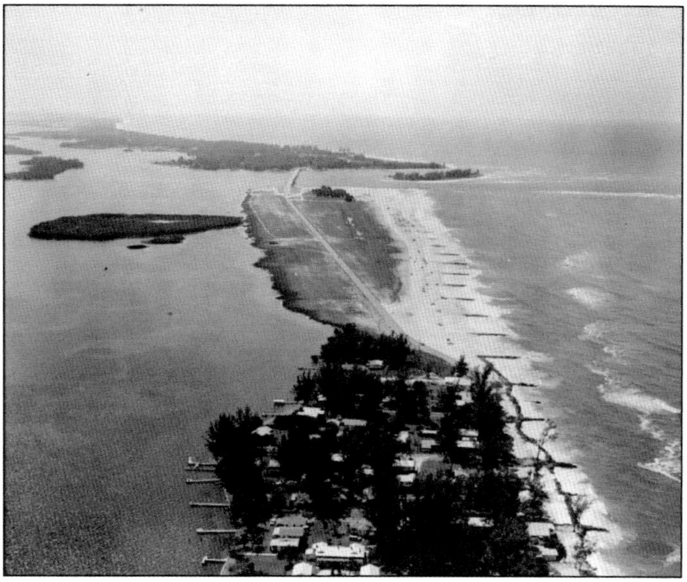

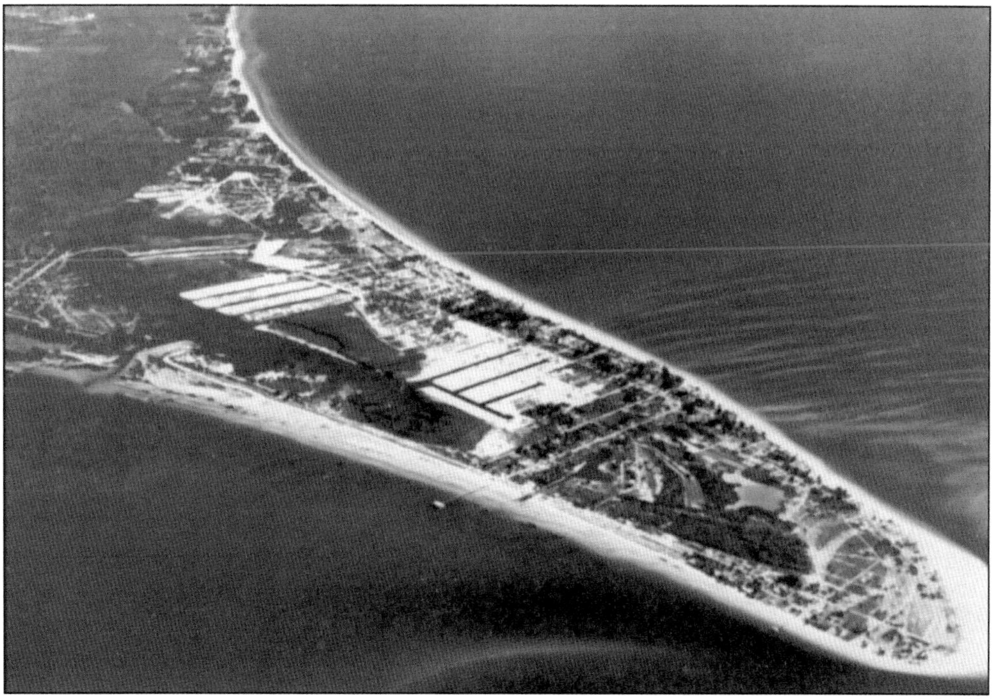

This view of the north end of Anna Maria Island from the 1960s shows the development reaching into Bimini Bay in Holmes Beach from the canal streets—Sixty-Sixth to Seventy-Fifth Streets—created by dredging sand and shell. Key Royale, on the left side of the photograph, shows signs of clearing for development. The Anna Maria and Rod & Reel Piers are visible at the bottom, and the long stretch of white beach on the Gulf of Mexico stands out.

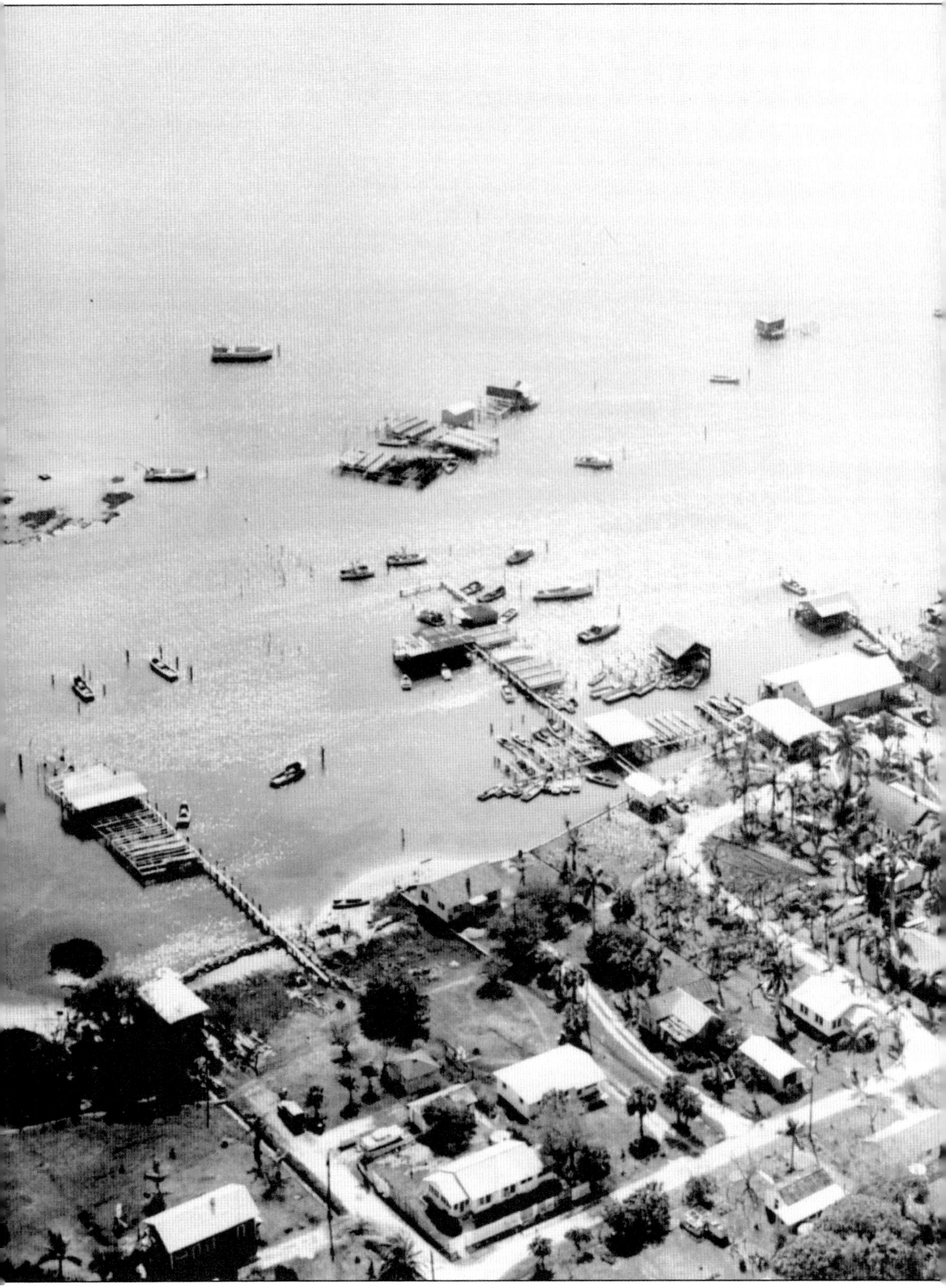

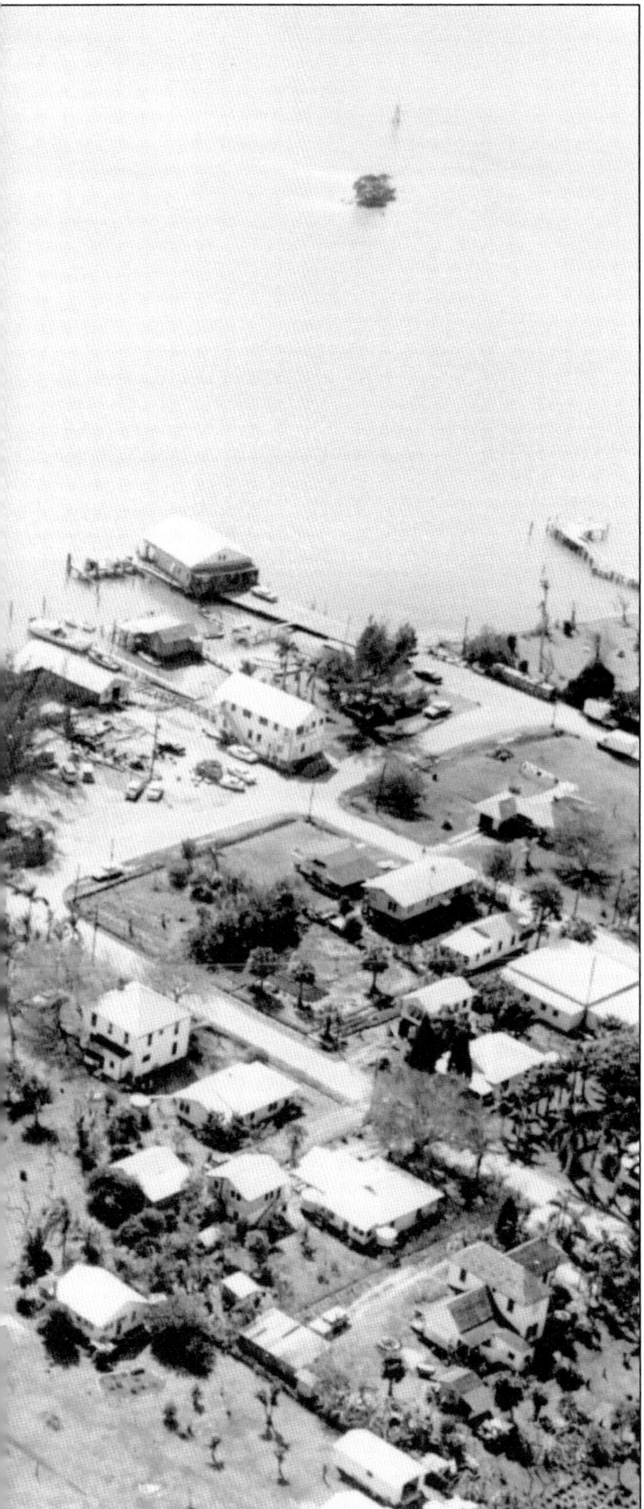

Just across Sarasota Bay on the mainland—a short ride on the Cortez Bridge that connects to Bradenton Beach—is the fishing village of Cortez. Its family-owned fish houses, situated on the bayfront, served a bustling commercial fishing industry until a statewide net ban in 1995 brought hard times to the village. Pictured here in the 1960s, the waterfront is dotted with fish-processing plants, boats, and net-drying storage racks.

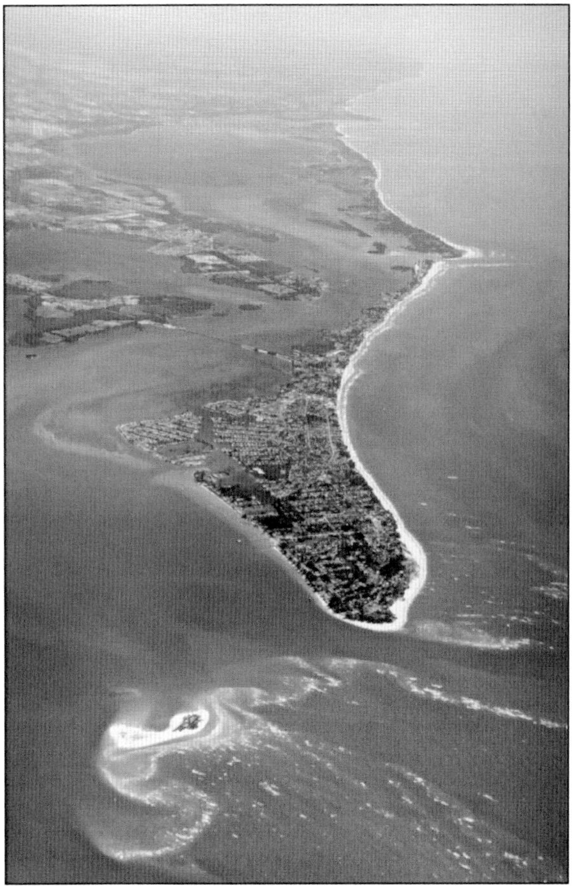

This view fast-forwards to 1987, and the seven-mile-long view of Anna Maria Island is white-sand beaches on the Gulf of Mexico, roads, canals, homes, and businesses. At bottom left is Passage Key, a wildlife refuge. Left of center are Perico Island and its growing home developments mixed with farmland; Cortez, a hopscotch of farmland; and, at the top, the long 17-mile expanse of Longboat Key, leading to Sarasota. (Photograph by Jack Elka, courtesy of the *Islander.*)

In 2014, the fascination for aerial views of Anna Maria Island and the surrounding azure waters grew exponentially, as did their popularity with visitors and newcomers. This view looks south from what is known as Bean Point, so named for the first homesteader, George Bean. (Photograph by Jack Elka, courtesy of the *Islander.*)

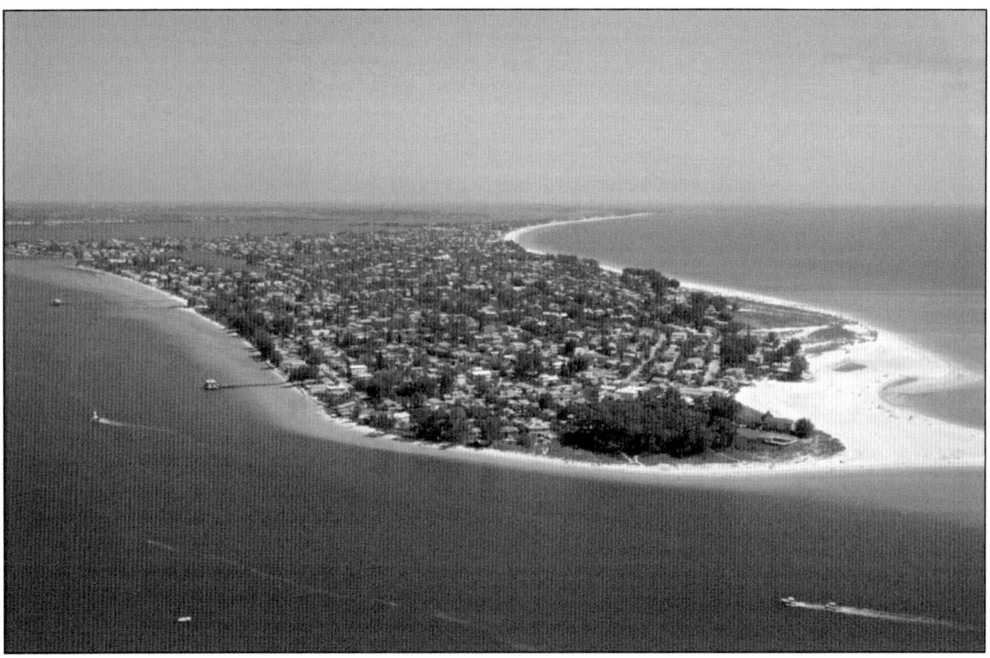

Seven

Bridges, Piers, Steamers

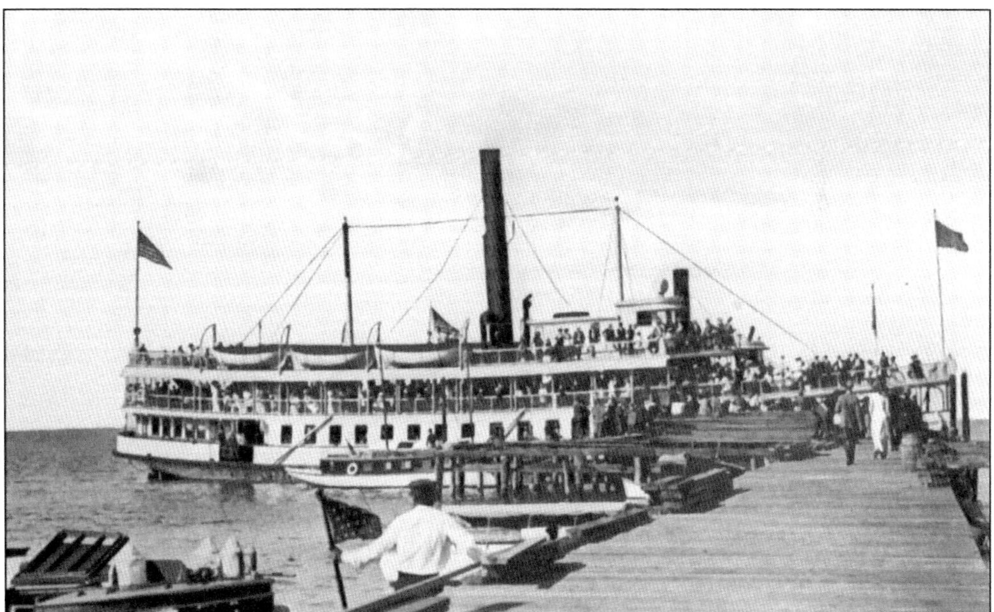

The Anna Maria Beach Pier was still under construction in 1910 when these visitors arrived aboard a steamer boat to walk the beach and enjoy the palm trees and gulf waters. Most visitors came to the island from Tampa at the beckoning of land-sales brochures and cottage builders. (Courtesy of the *Islander*.)

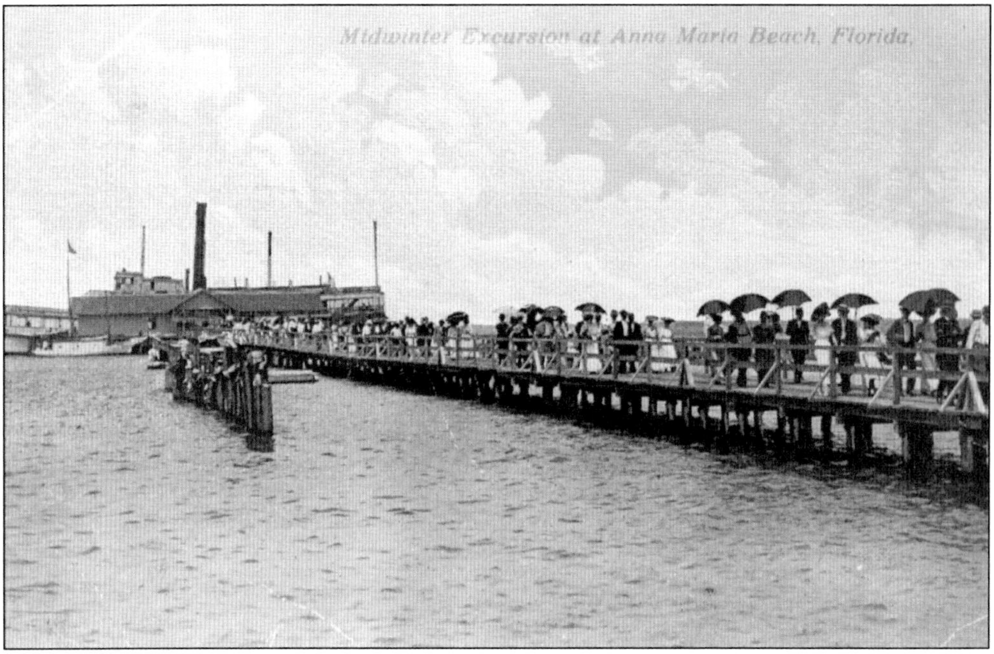

Passengers carrying parasols stream ashore in 1910 from the steamer *Favorite* while docked at the Anna Maria Beach Pier to visit Anna Maria Island—mostly overgrown with plants and trees but ripe for development. The steamboats most often carried eager buyers and day-trippers from Tampa looking to invest in a beach cottage and the island's tourist market. Smaller boats are moored to the pier landward of the *Favorite*.

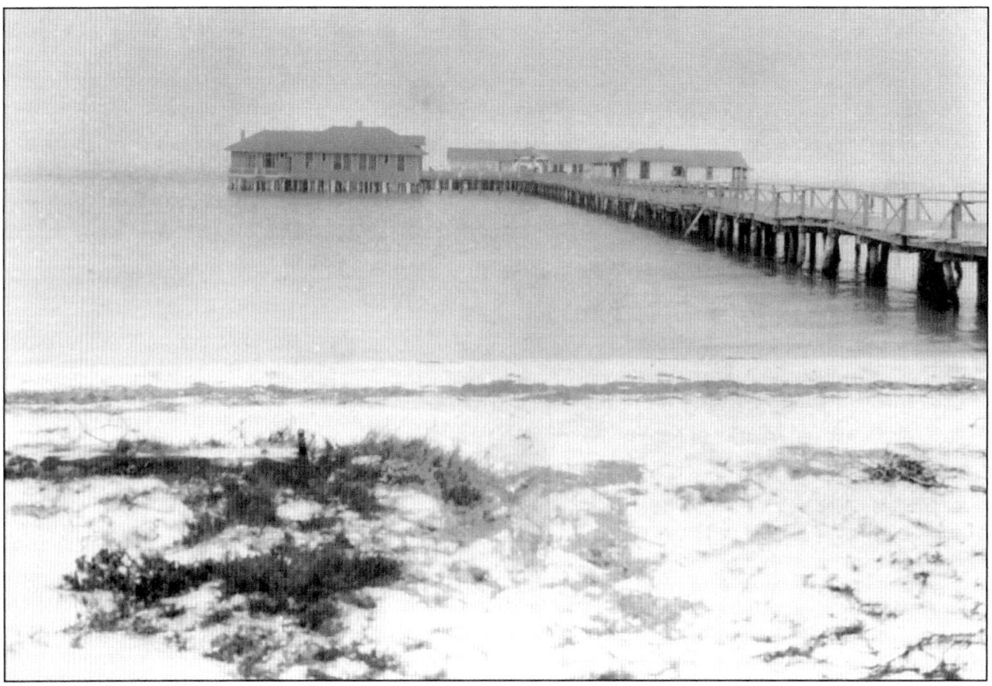

The Anna Maria Beach Pier fell into disrepair by the late 1910s, the result of being battered by storms. The two homes on either side of the pier were later removed, before the 1921 hurricane struck.

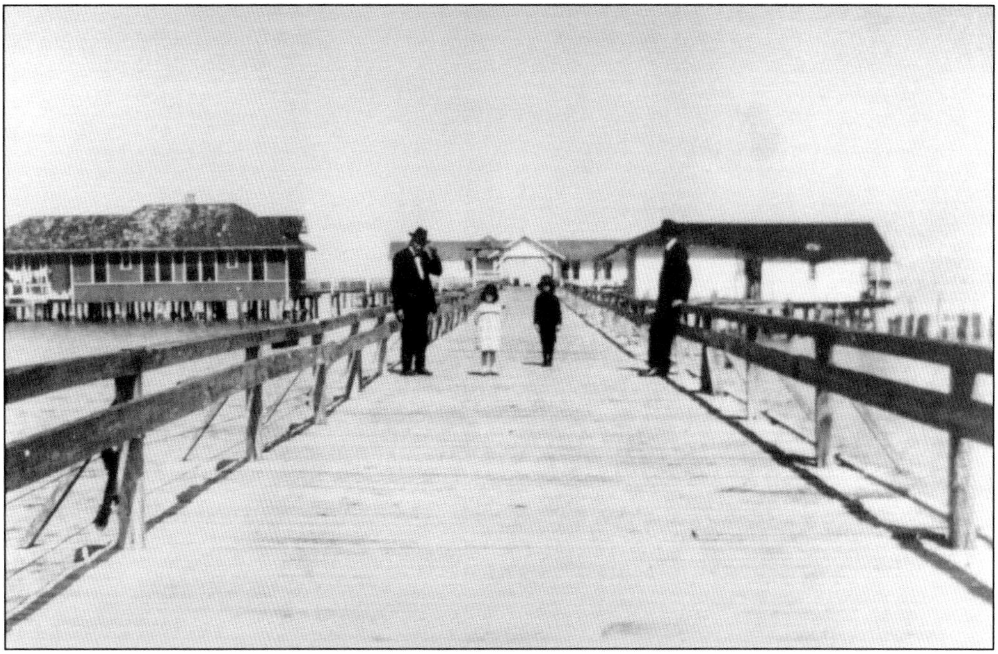

Two men and two young children walk the planks along the pier—minus the steamer boats that arrived bringing crowds of people to enjoy the beaches almost daily in the late 1910s.

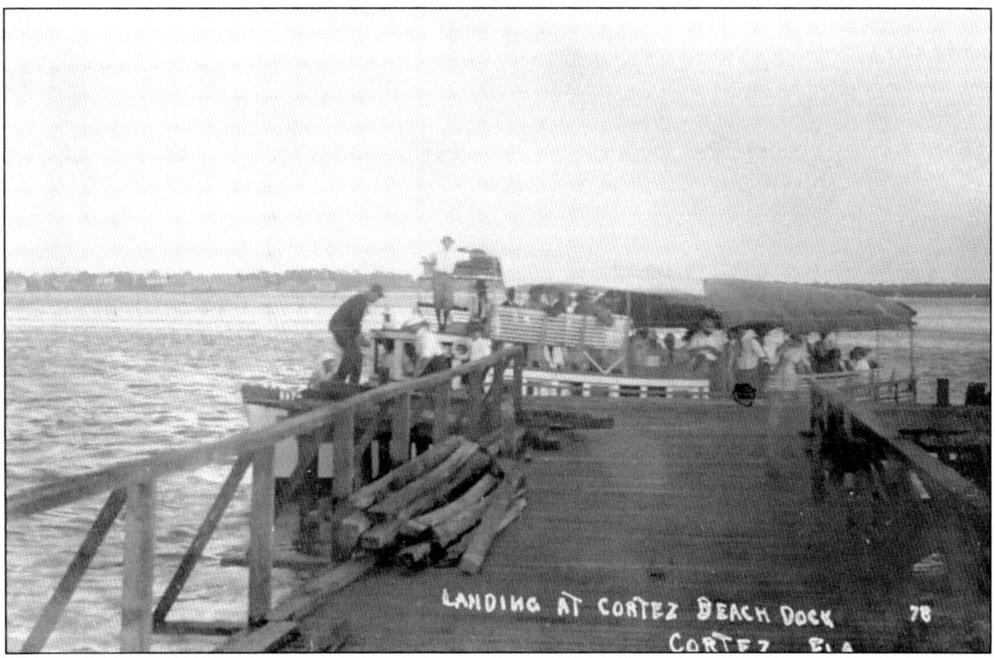

A boat lands in February 1916, five years before the wooden Cortez Bridge was built, at a wharf at Cortez Beach in south Bradenton Beach, ferrying people between Cortez on the mainland and Anna Maria Island.

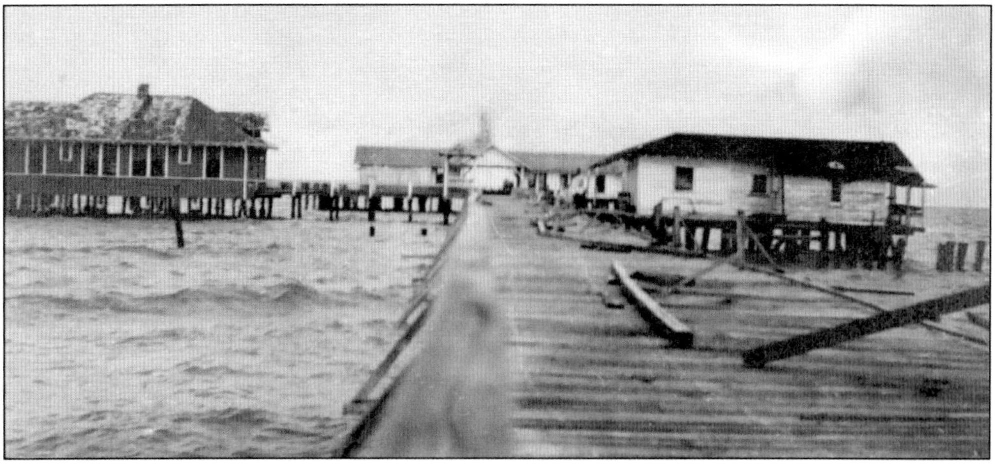

Damage to the Anna Maria Beach wharf—later named the Anna Maria City Pier—and the two homes built near the T-end in Tampa Bay is evident after a 1921 hurricane wrecked havoc. The homes were later removed.

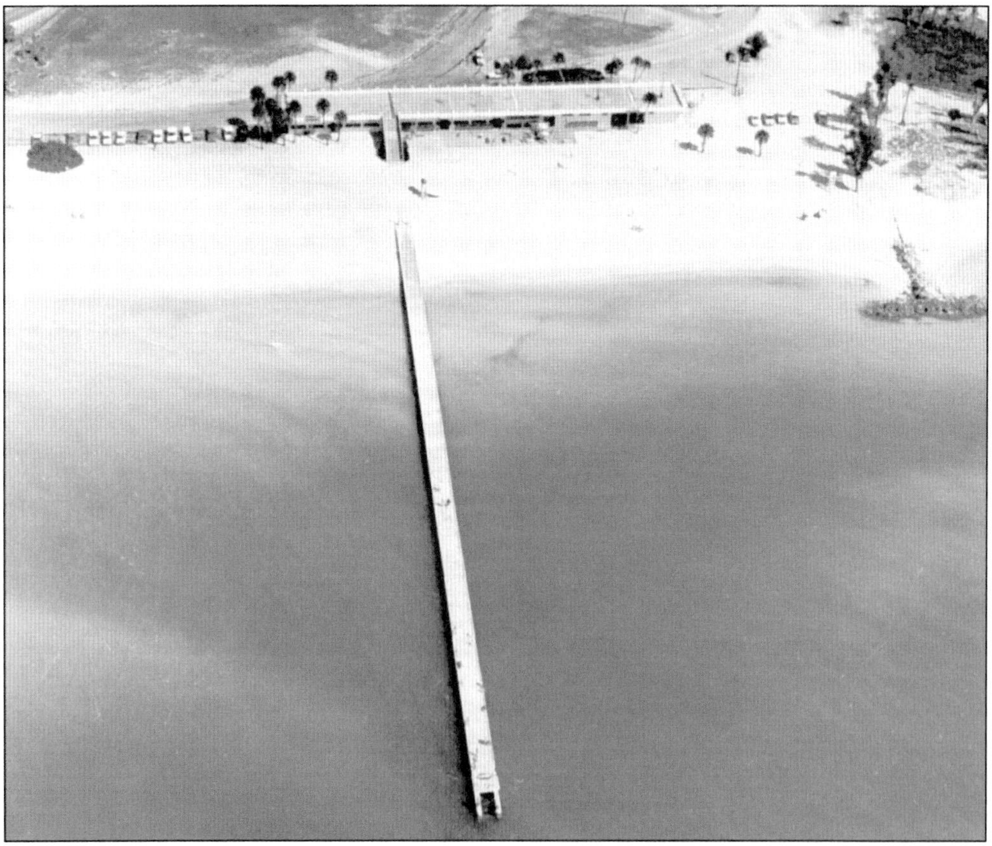

The Manatee County Public Beach is pictured in this 1964 image, which shows the new pavilion complete with a rooftop for dances and parties at night and a cascading stairwell from the roof to the beach, which leads to the pier and Gulf of Mexico. A patio on the west side provides dining space for the snack bar and the open pavilion was used by guests for events, parties and picnics. The pavilion now is home to a gift shop and the Anna Maria Island Beach Café.

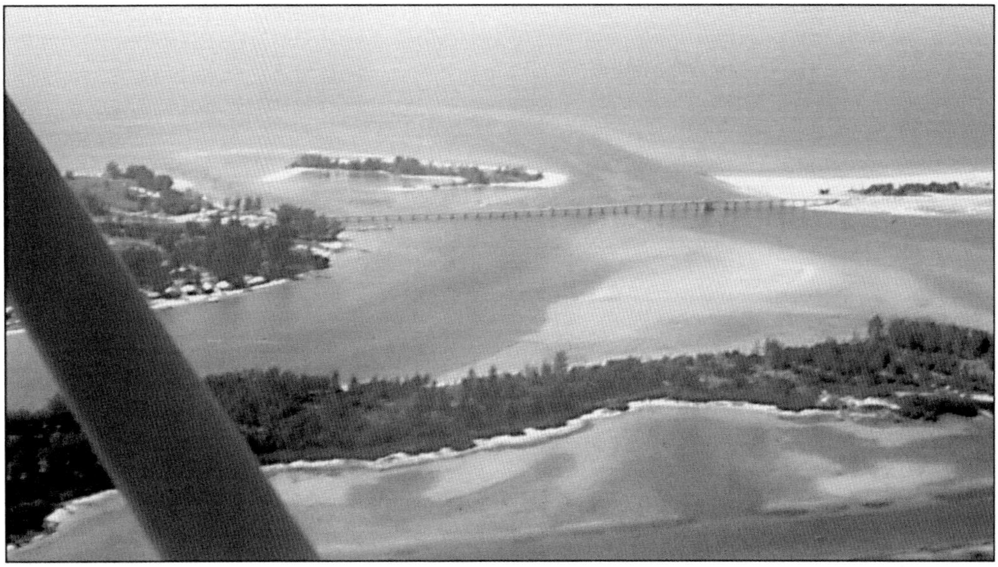

The newly completed Longboat Pass Bridge, pictured in 1961, carries vehicles to and from Bradenton Beach and Longboat Key. This bridge, along with its sister bridges at Cortez Road and Manatee Avenue, linking Anna Maria Island to the mainland, were part of Manatee County's 1955–1957 bridge program.

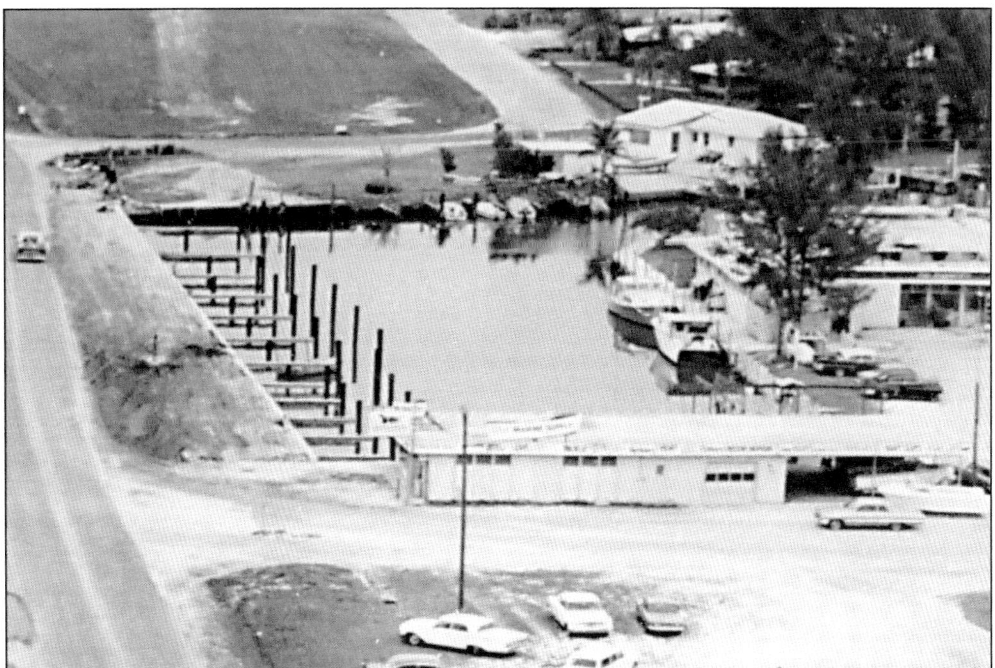

An aerial view in 1970–1971 of Watson's Bayou and Pete Reynard's Yacht Club Restaurant shows a marine-supply store and boat-service area in the foreground as well as plenty of dock space along a barren Marina Drive (no curb, no sidewalk) as a car at the left heads north. At the top of the photograph is the tip of the Holmes Beach Airport runway. At the top right is a home that also served as a marina and service station.

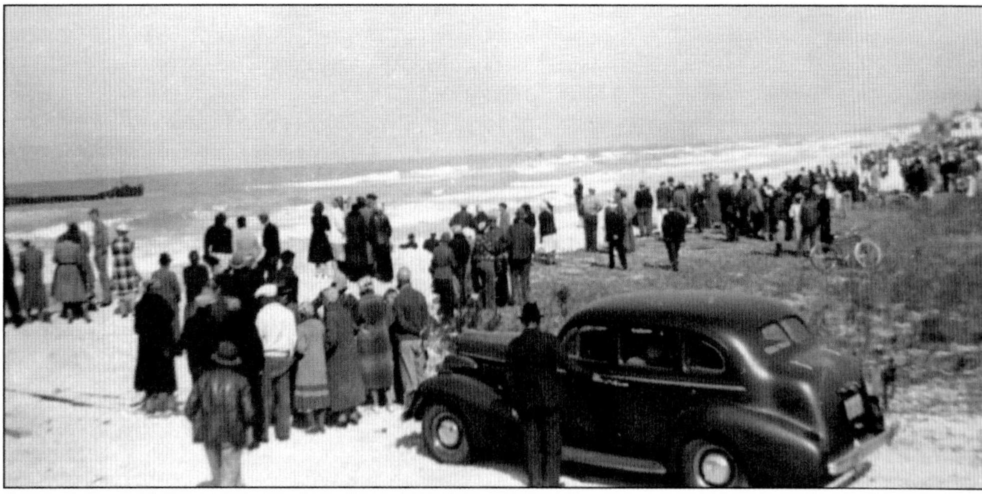

Spectators gather along the beach in Bradenton Beach in 1940 to witness the sinking of the 300-foot-long molasses barge *Regina*. It was a converted tanker, loaded with 350,000 gallons of Cuban molasses, when caught by stormy seas. Clayton Adams of Cortez and other local men were credited with rescuing the crew as the temperature dropped below 40 degrees. The ship's cook, Severino Canisares, and mascot, a German shepherd dog, died trying to swim to shore. The water and the beach were filled with brown globs of molasses for months. The site, north of Cortez Road, is now designated a Florida Underwater Archaeological Preserve.

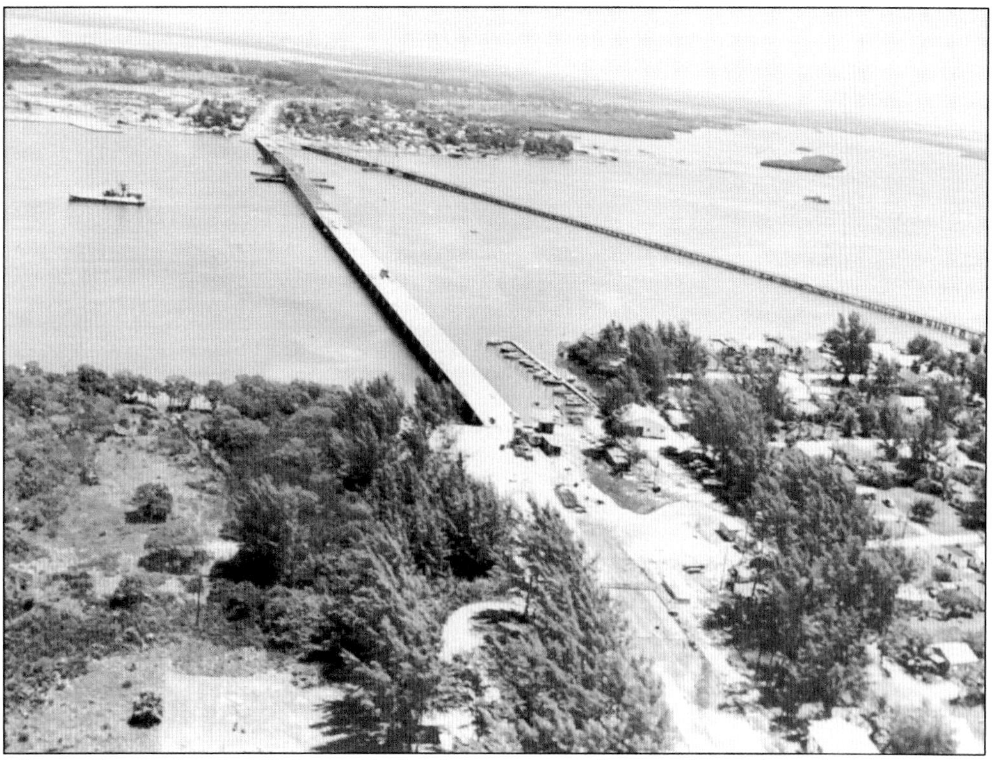

The nearly completed 1957 Cortez Bridge, left, is seen in this aerial view from above Bradenton Beach, looking eastward across Sarasota Bay to Cortez Village. The rickety 1921 wooden Cortez Bridge was still in use while the new bridge was under construction.

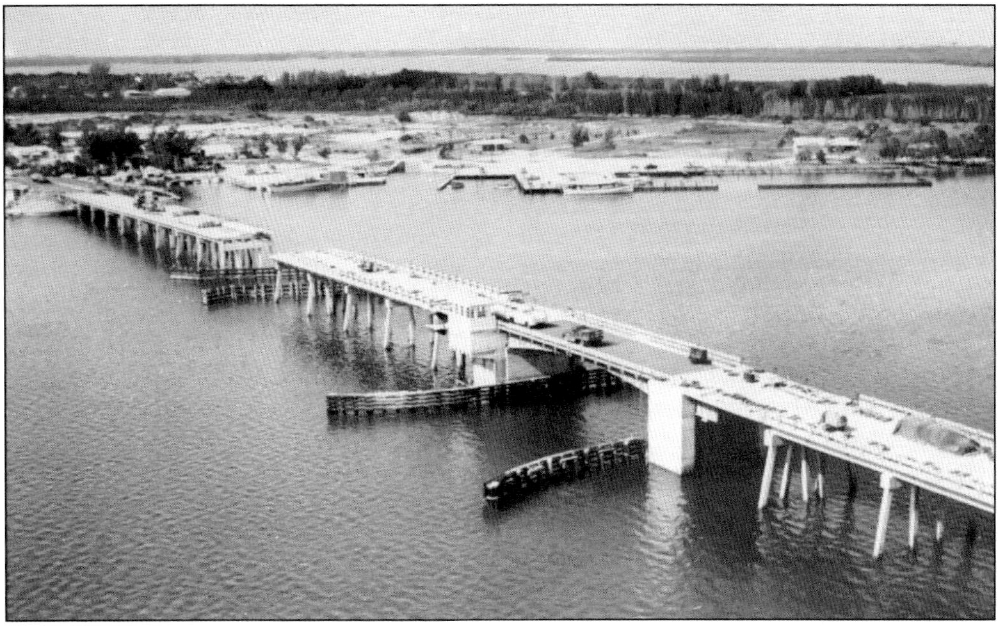

Construction is almost completed on the new bascule bridge linking Cortez to Bradenton Beach. With one section to finish on the new bridge, the old wooden bridge that opened in 1921 would soon be removed on the Cortez side but will remain for a fishing pier at the end of Bridge Street in Bradenton Beach. This view is looking toward Cortez, with few homes built around the new bridge landing area.

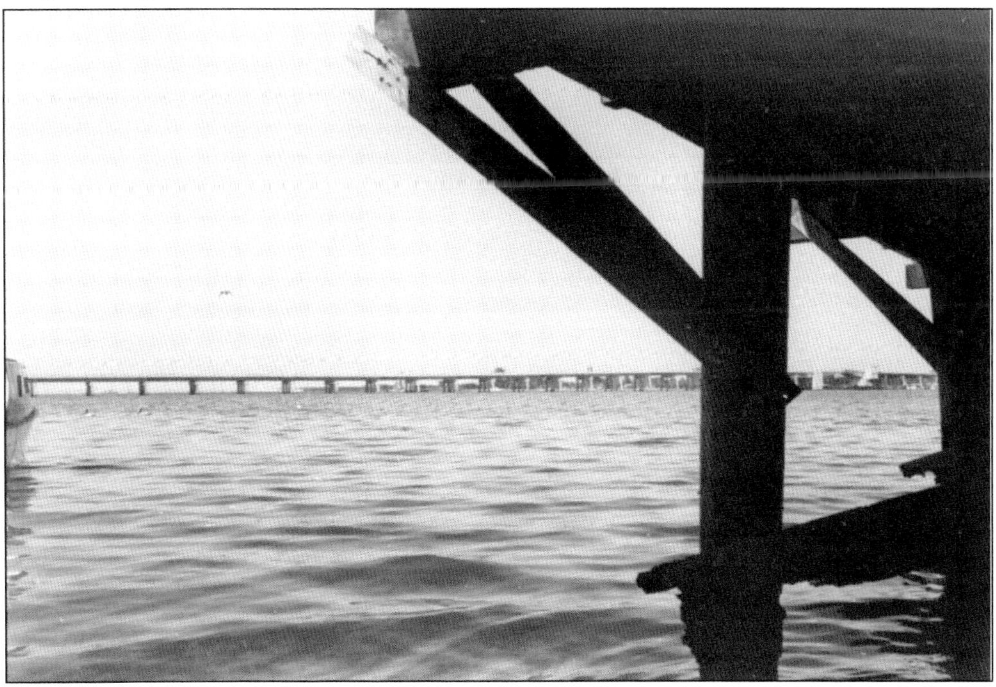

In a 1957 view looking northeast to Cortez from the pilings under the 1921 wooden Cortez Bridge, the new drawbridge spans Sarasota Bay. The landward portion of the old bridge on the island was salvaged for use as the Bradenton Beach Fishing Pier.

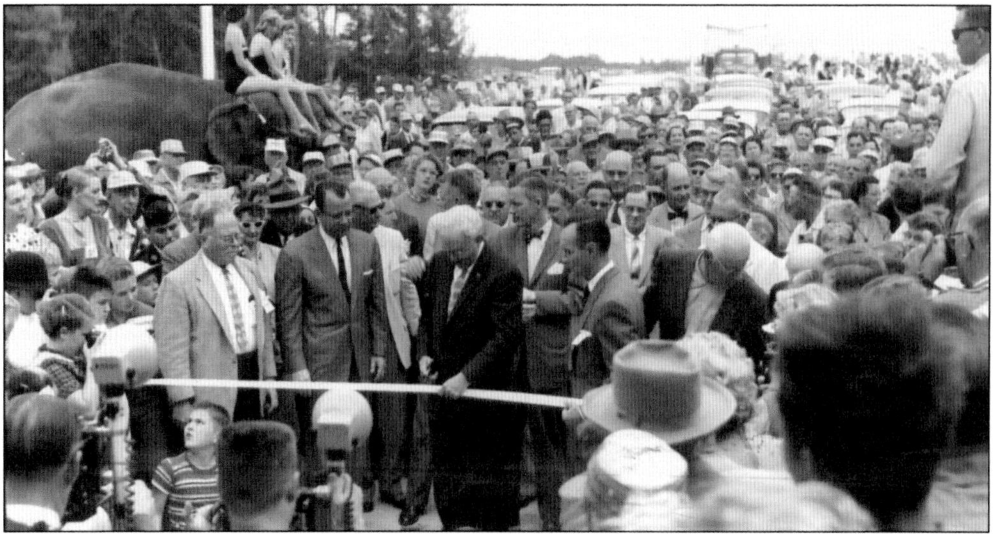

A celebration took place in March 1957 with the opening of the Cortez Bridge, replacing the one-lane wooden bridge. Elephants and bathing beauties were the first to cross the Cortez Bridge from Bradenton Beach landing to Cortez at the event. The Florida Department of Transportation opened three bridges linking to Anna Maria Island in 1957, but the celebration focused on the Cortez Bridge—the long-awaited replacement to what had been the only bridge to the island for 36 years. (Both, courtesy of the Florida Department of Transportation.)

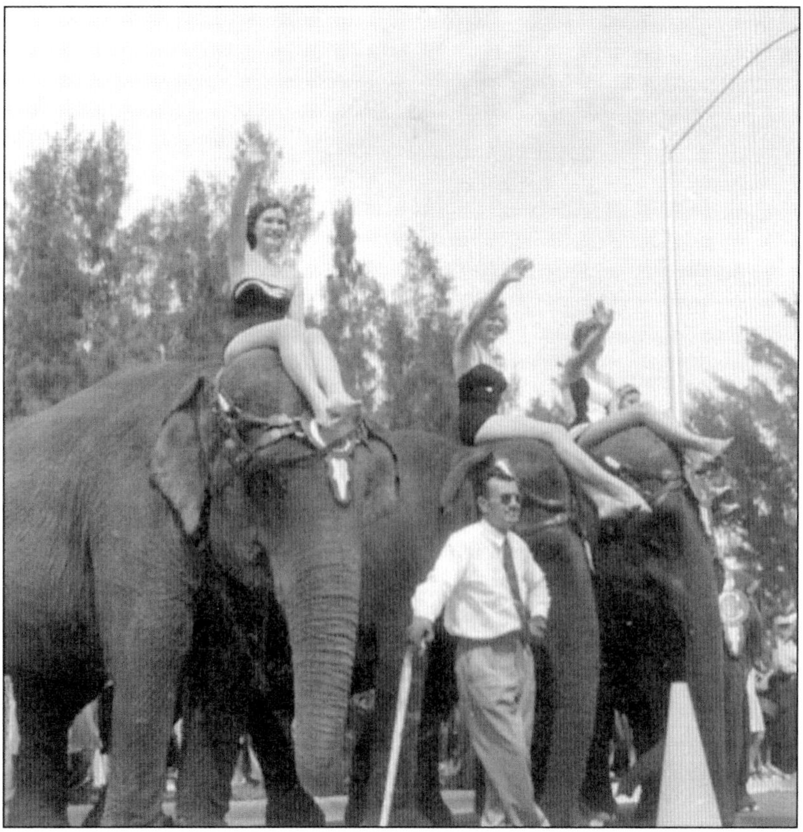

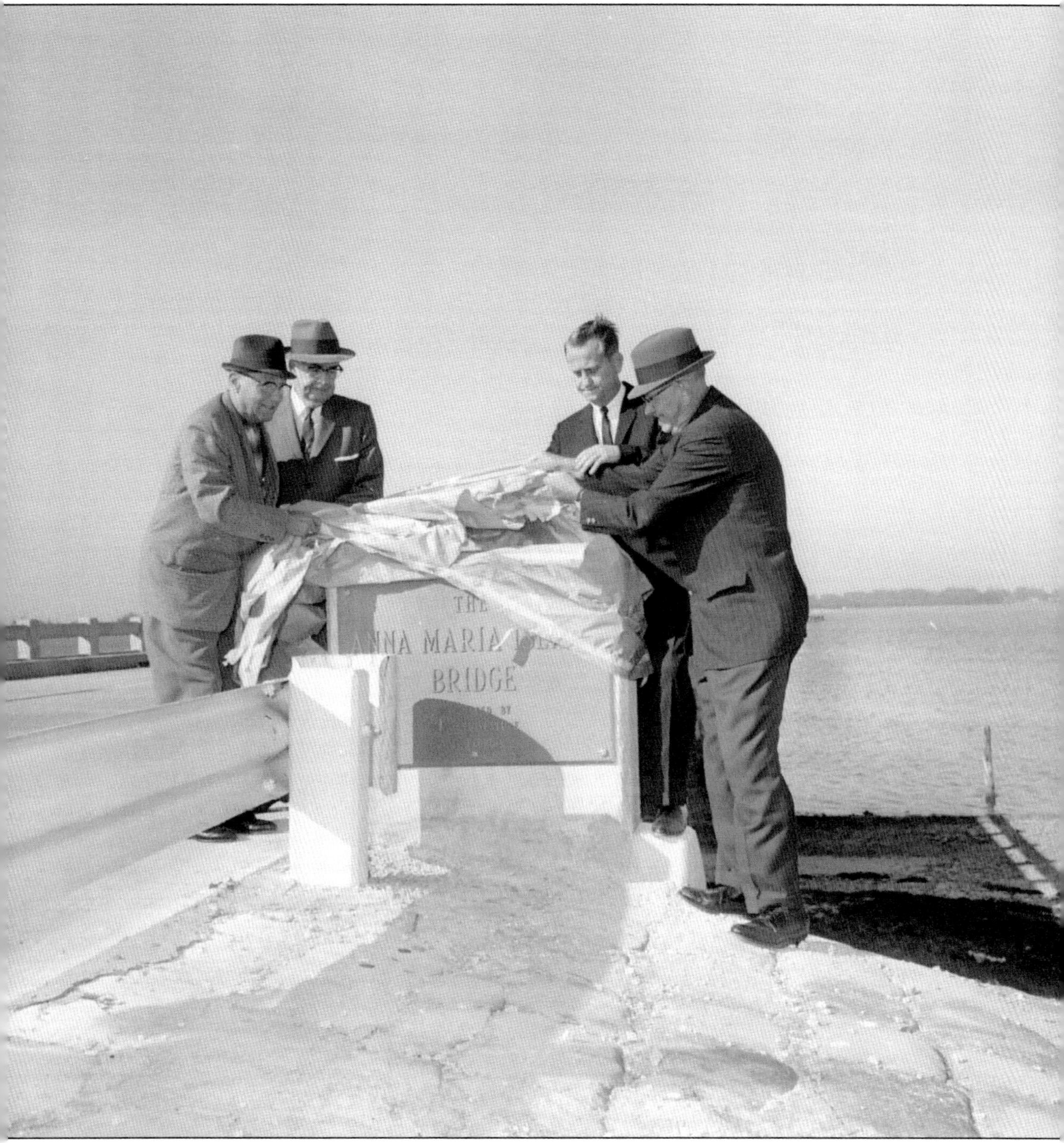

From left to right, Mayor Robert Kraft, Mayor Elmer Twist, Wilbur Boyd, and Mayor Harvey Meyer reveal the plaque for the Anna Maria Island Bridge on Manatee Avenue at a dedication in 1965. This bridge, along with its sister bridges at Cortez Road and on State Road 789, linking Anna Maria Island to Longboat Key, were part of Manatee County's 1955–1957 five-bridge program. The marker was erected eight years after the bridges were completed and opened.

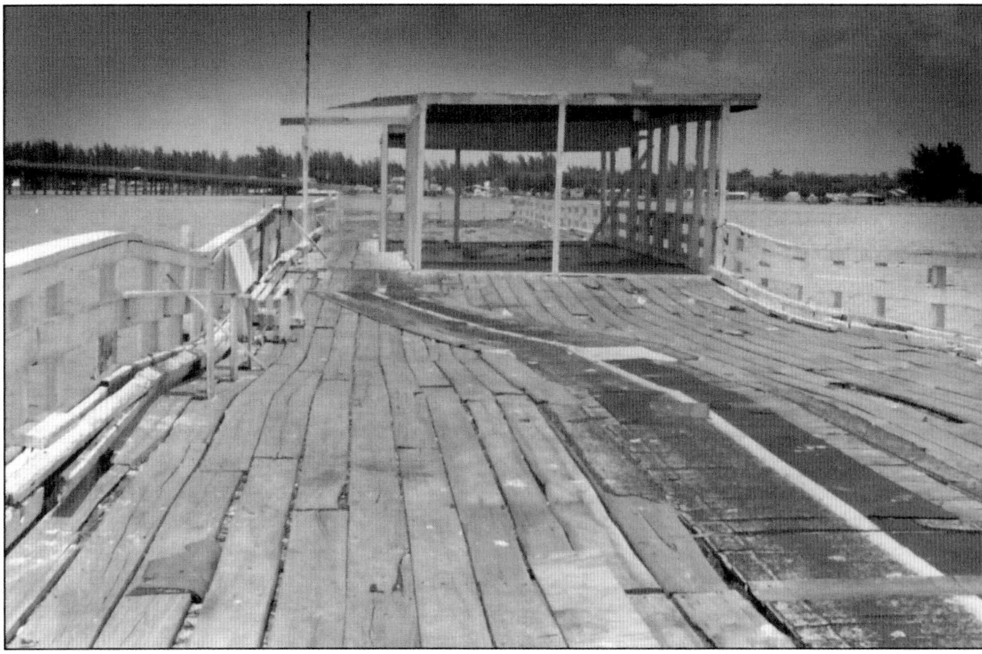

Pictured here are the remains of the 1921 wooden bridge, now shortened to a fishing pier where it connects to the Bradenton Beach waterfront. The pier was in dire need of repair in 1960. It got some repairs, and more rehabilitation was to come in the future, including a complete rebuild in 2014. (Courtesy of the *Islander*.)

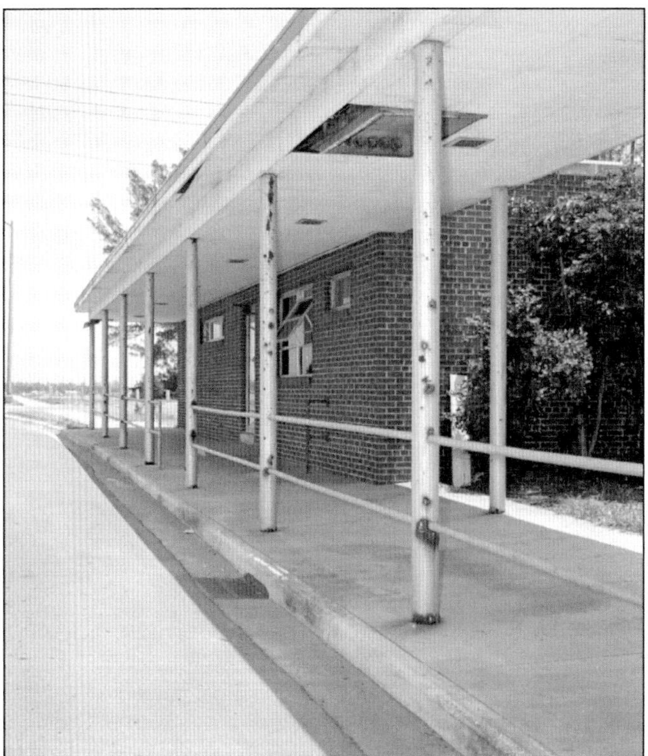

In 1970, with the cost of the Cortez Bridge recouped from 13 years of 10¢–25¢ tolls paid by users, the Bradenton Beach Police Department used the former toll booth as a city jail. It was later torn down, but the police department remains nearby, along with the public works department and a new cellular communications tower that became operational in 2015.

By the late 1960s and early 1970s, the Anna Maria Beach Pier had become city property and was named the Anna Maria City Pier. Opposite the foot of the pier across Bay Boulevard is the Anchorage tavern, while vehicles are parked along a row of erosion-control rock groins that reach into Tampa Bay to help preserve the shoreline at the Lake LaVista inlet on the left side.

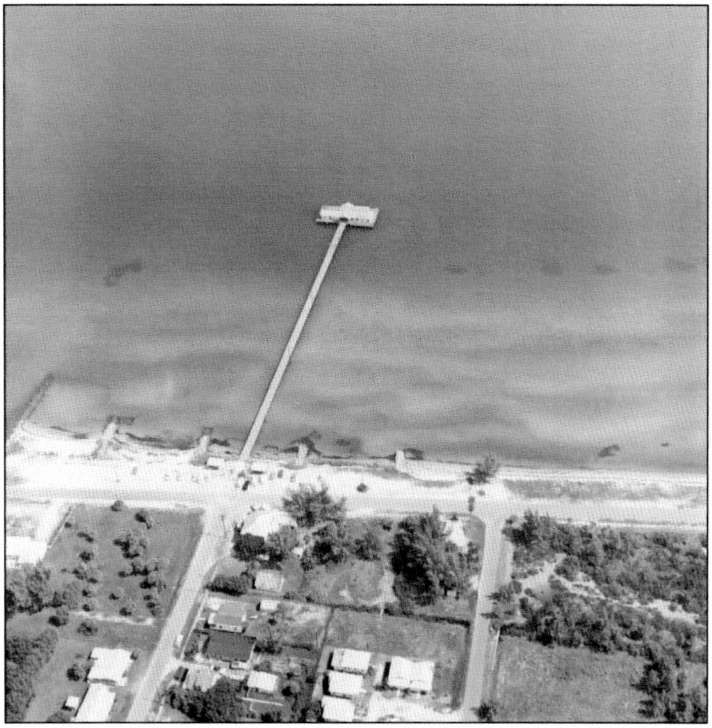

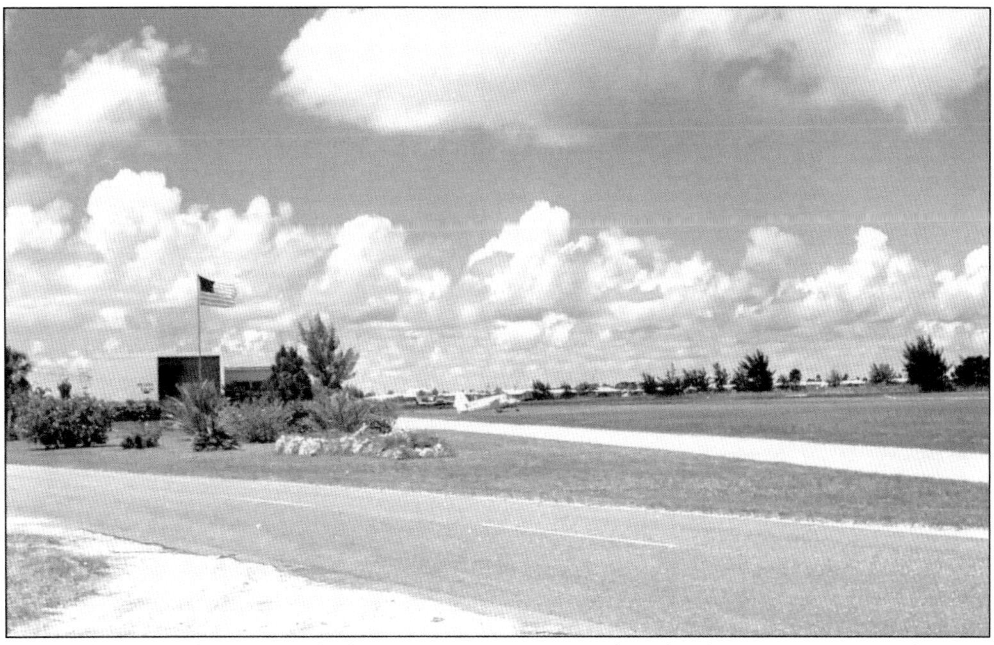

The Holmes Beach Airport, built in 1947, was positioned on land on Marina Drive donated to the city by residential developers. Several adjacent homeowners maintained private planes in hangars attached to their homes. It closed in the early 1970s, and over the next decades the property became host to a new station for West Manatee Fire Rescue District, a Manatee County Library branch, a new Holmes Beach City Hall, Pete Lannon Skate Park, Birdie Tebbetts Field, a dog park, and a soccer field.

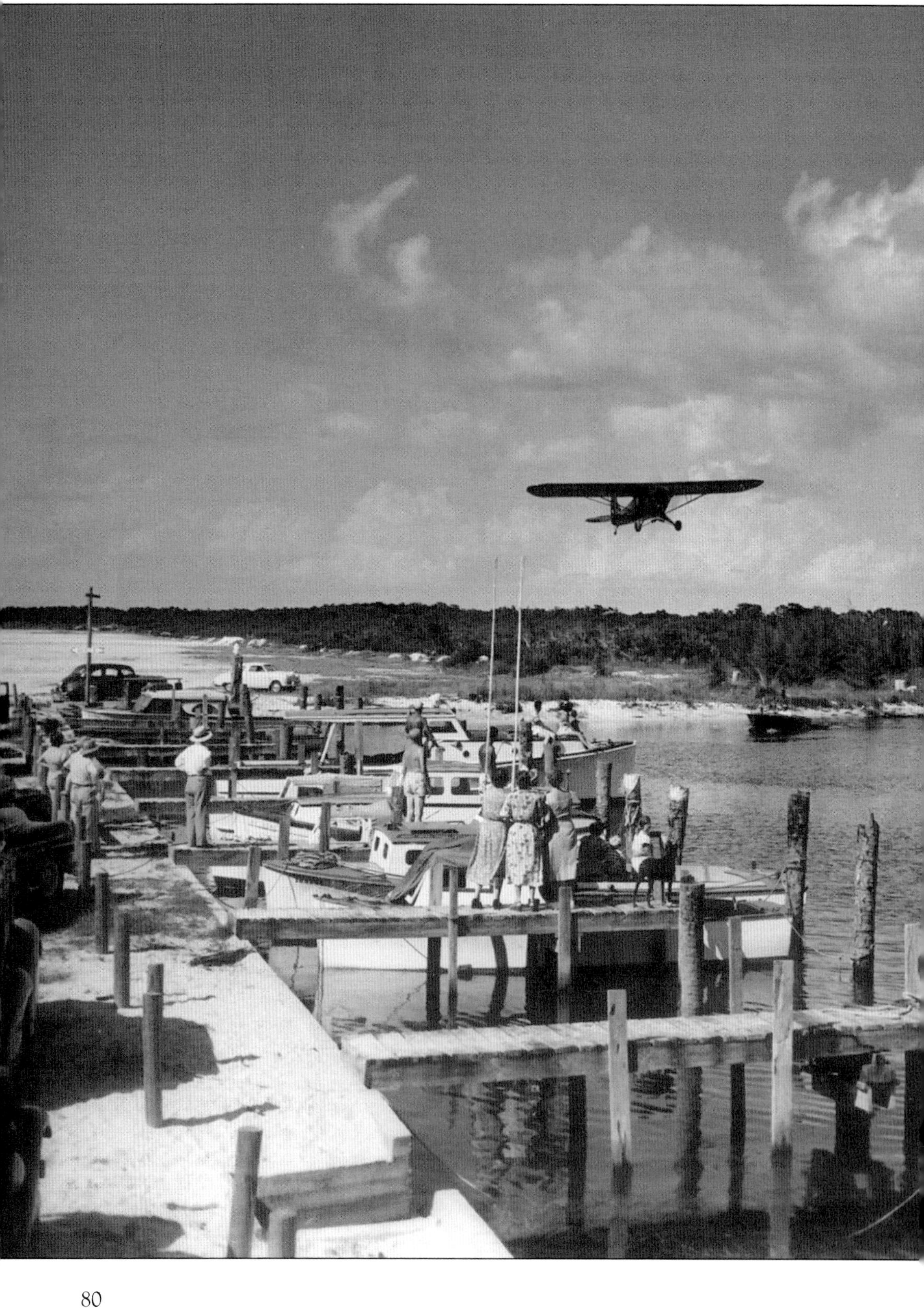

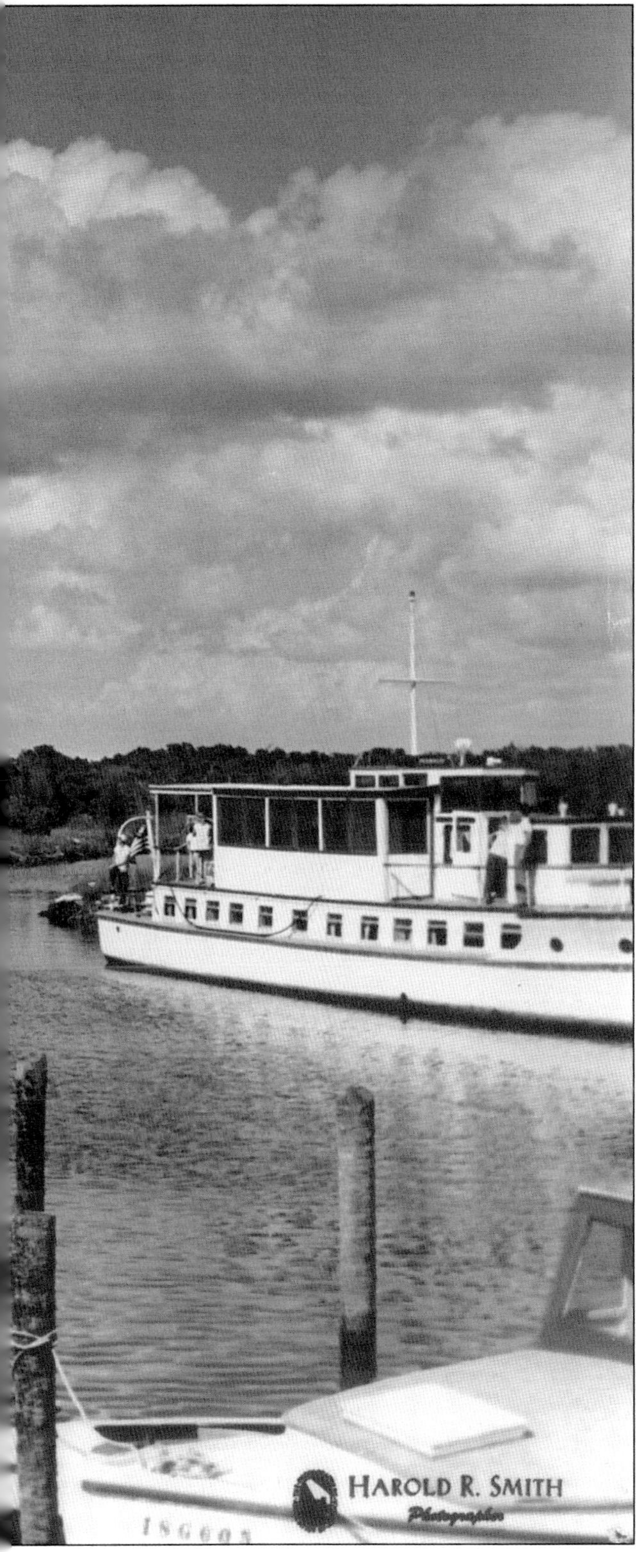

With only one bridge to the island, to the south in Bradenton Beach, the Holmes Beach Airport was likely responsible for much of the development that sprang up mid-island after the single shell-and-sand runway was laid out in 1947. This plane is taking off over Watson's Bayou, where docks serve large and small boats along what would become Marina Drive. (Courtesy of the Anna Maria Island Historical Society.)

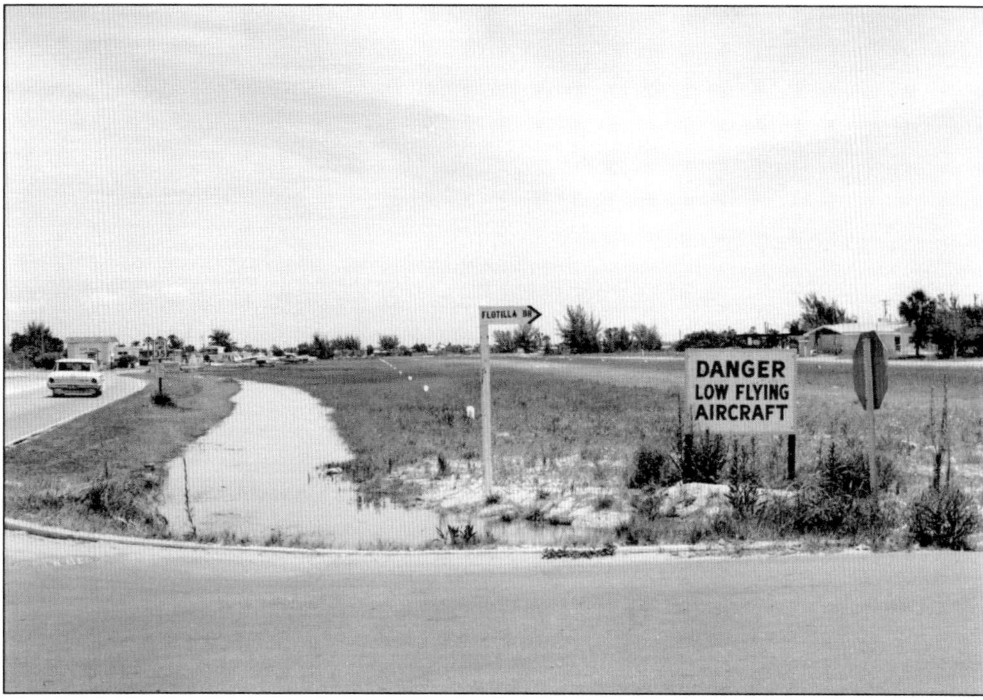

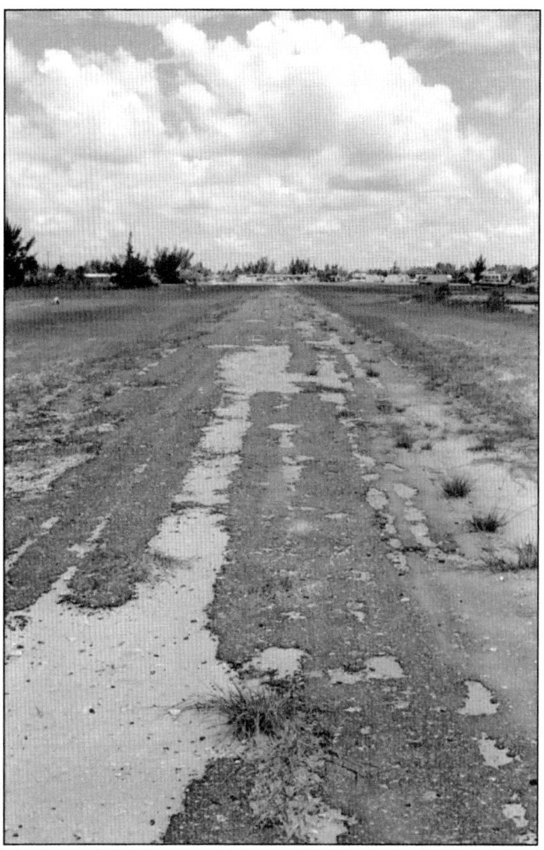

A danger sign is posted in 1972 at the intersection of Marina and Flotilla Drives in Holmes Beach on the south side of the field for the Holmes Beach Airport. Planes sit on the ground facing the runway. City hall (far left) has since been replaced, and what is left of the field is used for events, including arts and crafts shows and an annual Anna Maria Island Chamber of Commerce Cityfest. The area closest to the sign is home to the Island Library, and adjacent to that is a new city hall and police department.

Holmes Beach Airport, built in 1947, was on the brink of closure in 1972, following several accidents. In spite of a vote by residents to keep it open, the runway was in need of repair, and several transportation agencies wanted the airport closed.

Eight

Storm Season

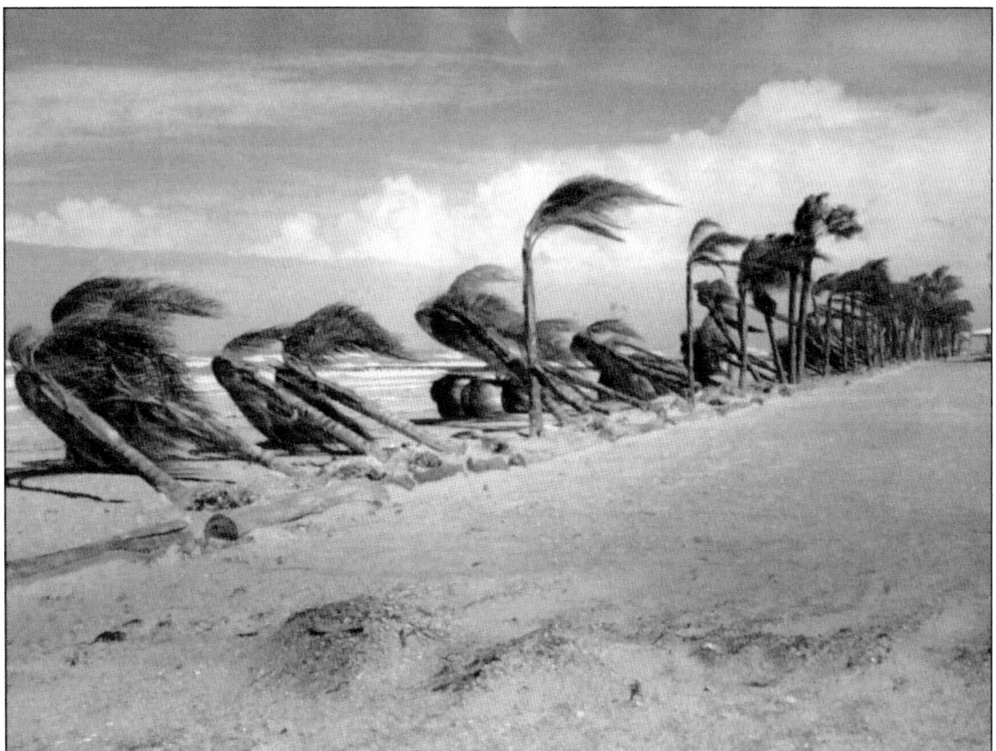

Mowed down like bowling pins, some newly planted graceful palm trees at Coquina Beach topple in the tropical storm–strength winds that sometimes visit Anna Maria Island's shore. (Courtesy of the *Islander*.)

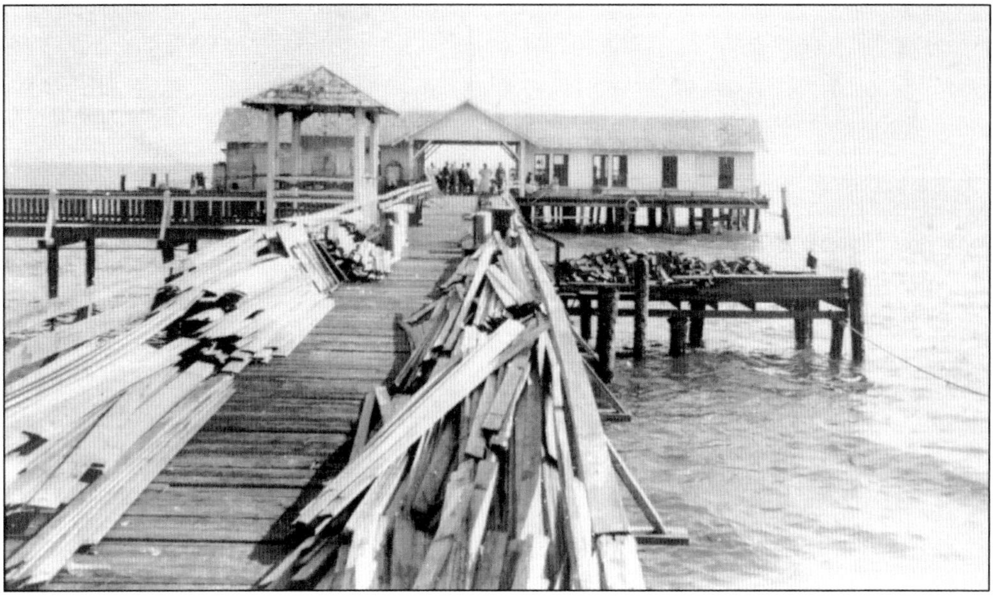

The Anna Maria City Pier, situated just south of the south entry to Tampa in the Tampa Bay channel, suffers damages from passing storms in the Gulf of Mexico. No direct hits by hurricanes have occurred on the island, but hurricane-force winds in the gulf can bring high surf and wind to the beaches.

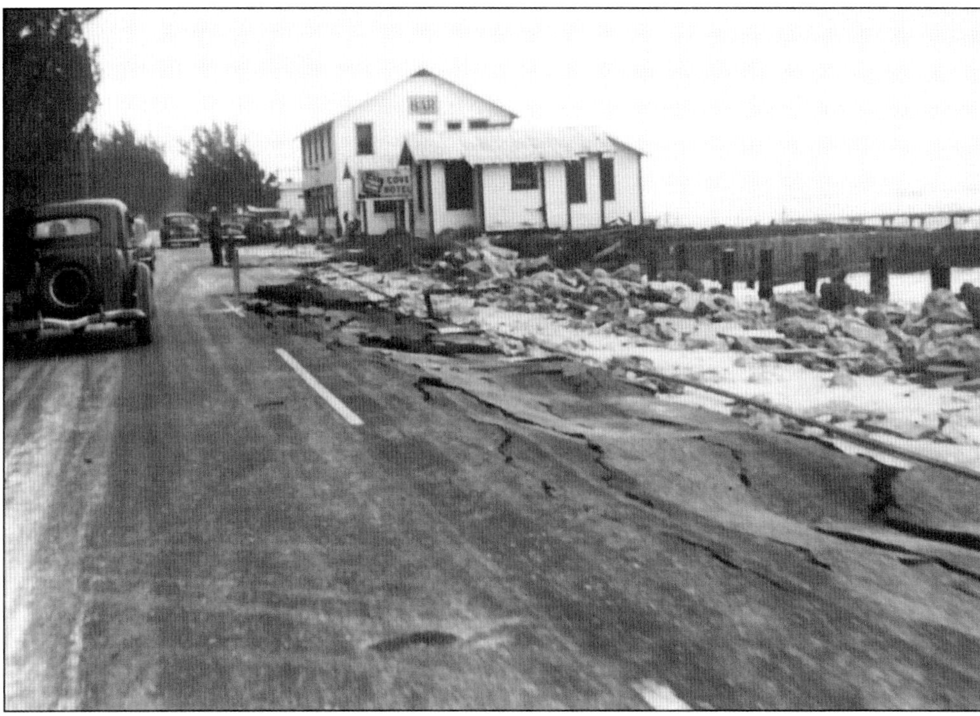

In 1950, the first year storms in the Atlantic Basin were given names, Hurricane Easy stalled early in September after crossing Cuba into the Gulf of Mexico. As it passed in the gulf, high winds and surf left the road crumbled in Bradenton Beach by the Cove Motel and Bar. (Courtesy of the *Islander*.)

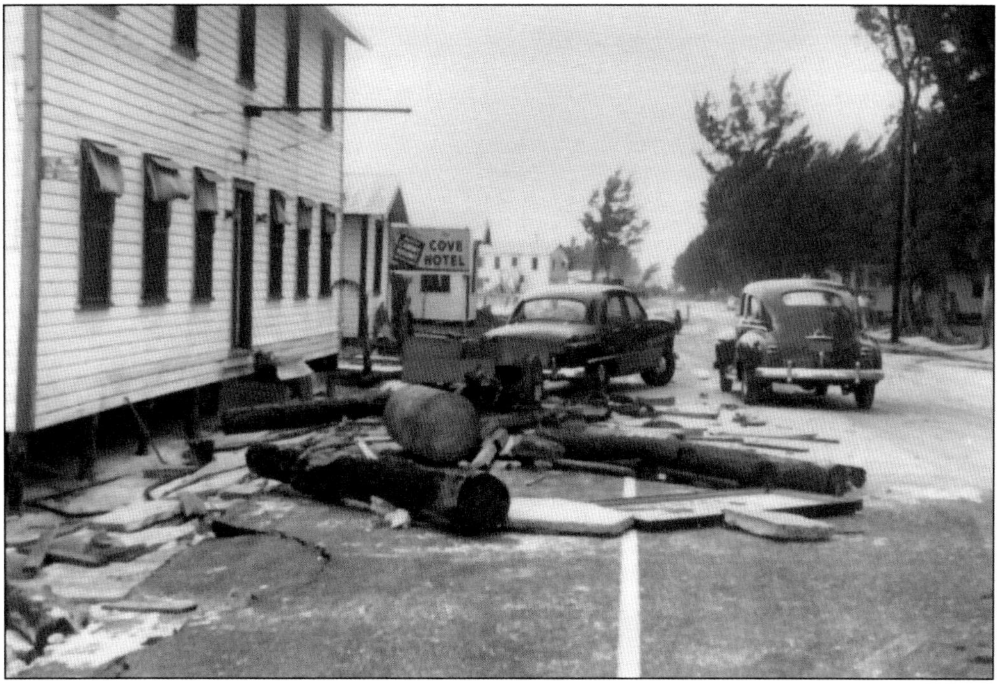

Another view of the Cove Motel in Bradenton Beach in September 1950 shows major structural damage after Hurricane Easy passed by Anna Maria Island in the Gulf of Mexico on the way from Cuba to Cedar Key, where it made landfall. (Courtesy of the *Islander*.)

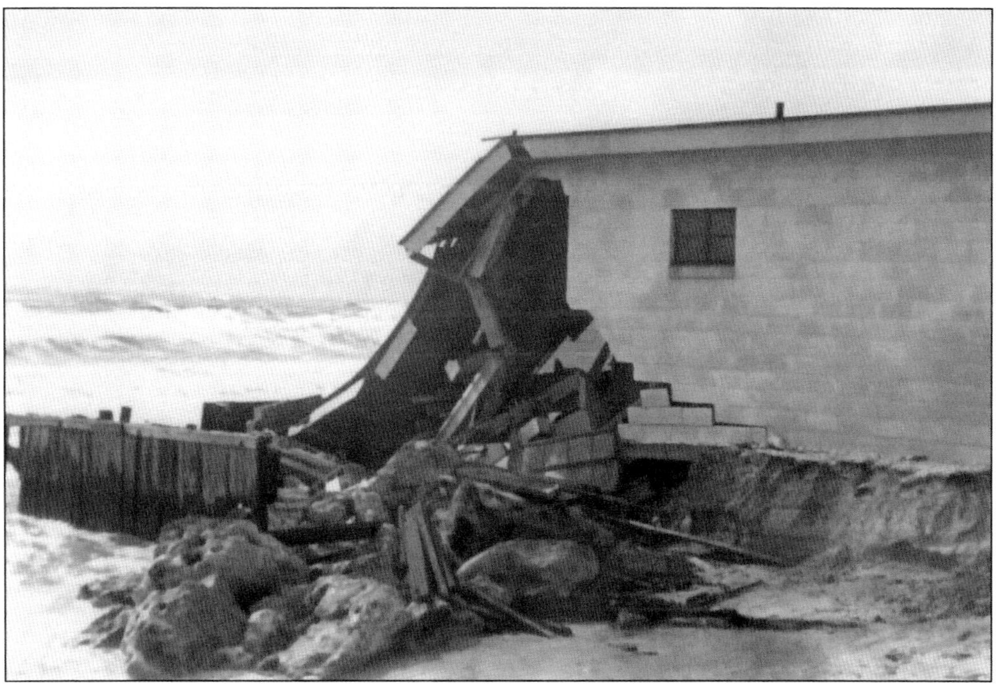

Pictured here is more damage from Hurricane Easy: a building that extended over the Gulf of Mexico shoreline was washed out at the foundation and crumbled from the bottom up in the large shoreline break that resulted from the storm. (Courtesy of the *Islander*.)

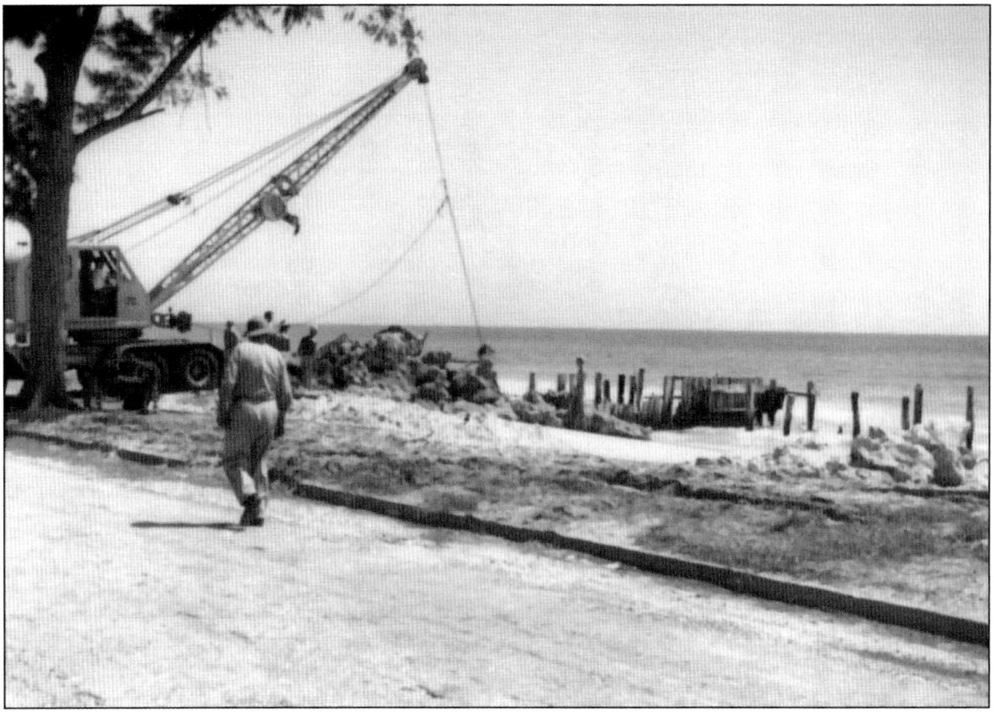

A contractor works to build a revetment in June 1949 to protect Gulf Drive/State Road 789 in Bradenton Beach, where storms threatened to wash out the road. Bradenton Beach made a concerted effort to get help for the main north-south artery from the Florida Department of Transportation upon incorporation in 1951. (Courtesy of the *Islander*.)

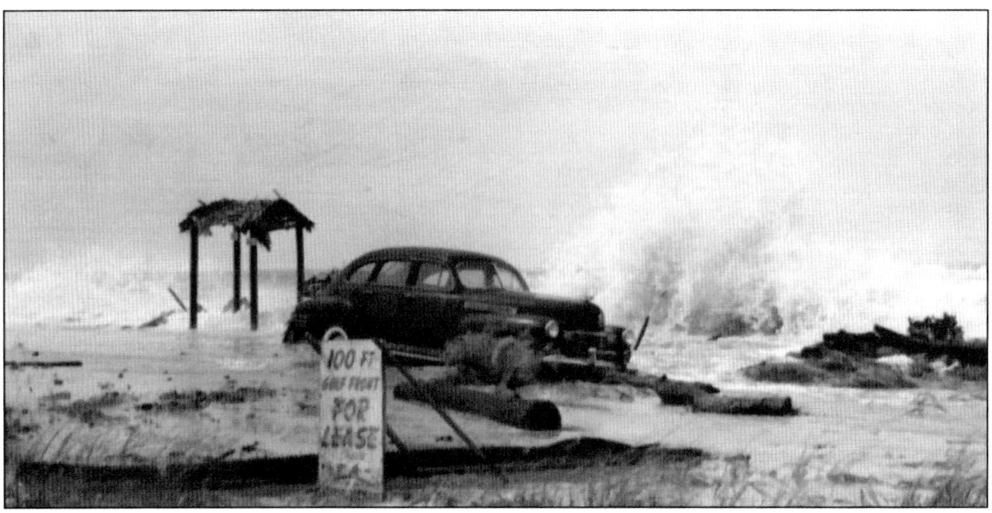

A car sits in a parking lot on the beach, which has been inundated with waves and surf that moved palm tree trunks aside and pushed debris landward. A sign offers the property for lease, but no price is named. (Courtesy of the *Islander*.)

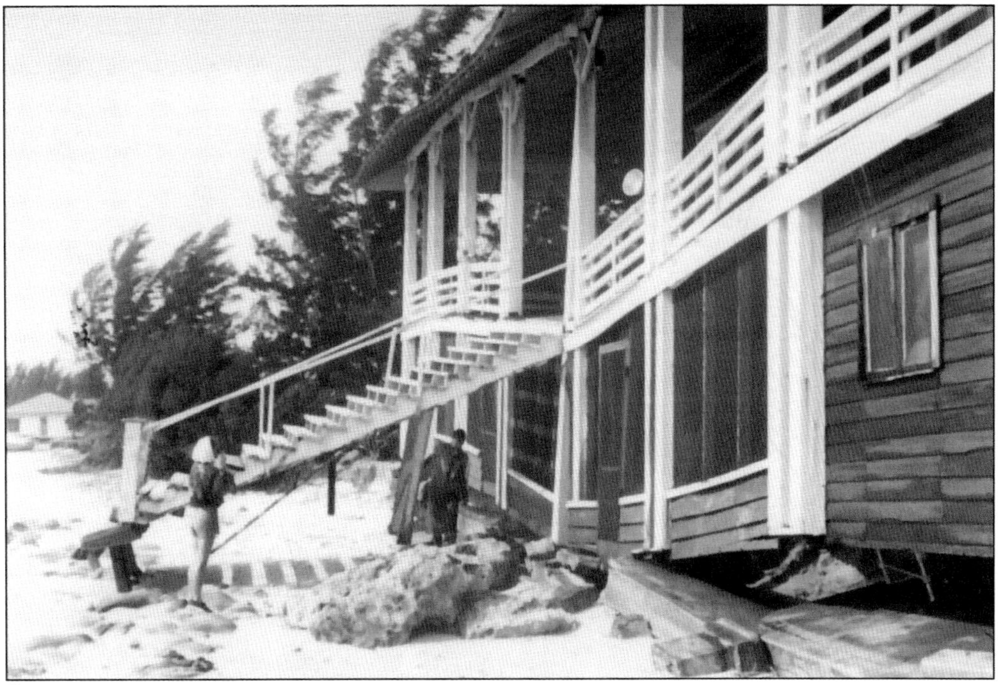

Hurricane Donna made landfall in September 1960 in Fort Myers, but its storm bands reached north across the state and through the Gulf of Mexico to damage the Gulf Park Hotel in north Bradenton Beach. (Courtesy of the *Islander*.)

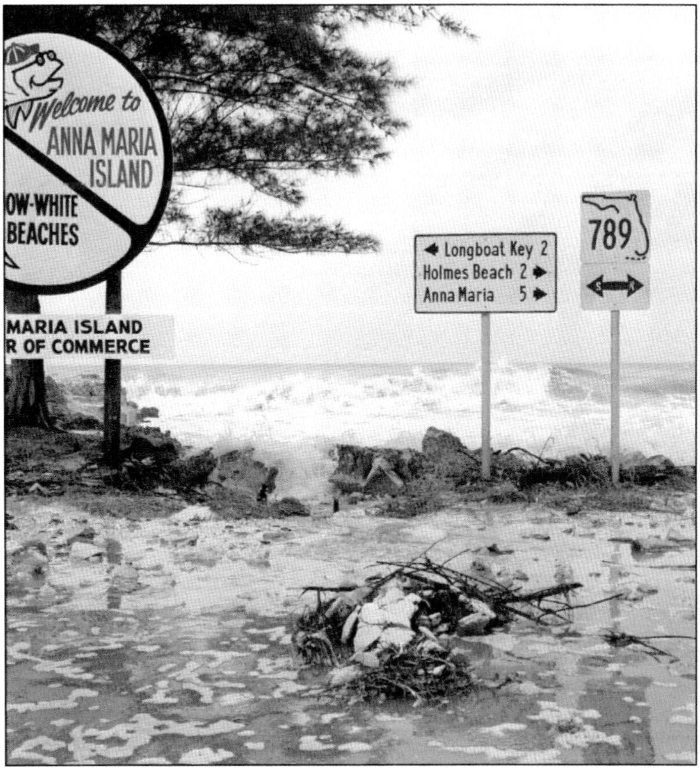

This picture of a chamber of commerce welcome sign at the entry on Cortez Road to the seven-mile length of Anna Maria Island was taken shortly after Hurricane Betsy passed in the Gulf of Mexico in September 1965. Gulf Drive/State Road 789 at the intersection with Cortez Road flooded often and was reinforced several times over with an extensive rock revetment and finally, in 1992, revitalization of the beach.

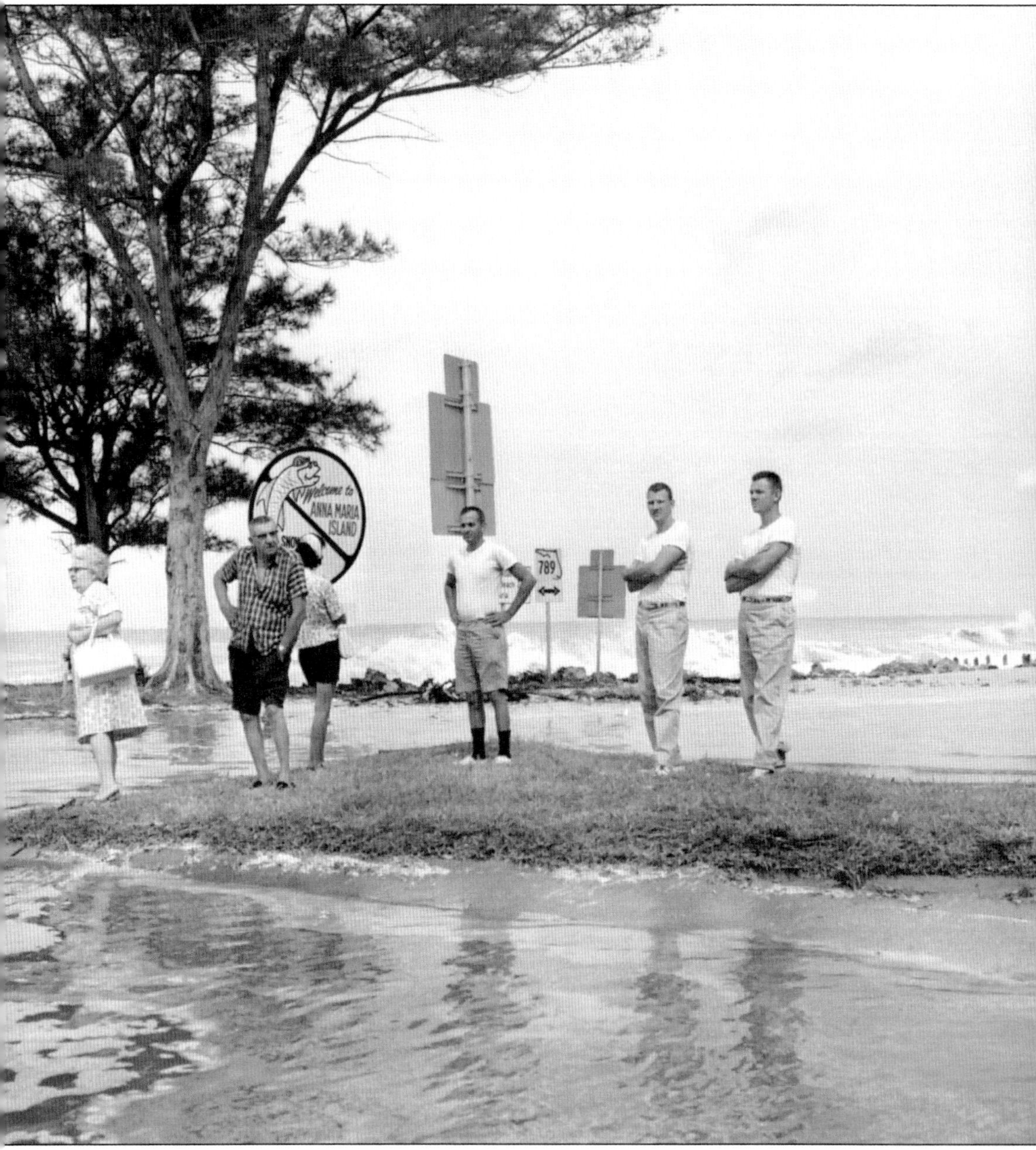

At the same Gulf Drive/State Road 789 intersection, some people look for a chance to cross the road; others survey the damage after the road was flooded by the tidal surge from Hurricane Betsy in 1965.

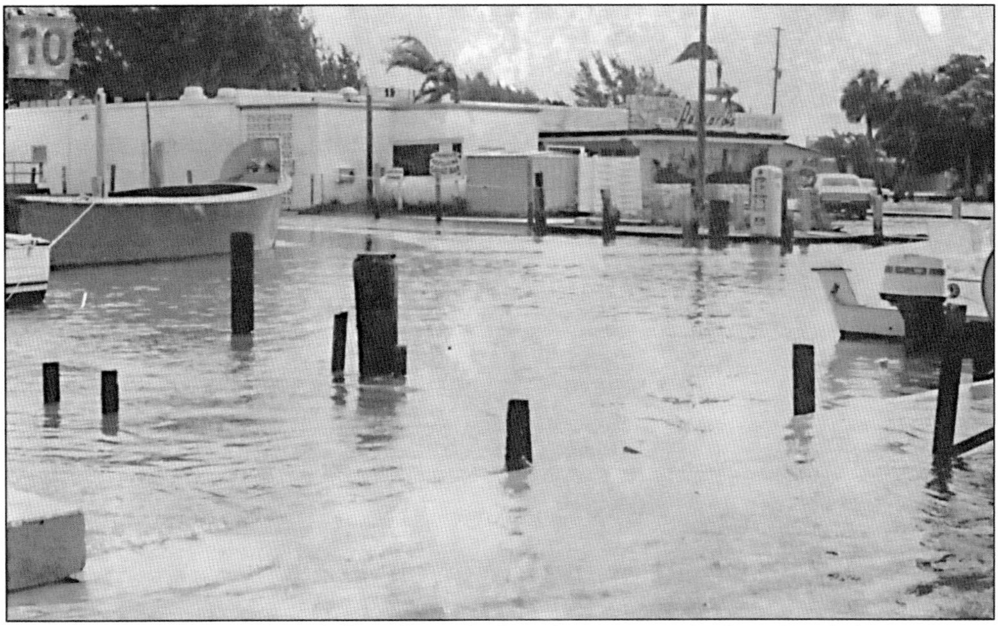

Storm water in the streets and the tide in the boat basin rise in Holmes Beach, bringing new meaning to waterfront dining at the landmark restaurant of the 1960s and 1970s, Pete Reynard's Yacht Club Restaurant. The boat basin provided dock space for charter-fishing captains and diners arriving by water to the restaurant, where a gas pump provided service to boaters. (Courtesy of the *Islander*.)

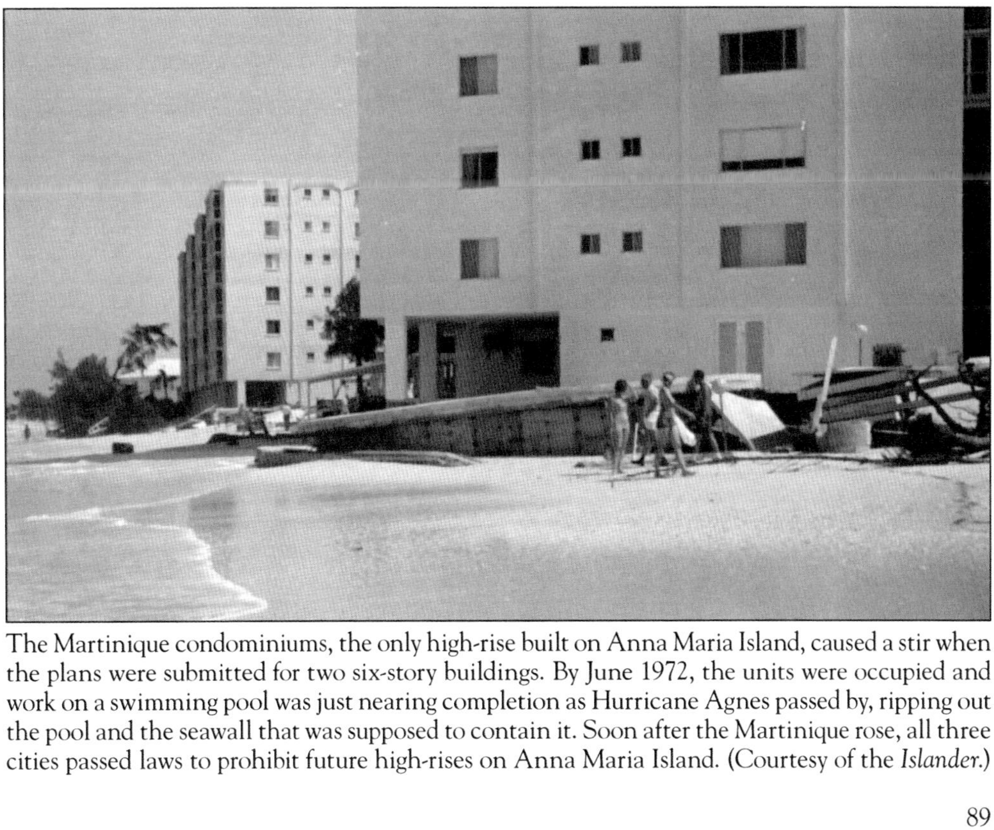

The Martinique condominiums, the only high-rise built on Anna Maria Island, caused a stir when the plans were submitted for two six-story buildings. By June 1972, the units were occupied and work on a swimming pool was just nearing completion as Hurricane Agnes passed by, ripping out the pool and the seawall that was supposed to contain it. Soon after the Martinique rose, all three cities passed laws to prohibit future high-rises on Anna Maria Island. (Courtesy of the *Islander*.)

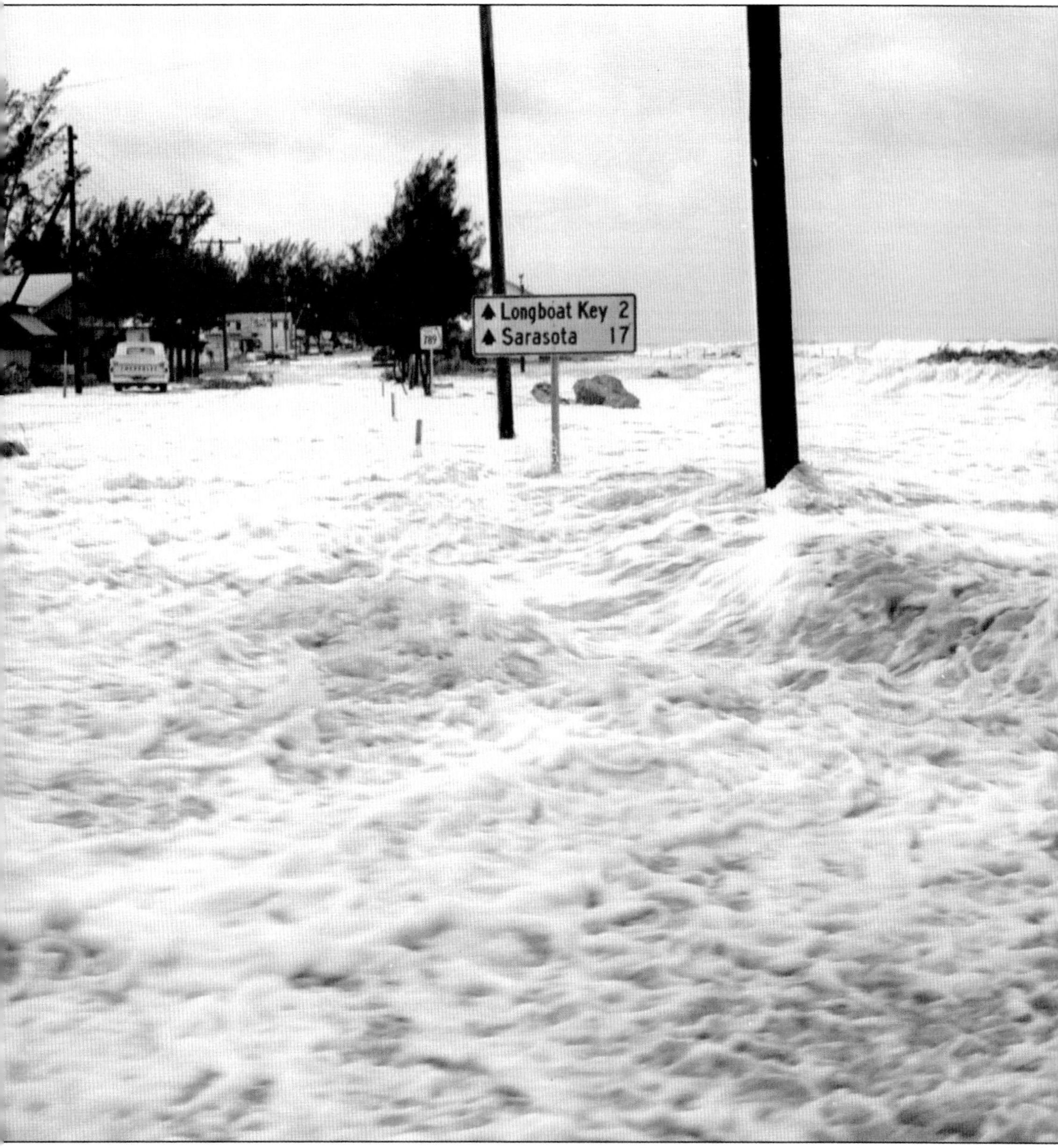

In September 1965, Hurricane Betsy left Gulf Drive in Bradenton Beach flooded in her wrath. The view in this photograph is looking south on Gulf Drive/State Road 789 just past the Cortez Road intersection. The Harbor House Restaurant is barely visible behind the Longboat Key–Sarasota sign. It still stands along the gulf as the Beach House Restaurant.

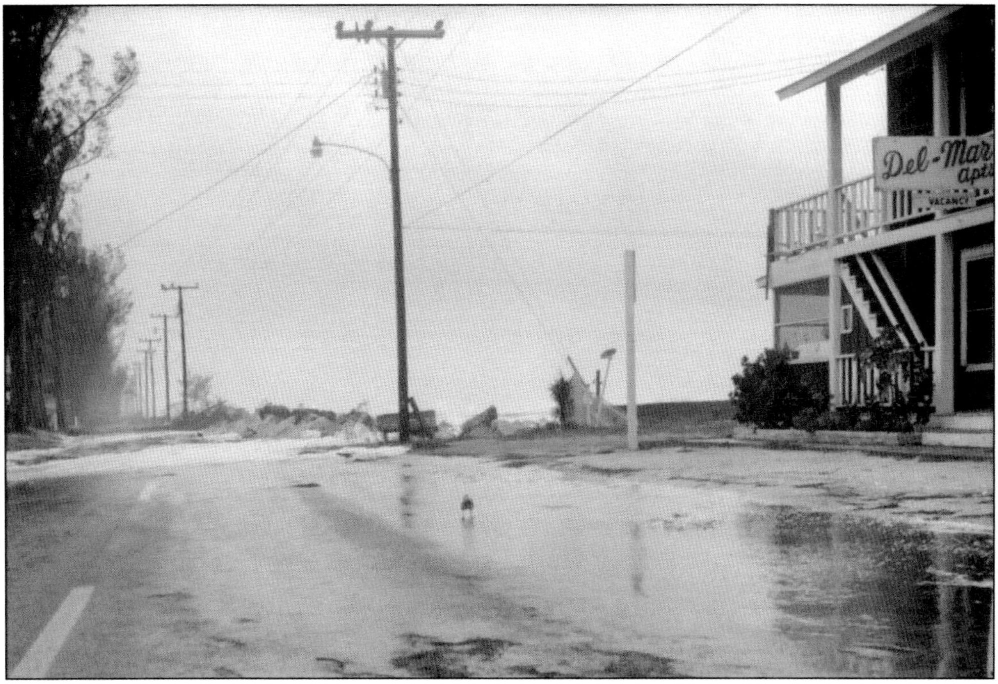

In June 1966, Hurricane Alma brushed by Anna Maria Island, leaving in its wake of high surf a washed-out Gulf Drive/State Road 789 just south of the Del Mar Apartments at Cortez Beach in Bradenton Beach.

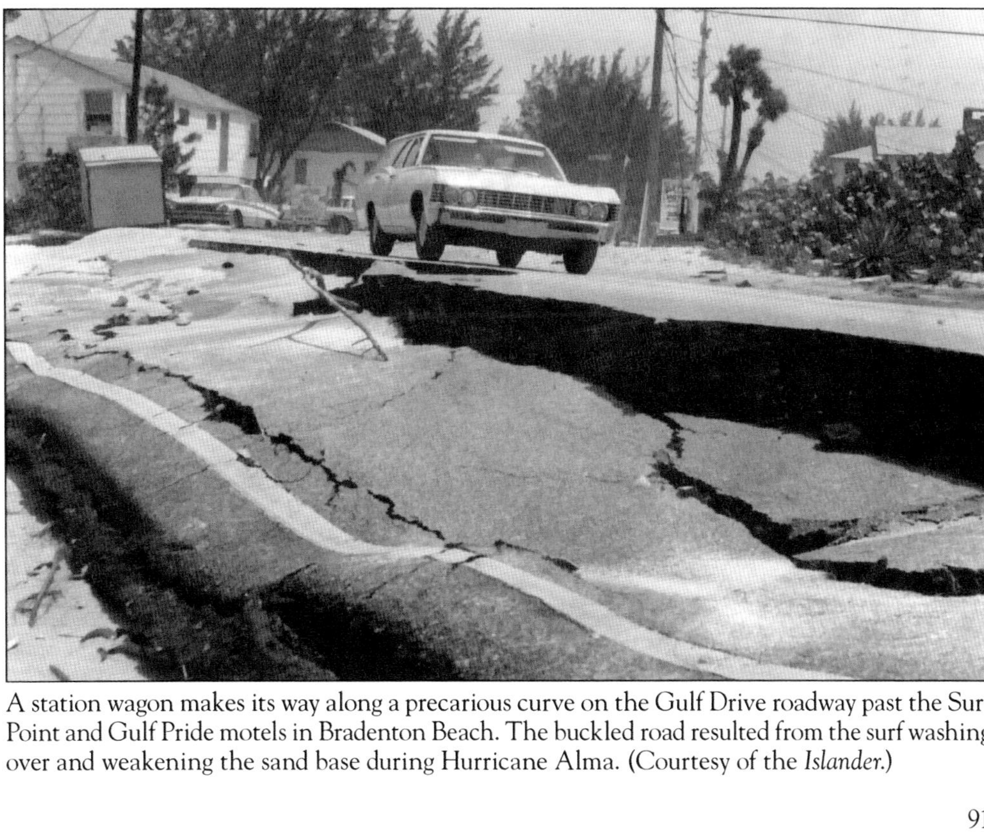

A station wagon makes its way along a precarious curve on the Gulf Drive roadway past the Surf Point and Gulf Pride motels in Bradenton Beach. The buckled road resulted from the surf washing over and weakening the sand base during Hurricane Alma. (Courtesy of the *Islander*.)

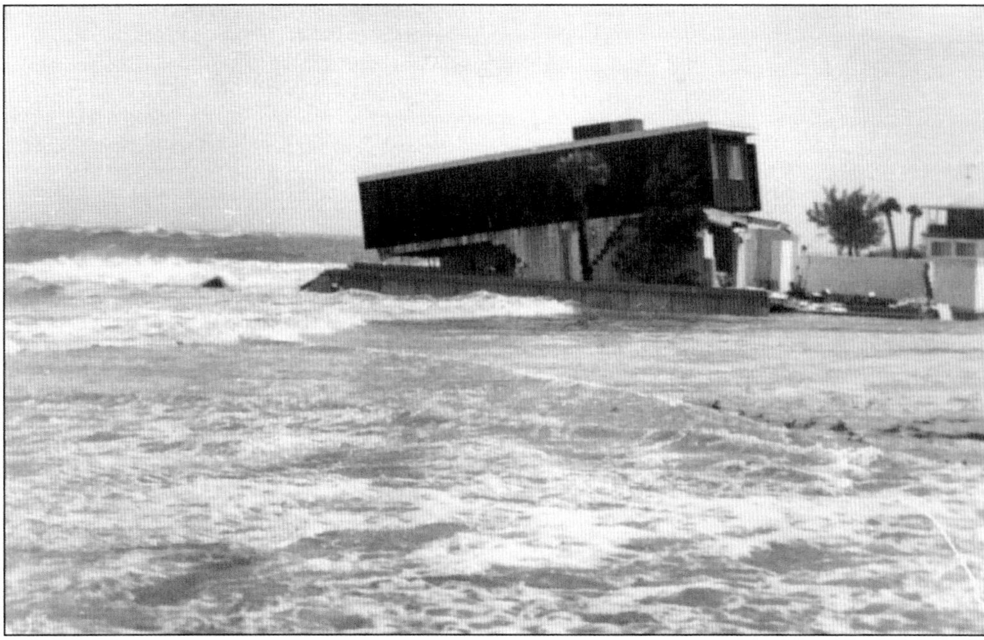

Hurricane Agnes brushed by Anna Maria Island in June 1972 in the Gulf of Mexico and left this beachfront home teetering at the edge of the surf— in spite of a seawall. The storm caused property destruction and extensive beach erosion.

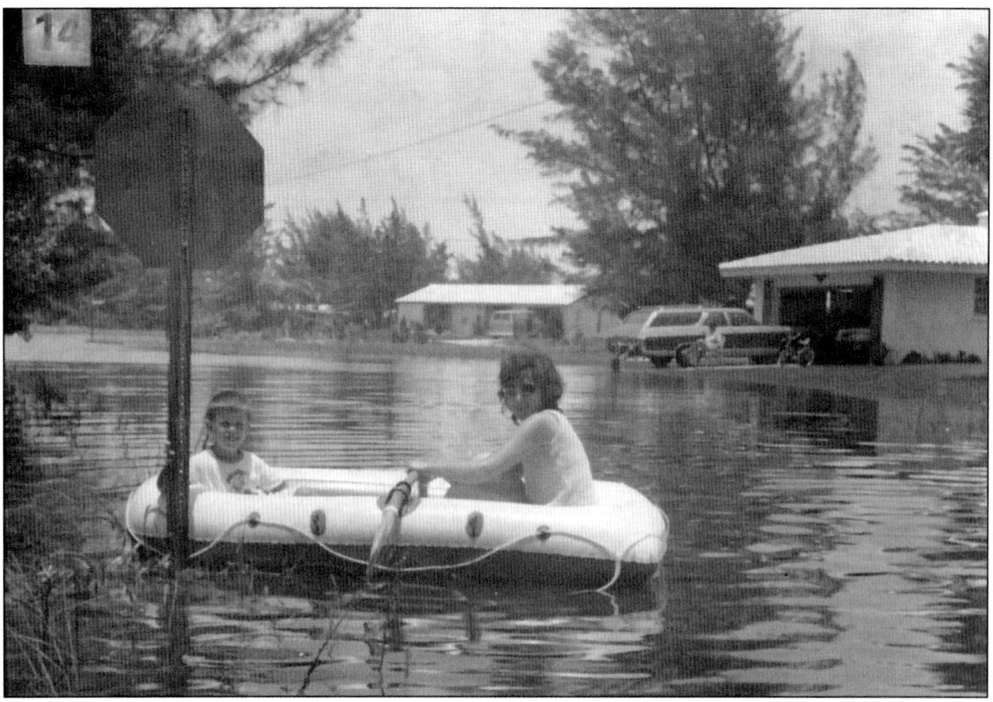

After Hurricane Agnes passed by Anna Maria Island in September 1972, this pair of adventurers took to the street, Holly Road in Anna Maria, in an inflatable dinghy to row around their neighborhood. In fact, rowing canoes, dinghies, rafts, and surfboards in the streets became a common practice for youngsters on the island. (Courtesy of the *Islander*.)

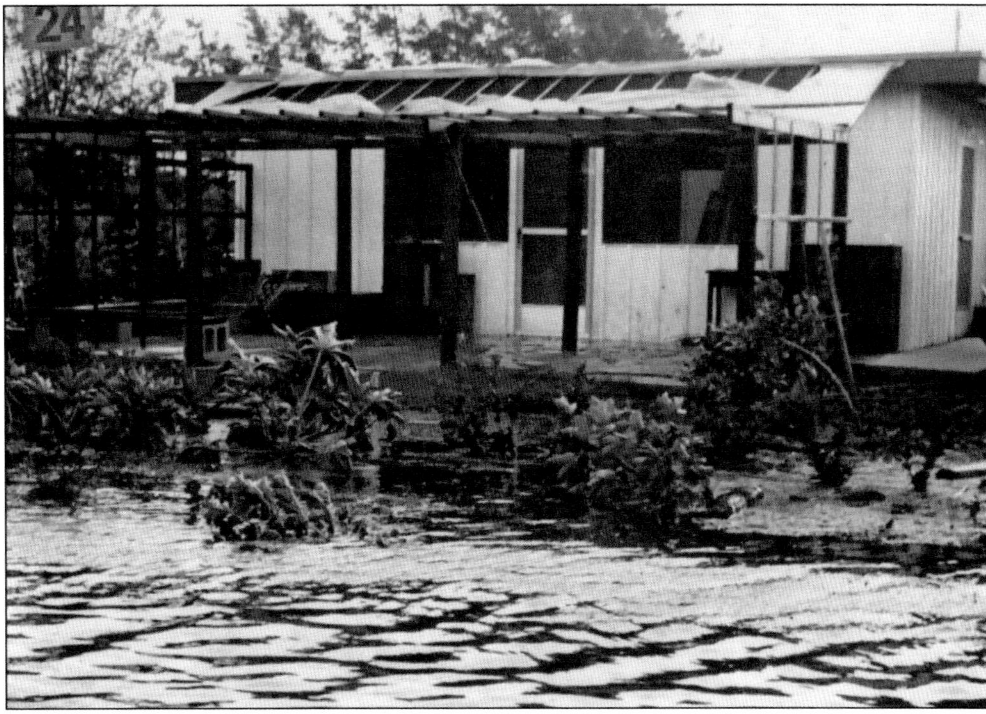

This house on Cedar Street in Anna Maria suffered damage and collected debris in the wake of Hurricane Agnes. The storm passed Anna Maria Island far out in the Gulf of Mexico but produced high wind shear and numerous tornados on its path to the Florida Panhandle. (Courtesy of the *Islander.*)

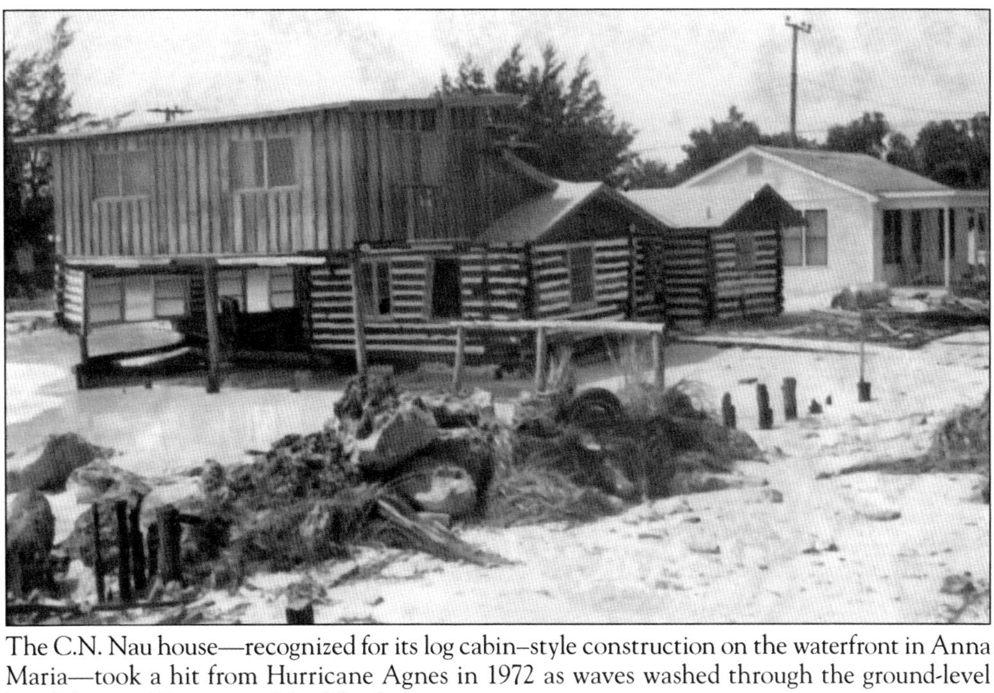

The C.N. Nau house—recognized for its log cabin–style construction on the waterfront in Anna Maria—took a hit from Hurricane Agnes in 1972 as waves washed through the ground-level beach house. (Courtesy of the *Islander.*)

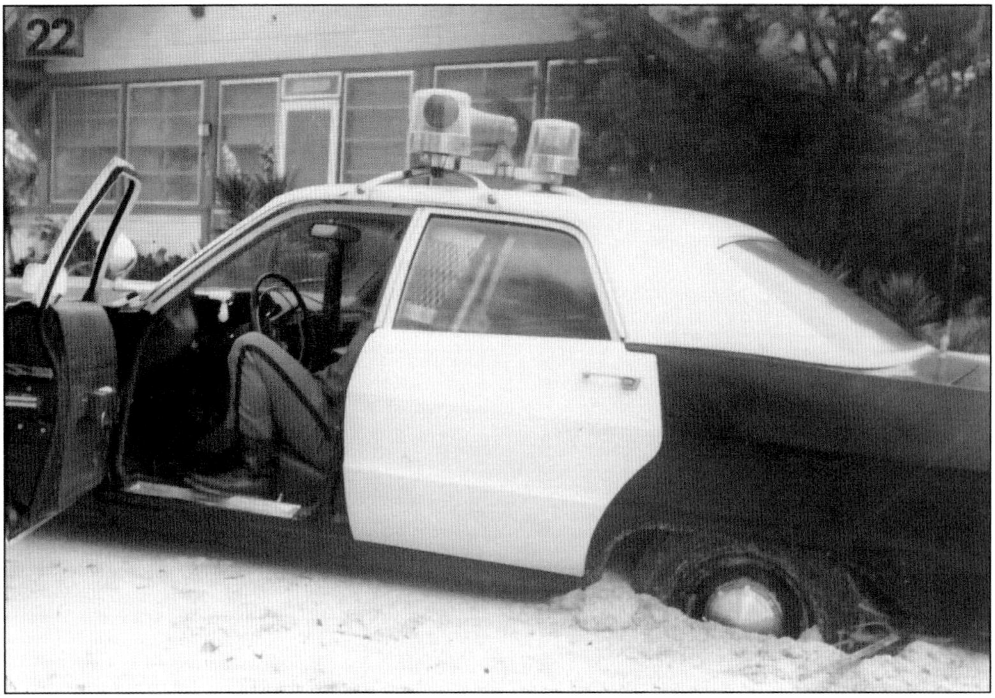

A police car on Gulf Boulevard in Anna Maria comes to a halt in sand washed onto the road from the high surf and storm surge resulting from Hurricane Agnes. (Courtesy of the *Islander*.)

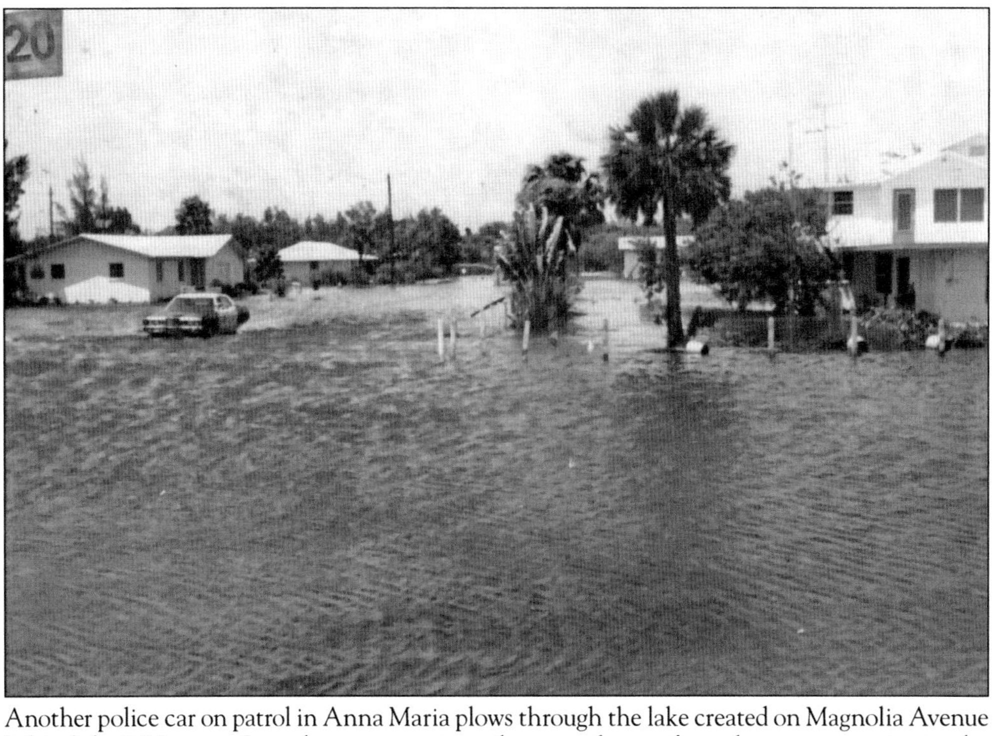

Another police car on patrol in Anna Maria plows through the lake created on Magnolia Avenue behind the IGA store. Some houses experienced waves of water from the streets coming in the doors. (Courtesy of the *Islander*.)

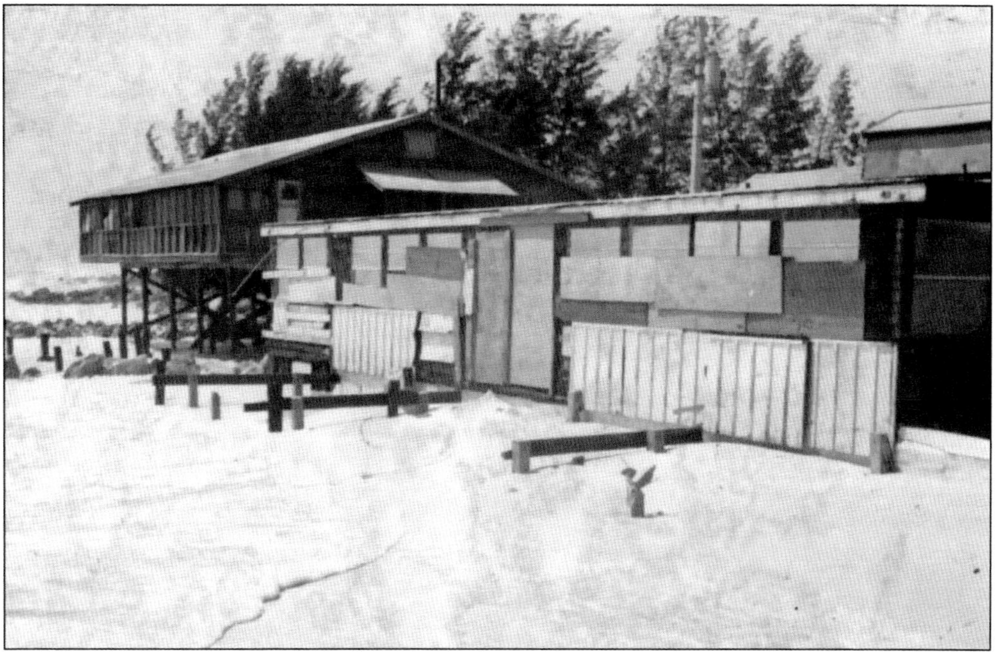

The now iconic Sandbar Restaurant on the beach end of Spring Street, although less well-known in 1972, has boarded its gulf-side windows in preparation for Hurricane Agnes. The stilt house to the left, north of the Sandbar, eventually gave way to the storm and was never rebuilt. (Courtesy of the *Islander*.)

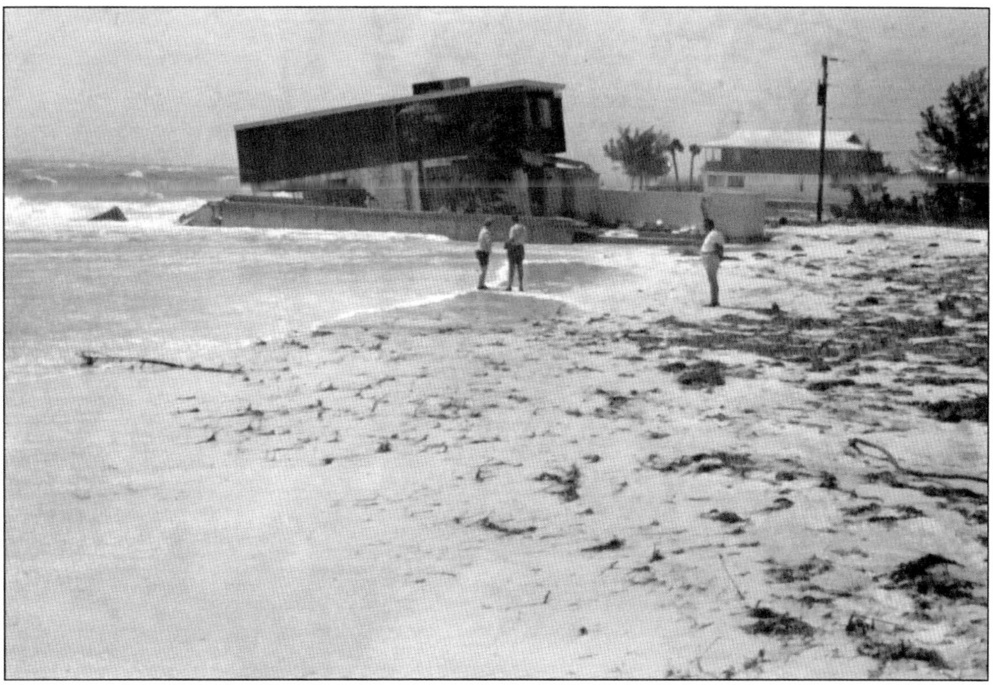

A house on the north shore of Anna Maria is surrounded by the exposed seawall, which was washed out by high surf. The lower level of the home also was washed out and damaged when Hurricane Agnes passed by Anna Maria Island in 1972. (Courtesy of the *Islander*.)

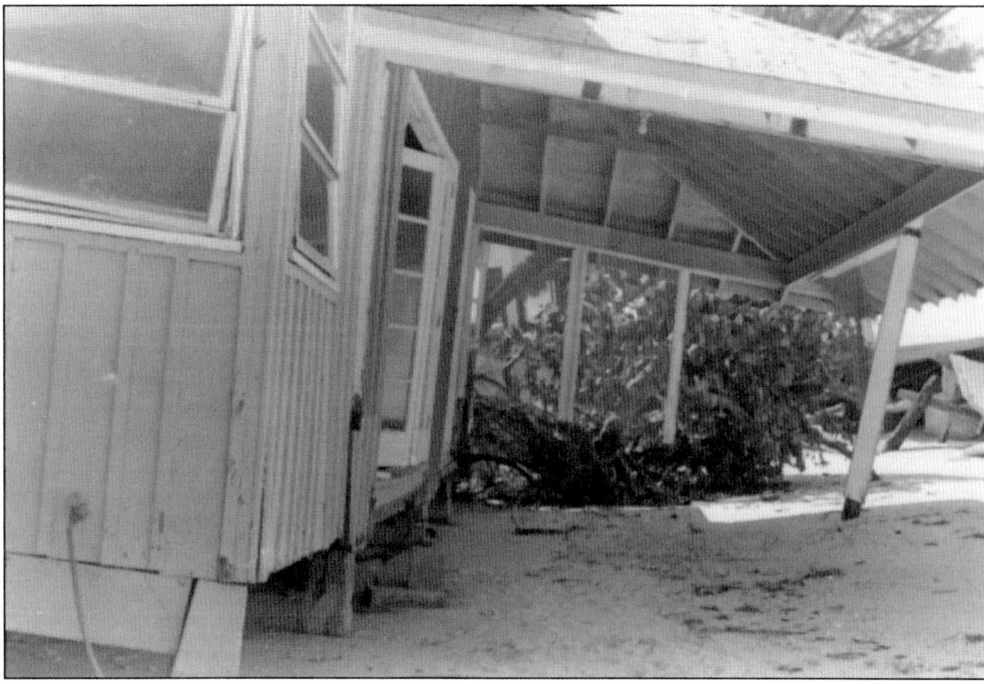

Another house in Anna Maria has taken on a tilt on the beachfront, where the high surf and storm surge from Hurricane Agnes in mid-June 1972 washed out concrete pilings and left the house leaning toward the water. (Courtesy of the *Islander*.)

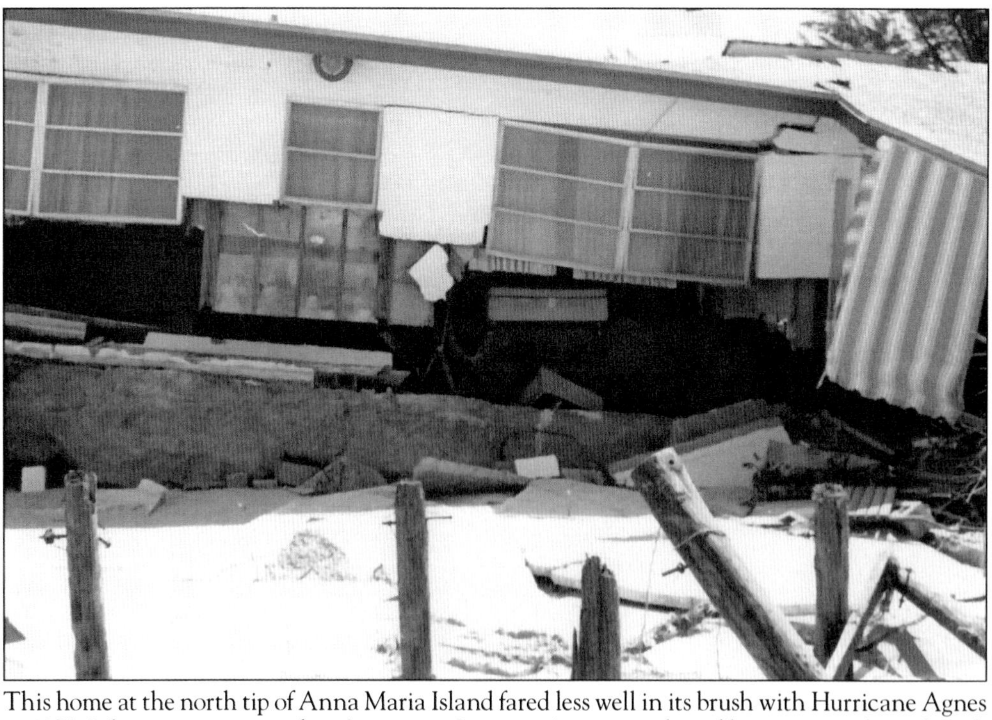

This home at the north tip of Anna Maria Island fared less well in its brush with Hurricane Agnes in 1972. It bears mentioning that Agnes—a Category 1 storm—plowed by on its northward track in the Gulf of Mexico some 300 miles from the island shoreline. (Courtesy of the *Islander*.)

Hurricane Agnes made its Category 1 strength known in Cortez at the boat docks adjacent to the Cortez Bridge, where most of the resident fishing boats had been moved inland for safekeeping. (Courtesy of the *Islander*.)

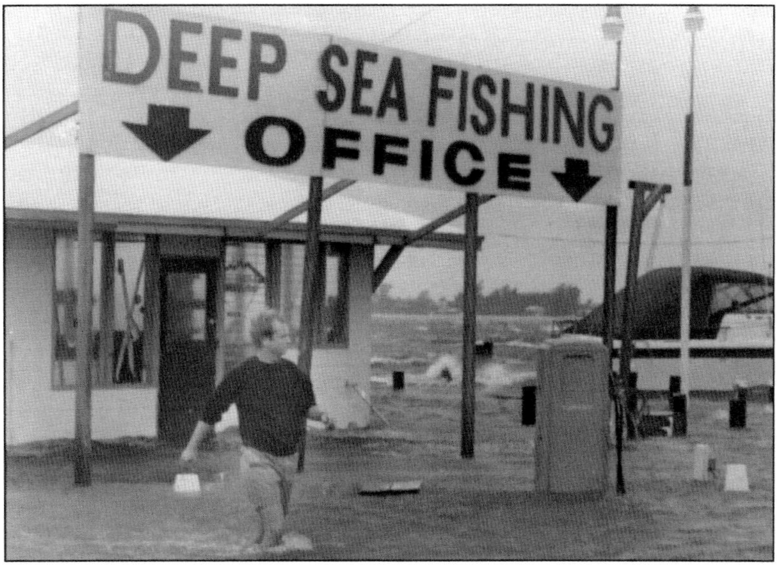

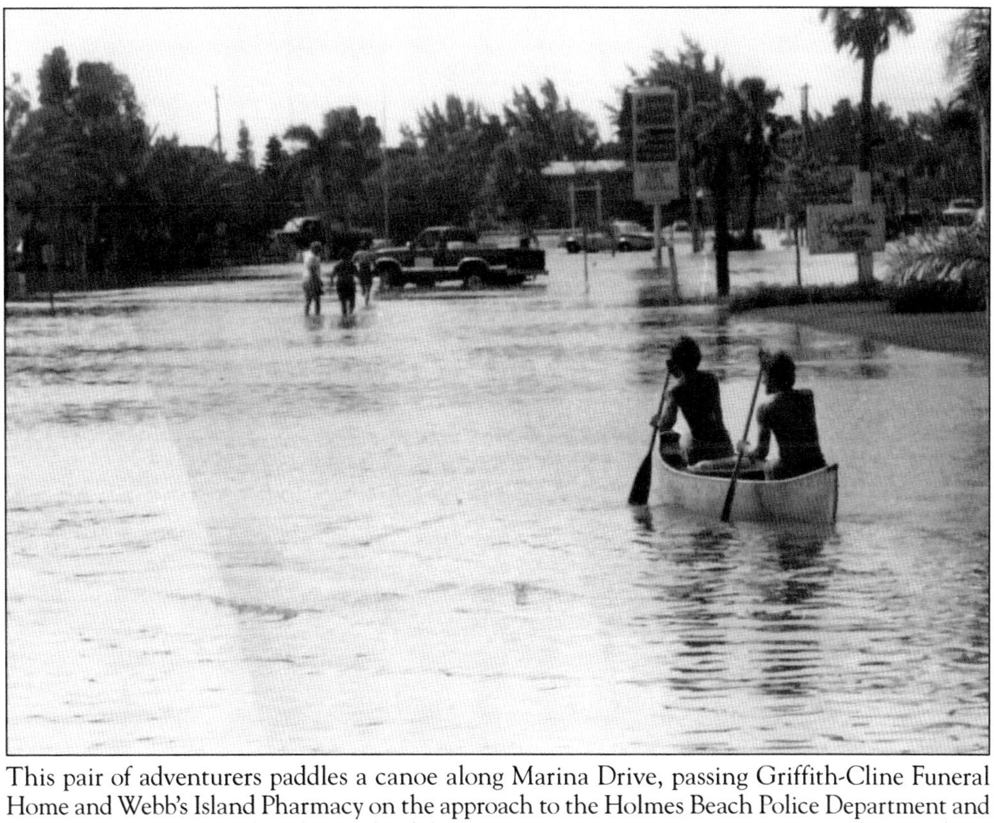

This pair of adventurers paddles a canoe along Marina Drive, passing Griffith-Cline Funeral Home and Webb's Island Pharmacy on the approach to the Holmes Beach Police Department and city hall on the left in the aftermath of the June 18, 1982, "No Name Storm." Striking without warning before daybreak, the storm managed to surprise weather forecasters, which accounted for the tropical system's lack of a name. (Courtesy of the *Islander*.)

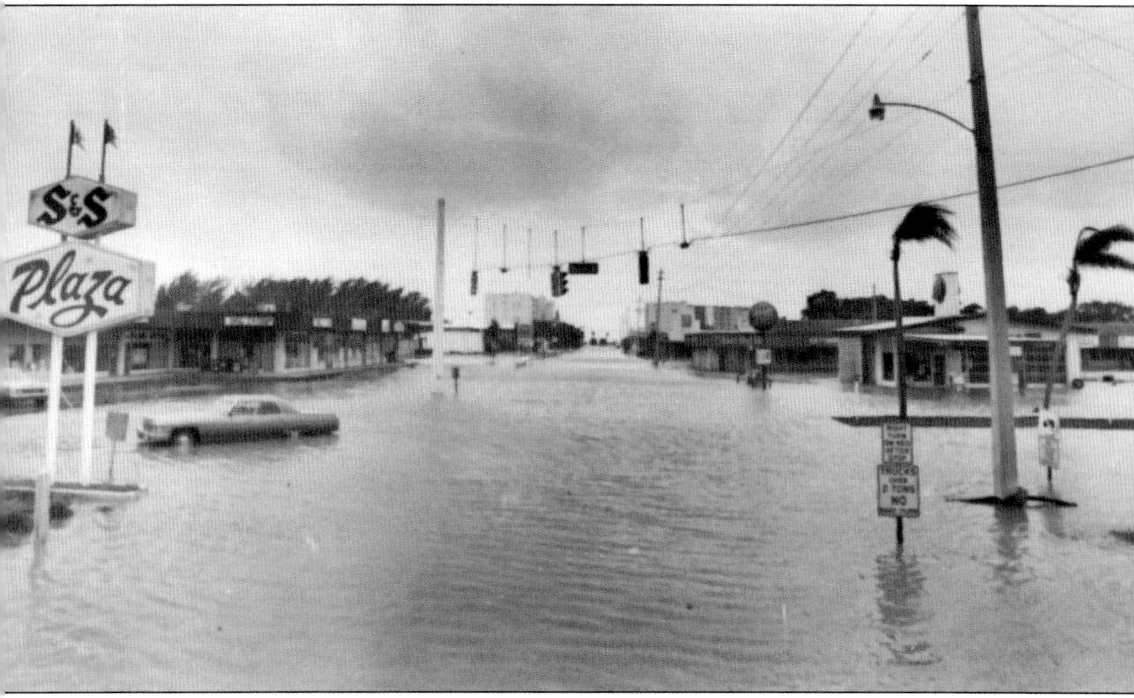

The No Name Storm of 1982 left the intersection of Marina and Gulf Drives, the main business center in Holmes Beach, inundated with water as, following the initial downpour, the high surf continued for much of the day. (Courtesy of the *Islander*.)

The Union 76 gas and service station at the corner of Marina and Gulf Drives in Holmes Beach was surrounded by water and unable to provide service for much of the day. Most of the island was without power, and almost no one had notice or warning before the storm arrived just before daybreak on June 18, 1982. (Courtesy of the *Islander*.)

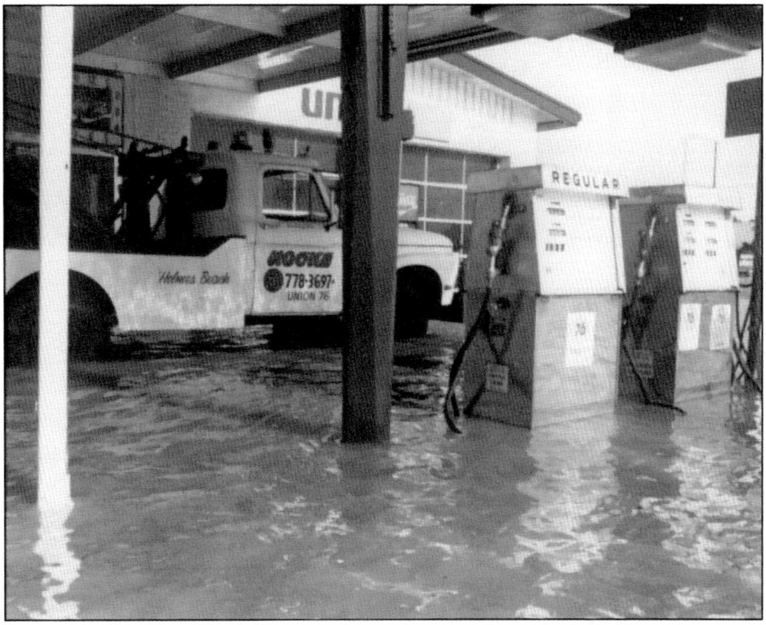

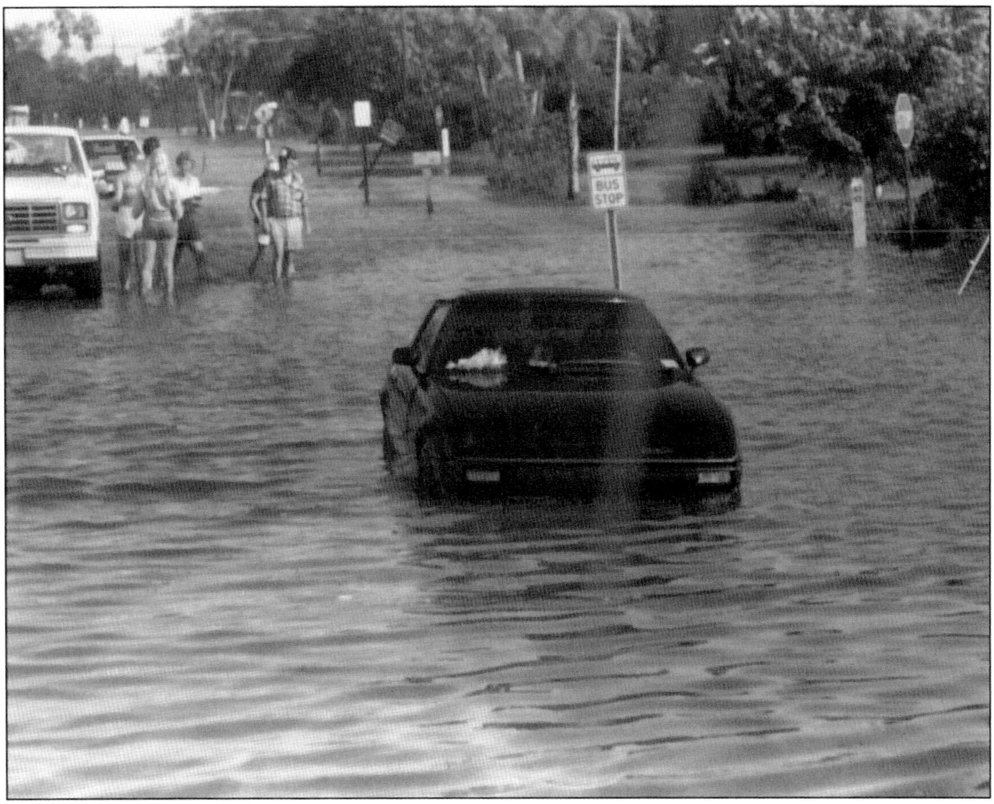

A car is stranded on Marina Drive at Sixty-Third Street in Holmes Beach, where some people walk near the center of the road in more shallow standing water and other people in a pickup truck ride through the flooded street that resulted from the 1982 No Name Storm. (Courtesy of the *Islander*.)

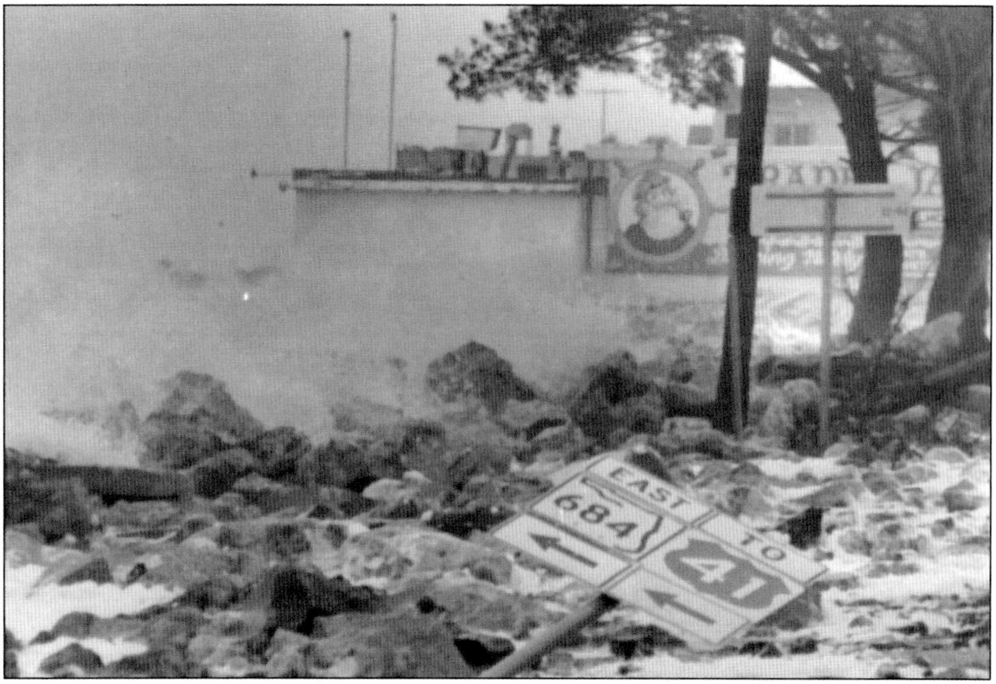

Trader Jack's Restaurant, now the Gulf Drive Cafe and Tiki Bar, at Ninth Street North and Gulf Drive/State Road 789 on the beach in Bradenton Beach, just a few blocks north of the Cortez Bridge, takes a licking from the high surf in Hurricane Elena, a Category 2 storm that stalled in the Gulf of Mexico. It went ashore in Biloxi, Mississippi, on Labor Day 1985. (Courtesy of the *Islander*.)

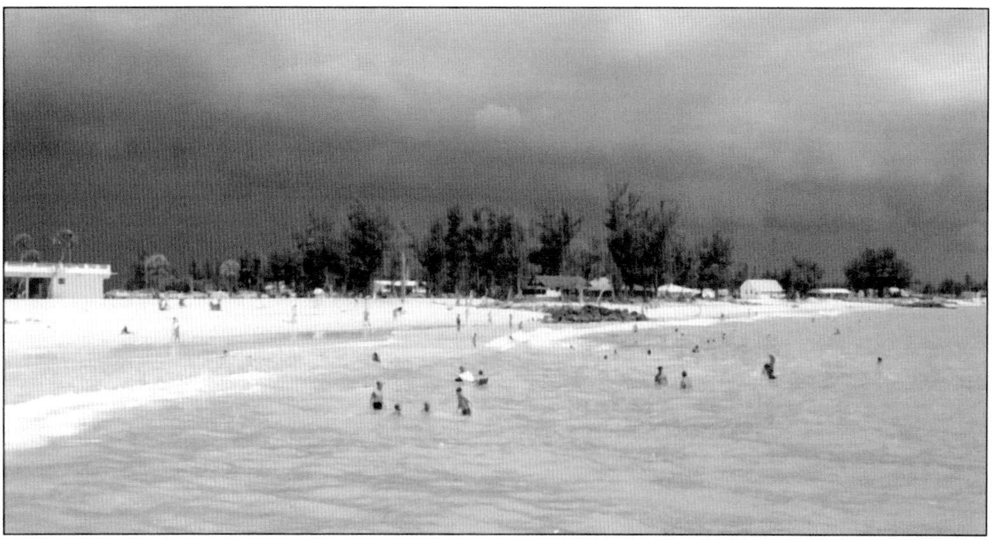

A storm rolls into Holmes Beach at the Manatee Public Beach, where people continue to swim and body surf. The rooftop pavilion was once the host to weekend dances. A double-wide stairway from the roof cascaded downward over the beachfront patio onto the beach, and a short walk over the sand led to the pier over the Gulf of Mexico, where strollers and fishers shared the wide deck. The food concession operated daily, serving breakfast, lunch, and dinner. The pavilion also included restrooms, showers, and lockers.

Nine

CAPTURED BY THE PRIVATEERS

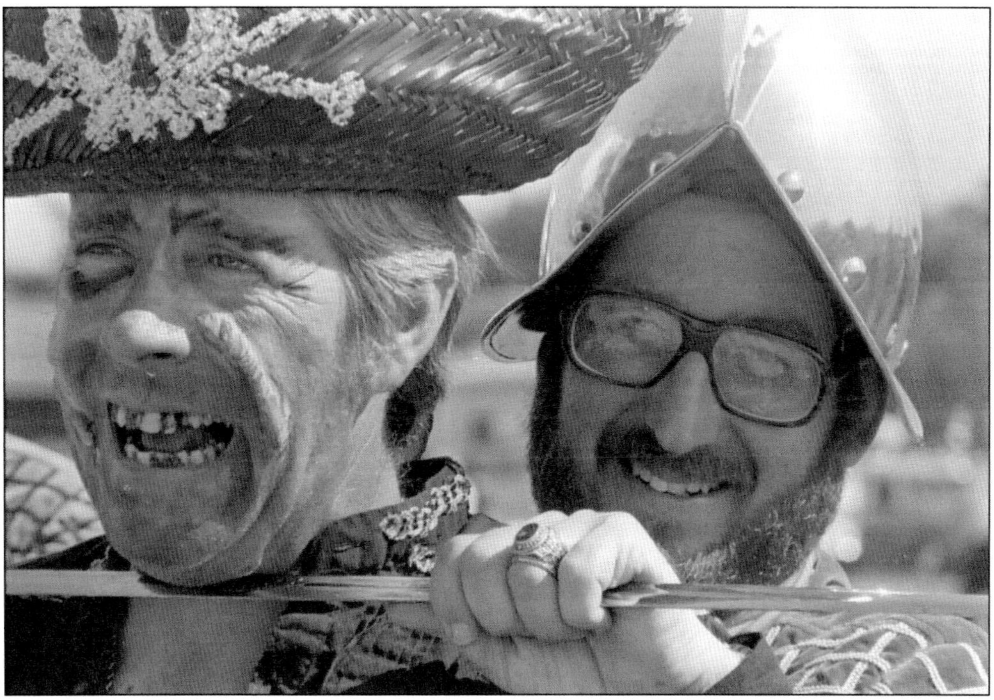

Held by a sword to his throat, a gnarly, desperate pirate calls for help in the bloody battle of 1977 between the Anna Maria Island Privateers and the DeSoto Conquistadors of Bradenton. The colorful battle put on by the two nonprofit organizations to conquer the three island cities was repeated annually for many years, as a part of the Hernando De Soto Celebration. There was much booty to be paid to gain the release from the conquistadors of citizens, officials, and pirate women and children.

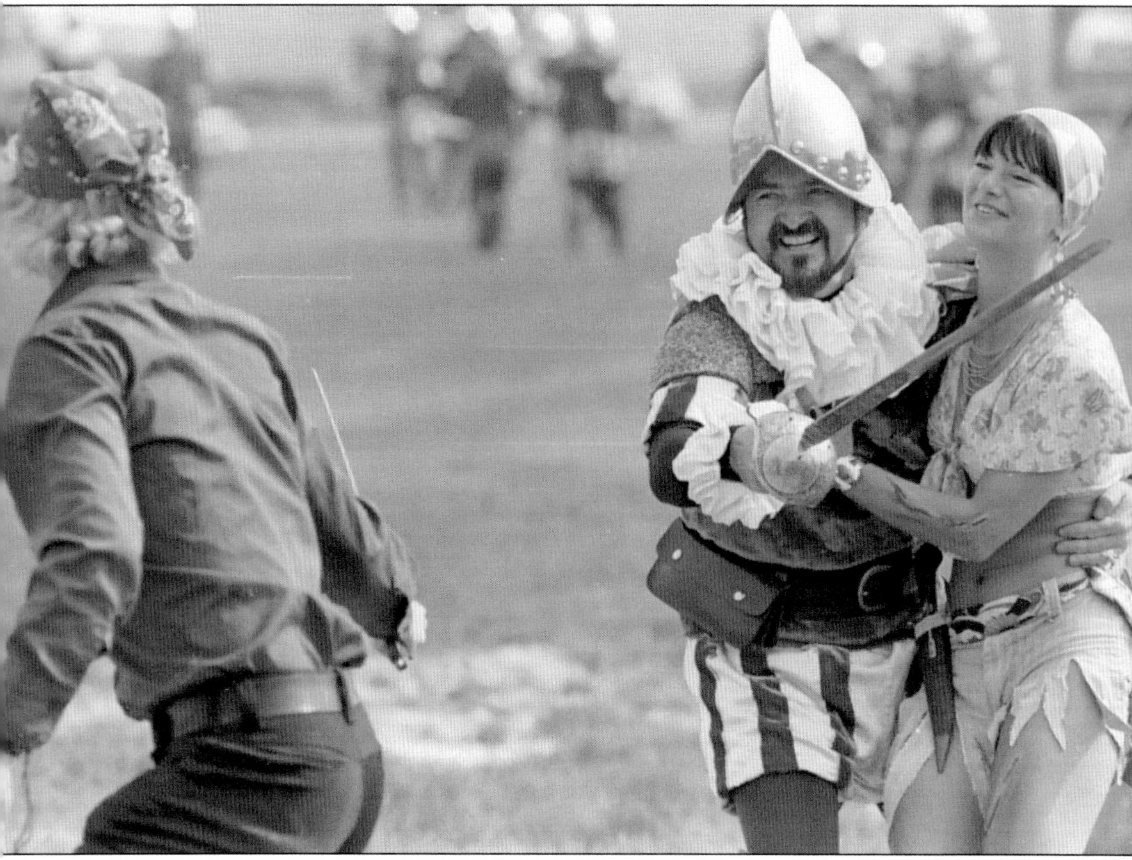

With sword drawn, a member of the DeSoto Conquistadors (right) captures an island woman as an Anna Maria Island Privateer attempts to defend her during a skirmish in Holmes Beach. The conquistadors came to overtake the privateers and conquer the city as part of their 1977 Hernando De Soto Celebration.

The Anna Maria Island Privateers put up a defensive fort in the field adjacent to Holmes Beach City Hall, the former airport field, to hold off the DeSoto Conquistadors during the Bradenton crew's annual attempt to conquer the city. Families and friends of the privateers, who come as spectators, often take part in defense of the city by harassing and distracting the conquistadors.

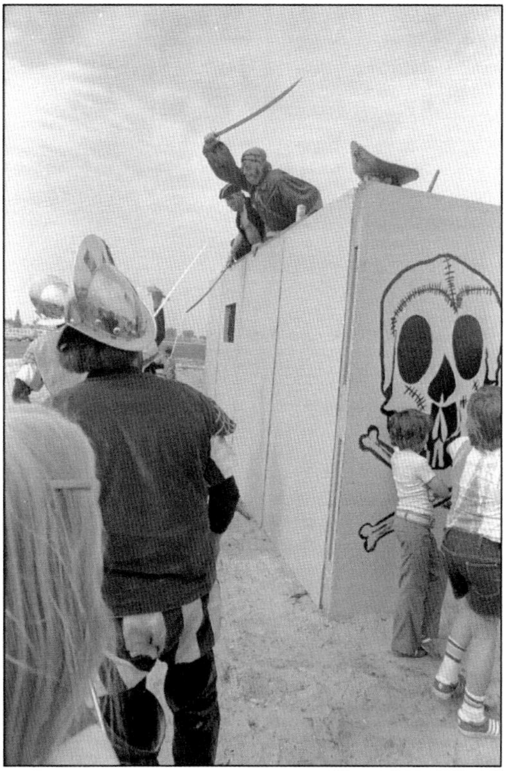

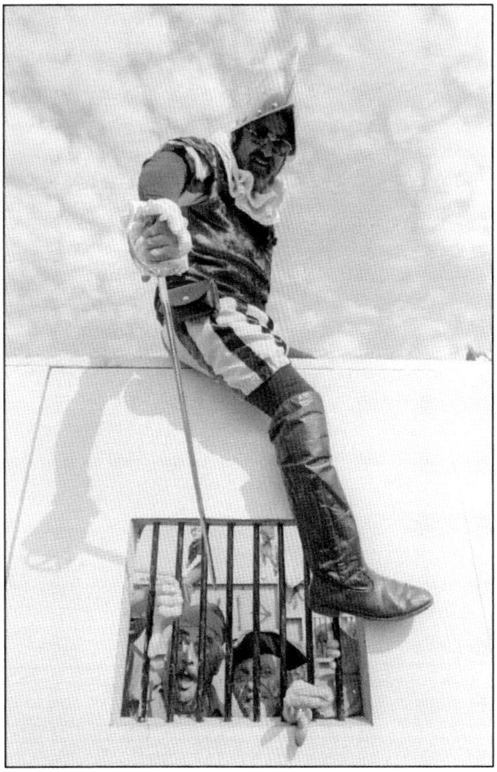

With his sword, a conquistador takes part in the 1977 capture of Holmes Beach and holds two privateers in a pokey, which previously served as the privateers' fort. The annual event marks the celebration of Hernando De Soto Day, including a fishing tournament, a bottle-boat regatta on Palma Sola Bay, and a grand parade in Bradenton.

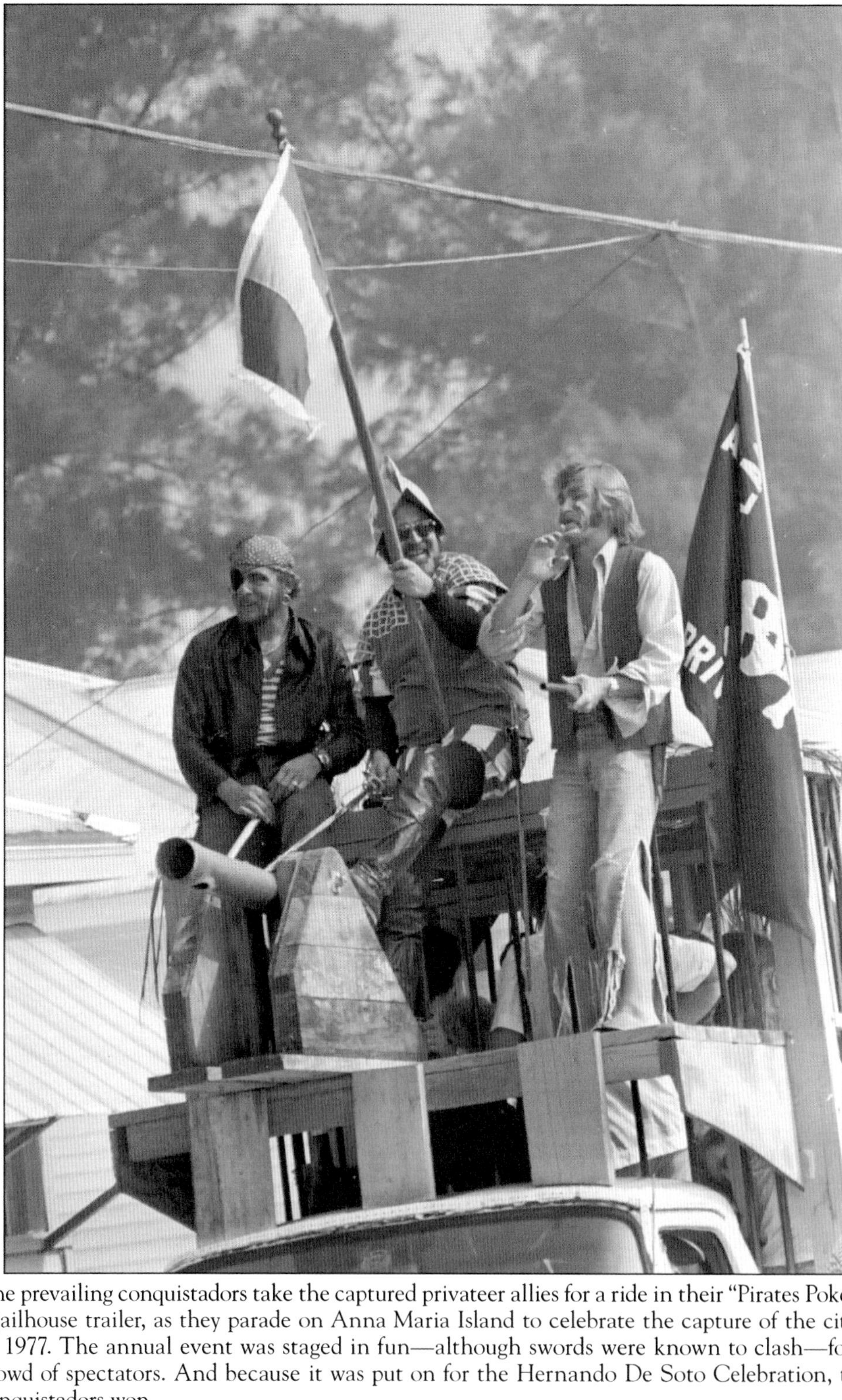

The prevailing conquistadors take the captured privateer allies for a ride in their "Pirates Pokey," a jailhouse trailer, as they parade on Anna Maria Island to celebrate the capture of the cities in 1977. The annual event was staged in fun—although swords were known to clash—for a crowd of spectators. And because it was put on for the Hernando De Soto Celebration, the conquistadors won.

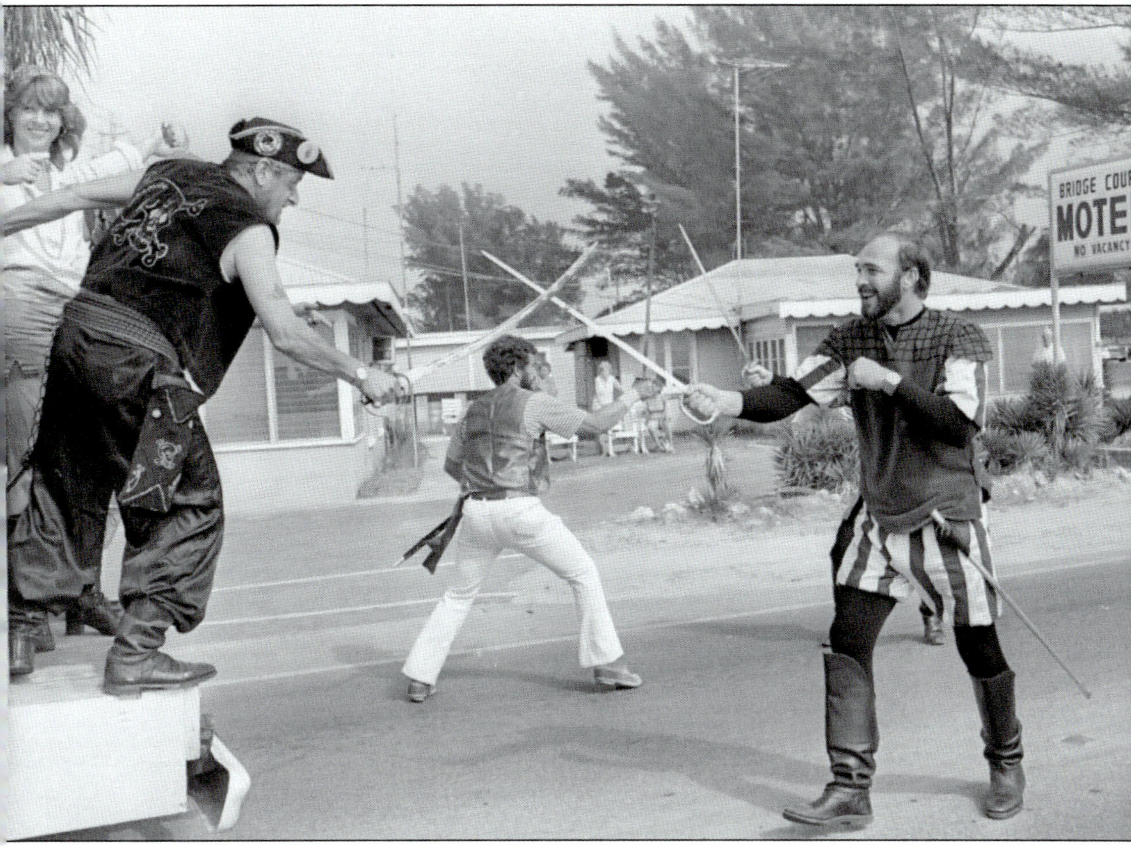

Several men from the conquistadors and the privateers leap to a sword fight in the street as the parade that followed the capture of the cities proceeds on Gulf Drive through Bradenton Beach. Recognized hanging onto the rear of the jail float is Patty Davis, who still resides on the island. While women were allowed at celebrations, in 1977, the privateers, established in 1971, allowed no female members.

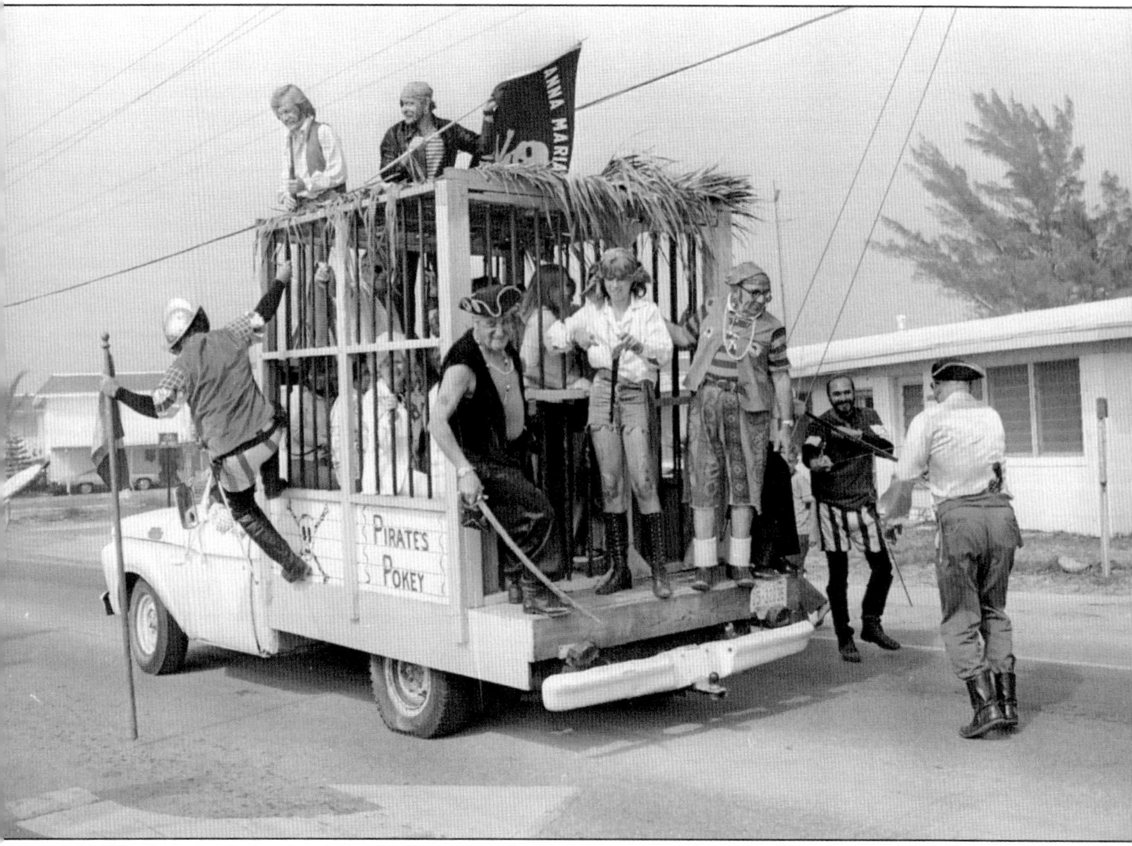

The "Pirates Pokey" is filled with innocent citizens captured in 1977 by the DeSoto Conquistadors, as Anna Maria Island Privateers attempt to defend and release them. The pokey ride led from Bradenton Beach to Holmes Beach—where the sword fights continued at the city field before the crowd that gathered for the event—to the Anna Maria City Pier. It was all part of Bradenton's celebration of Hernando De Soto Days.

Patty Davis of Anna Maria Island and a friend of the privateers is captured and offered for ransom by the DeSoto Conquistadors on a stage complete with gallows to punish those who fought against them in their capture of the city. The long-standing rivalry between the scruffy do-good privateers and the well-dressed and armed conquistadors, begun in 1971, continues to this day.

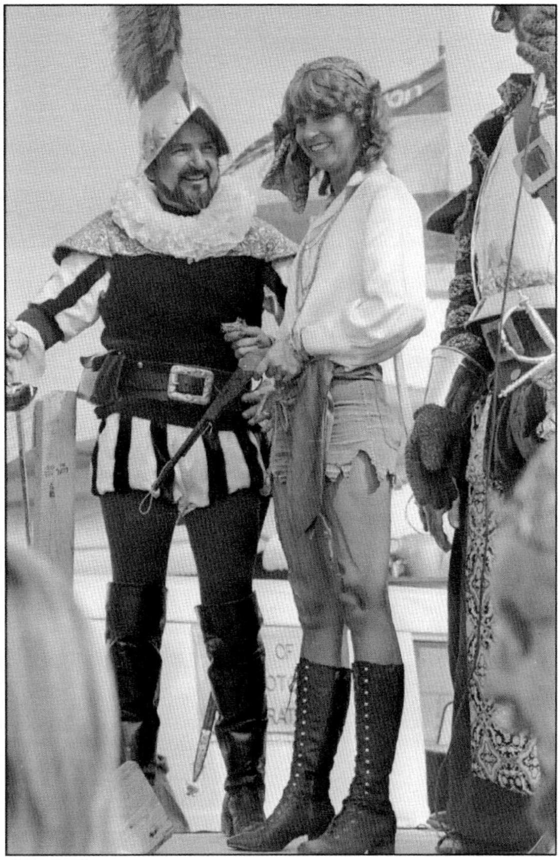

The DeSoto Conquistadors' annual conquest on Anna Maria Island culminated on the beach in 1979, where gallows had been constructed for the (mock) hanging of the captured privateers—their punishment for resistance. Both the privateers and the conquistadors made demands for booty, as the nonprofit organizations continue in their endeavors to this day, although the conquistadors ceased pillaging the island in the late 1980s.

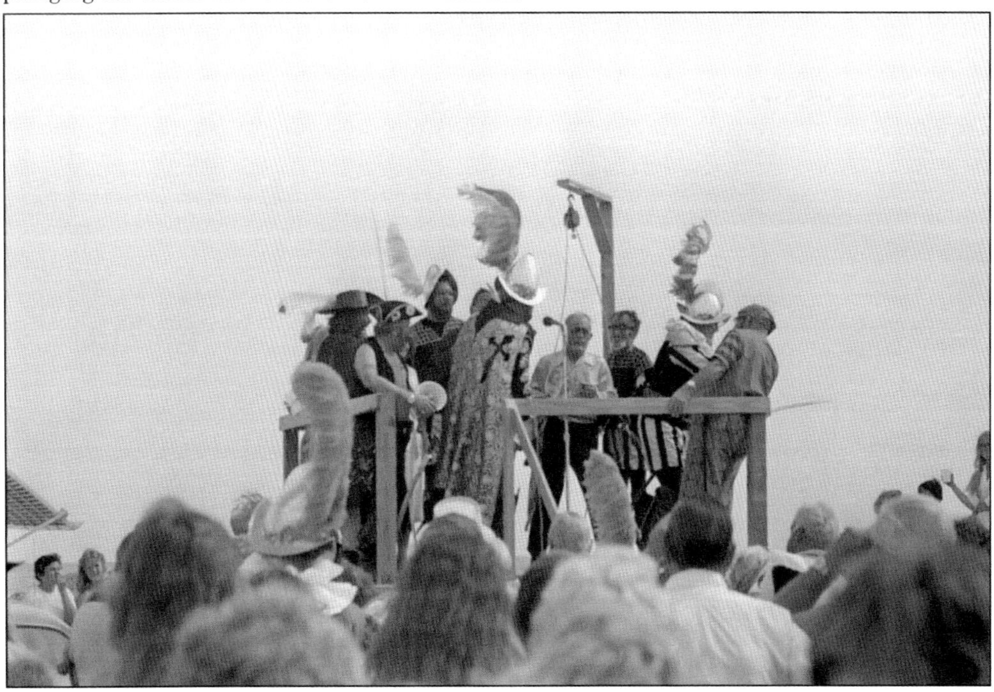

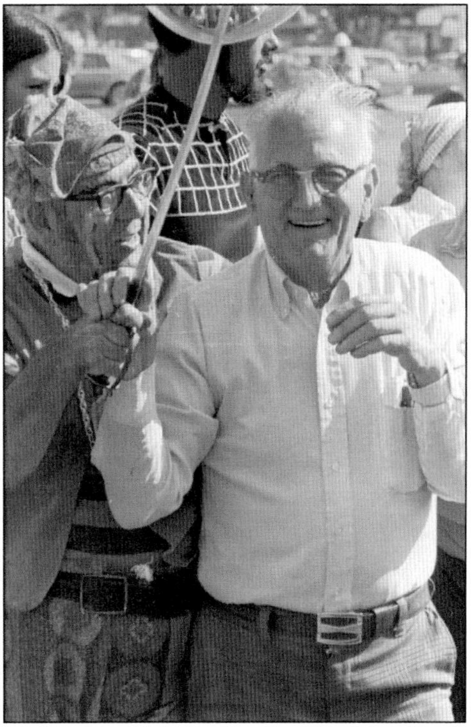

A privateer leads former Anna Maria mayor Ernie Cagnina—captured by the scoundrel DeSoto Conquistadors and forced to take up a sword against his fellow islanders—from the fray after the booty is paid for his release. The event was a fun fundraiser for the crews, who spread their wealth and booty by helping the youngest pirates enjoy their upbringing on the beach. The privateers joined former Holmes Beach police chief Snooks Adams in hosting Kids Day at Bayfront Park, a day of games and treasure hunting and free hot dogs and sodas.

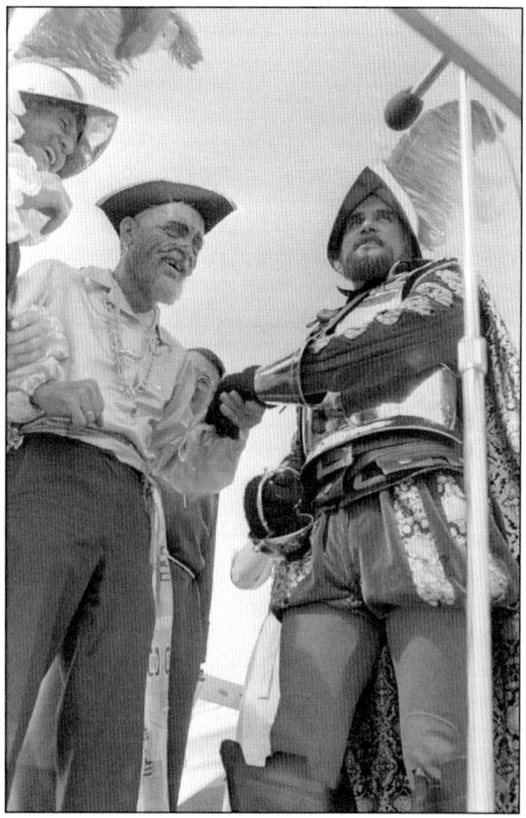

The DeSoto Conquistadors lead their prime capture, a bedraggled pirate, from the defeated crew of Anna Maria Island Privateers to his finish at the gallows, where a booty was demanded for his release along with all the citizens, city officials, pirates, men, women, and children they captured in the looting of the island.

Ten

One Island, Three Cities

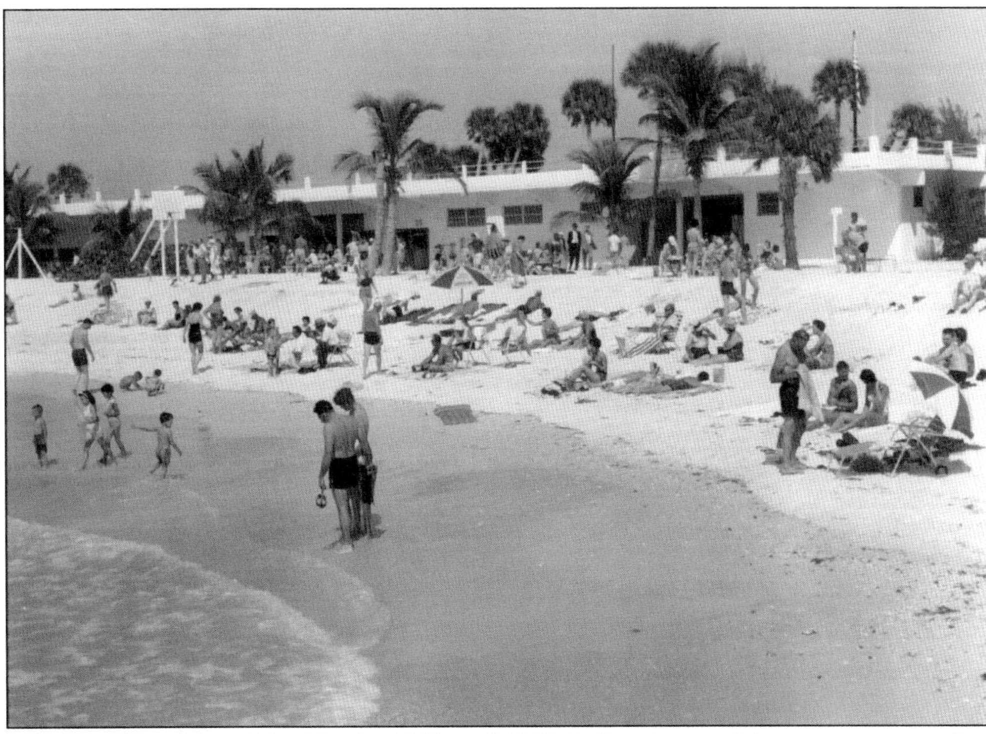

A hub on Anna Maria Island by the 1950s and 1960s for beachgoers, fishers, swimmers, surfers, and sunbathers, the Manatee Public Beach pavilion served hundreds of people daily. A snack bar opened for coffee at sunrise and closed at sunset. Dances were held on the rooftop after the sun went down on the weekends. A basketball hoop stands in the sand. Swimmers and sunbathers are abundant. (Courtesy of the *Islander*.)

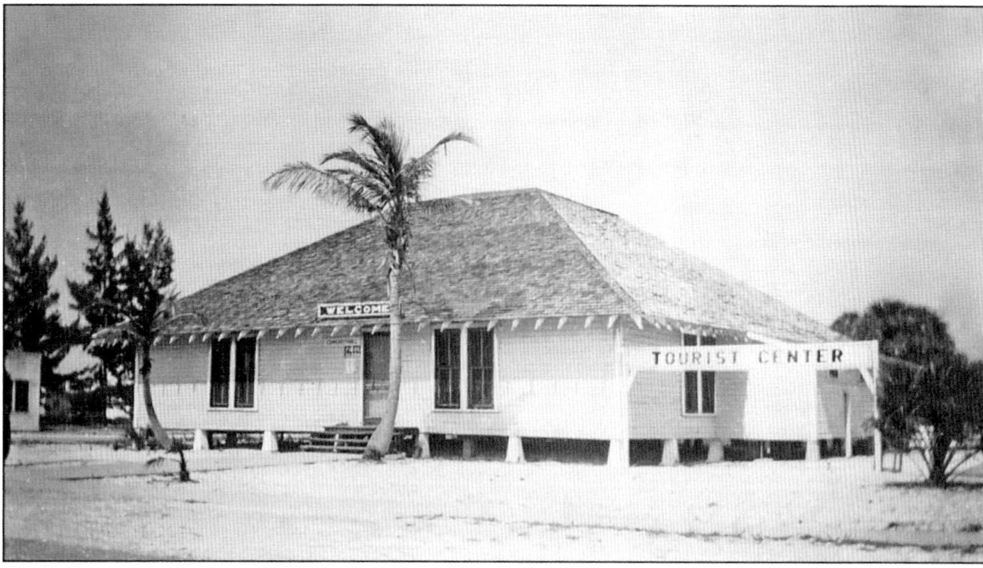

This building is one of the oldest on Anna Maria Island. Once the home of William H. Gillett, it was originally located in Parrish. In 1912, it was barged on the Manatee River across Tampa Bay to Anna Maria. It was first used as a sales office by the Anna Maria Beach Development Company, which brought prospective buyers by steamship from Tampa. Following the city's incorporation in 1923, the building was used as a church, city offices, classrooms, and a social hall for World War II soldiers. Since 1949, it has served as the theater for the nonprofit Island Players. (Courtesy of the *Islander.*)

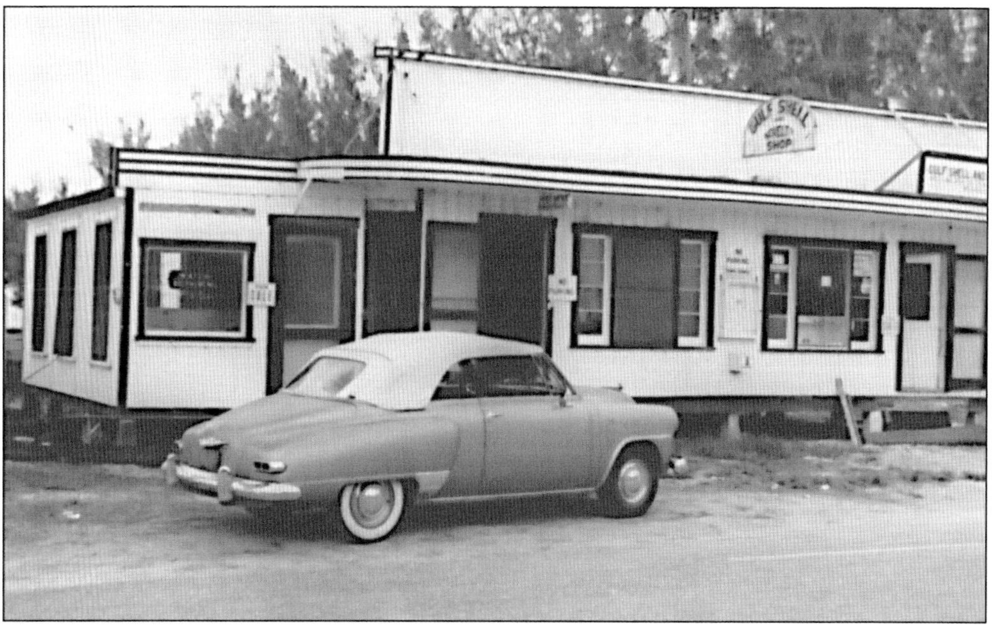

This building in Bradenton Beach housed what likely was the first shell shop on the island—Gulf Shell and Novelty Shop. To the left of the shell shop, there is a small post office with several No Parking signs, and the watch-repair shop has a For Sale sign tacked to the building. And what is that car parked in front? A 1950s Studebaker convertible with a Manatee County tag. (Courtesy of the *Islander.*)

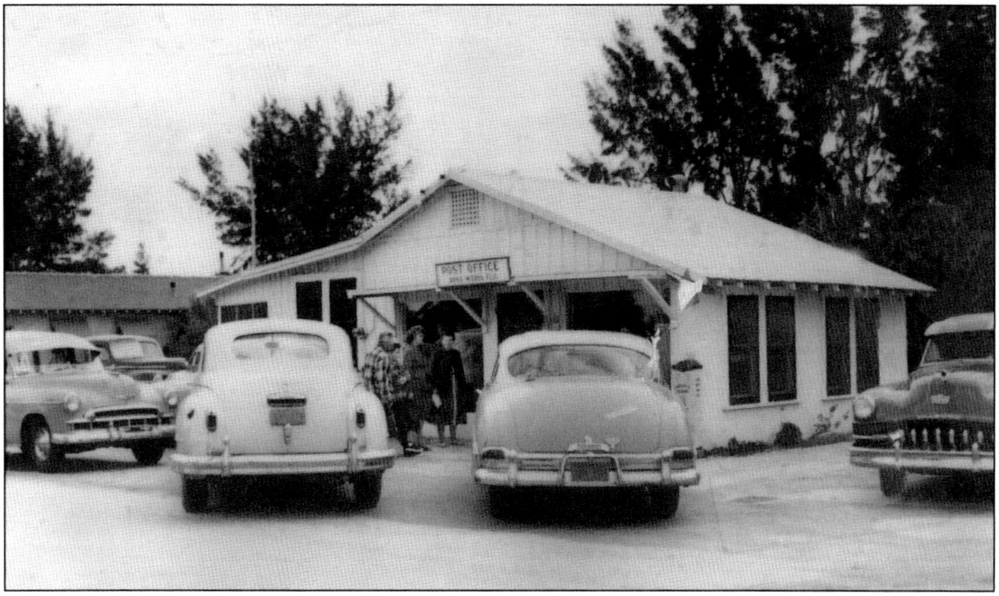

The first post office on Anna Maria Island operated in the city of Anna Maria starting in 1914. It was at the corner of Gulf Drive and Spring Avenue. A replacement, opened in 1955, was constructed behind the original building, which was razed to make way for parking. (Courtesy of the *Islander.*)

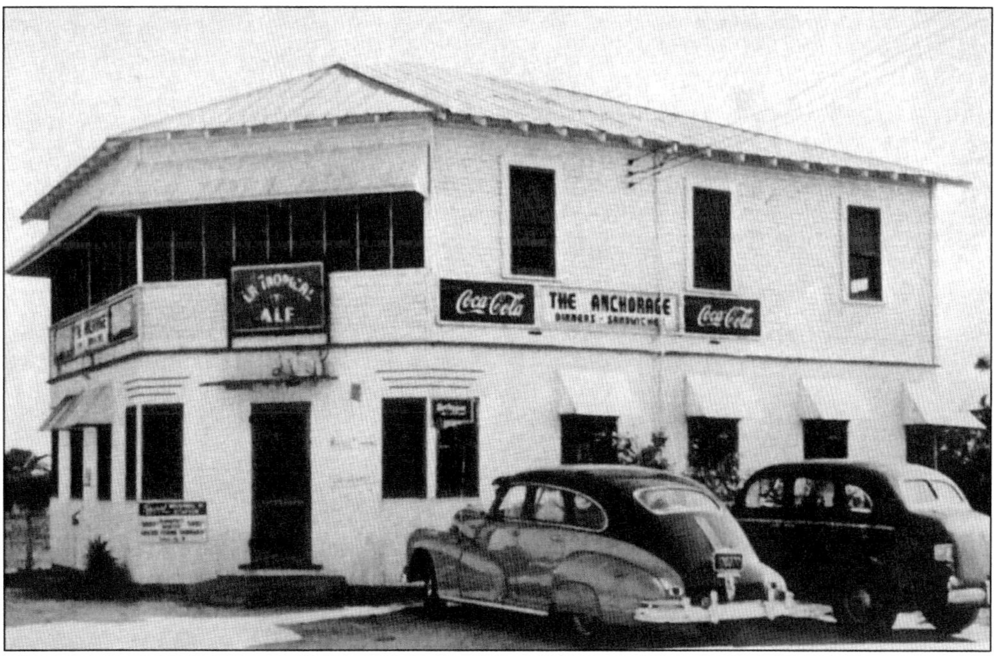

The Anchorage, at the corner of Bay Boulevard and Pine Avenue, opposite the landing to the city pier, was a popular spot in the 1950s and 1960s in Anna Maria. It was known for good sandwiches, cold beer, and tropical ale. After it fell into disrepair and was demolished, it was followed by a new Fast Eddie's Place in the 1980s. But Fast Eddie Porter fell on hard times, and his restaurant also was demolished to make way for Bayview Plaza, home today to several shops and the local post office. (Courtesy of the *Islander.*)

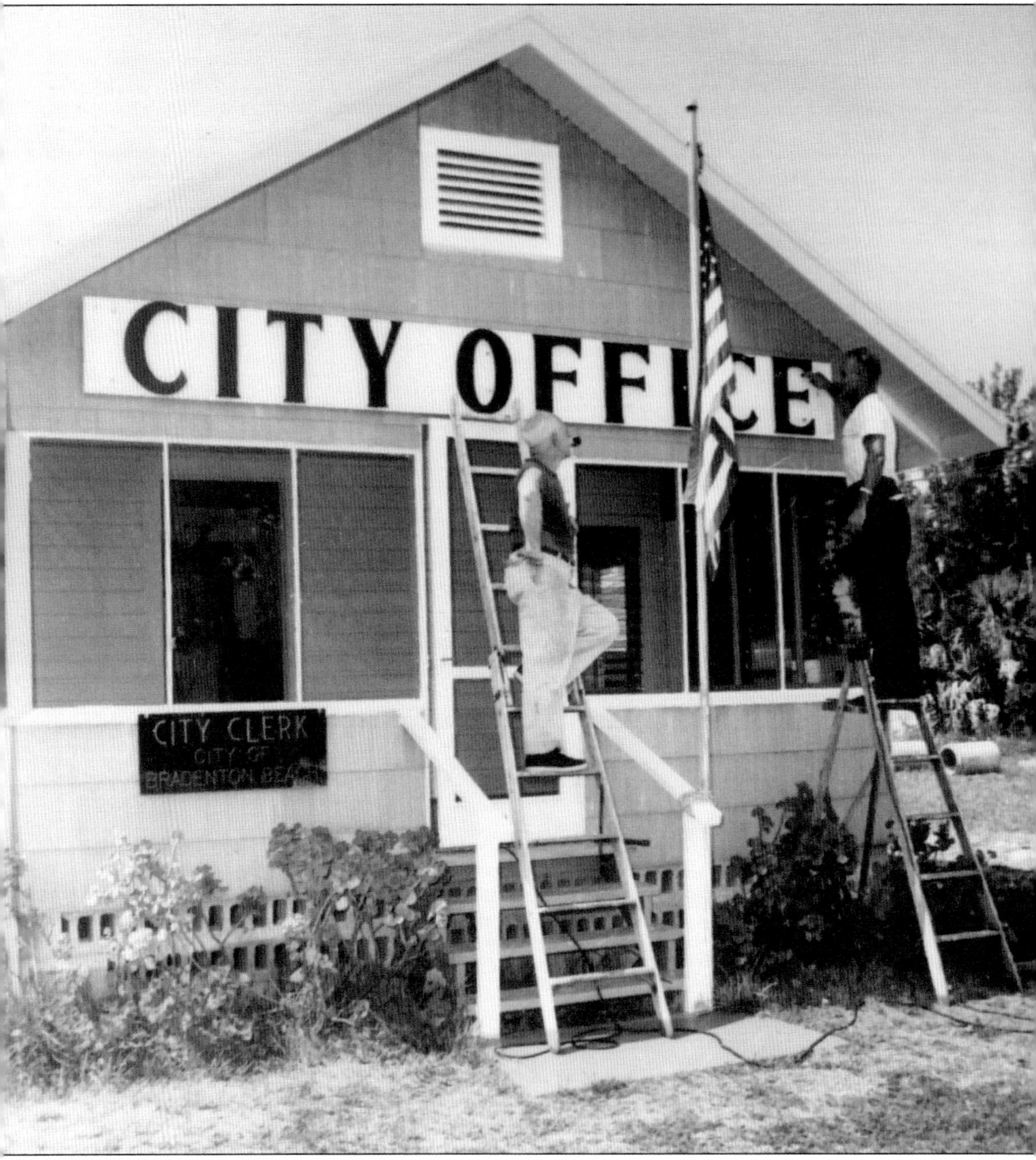

Bradenton Beach City Hall gets a sprucing up in the 1950s. The city incorporated in 1951, following a vote of 84 property owners at a meeting in the volunteer firehouse. Bernie Wagaman was elected mayor among those gathered for the event. By election time in November 1952, the city had grown to 233 voters. (Courtesy of the *Islander*.)

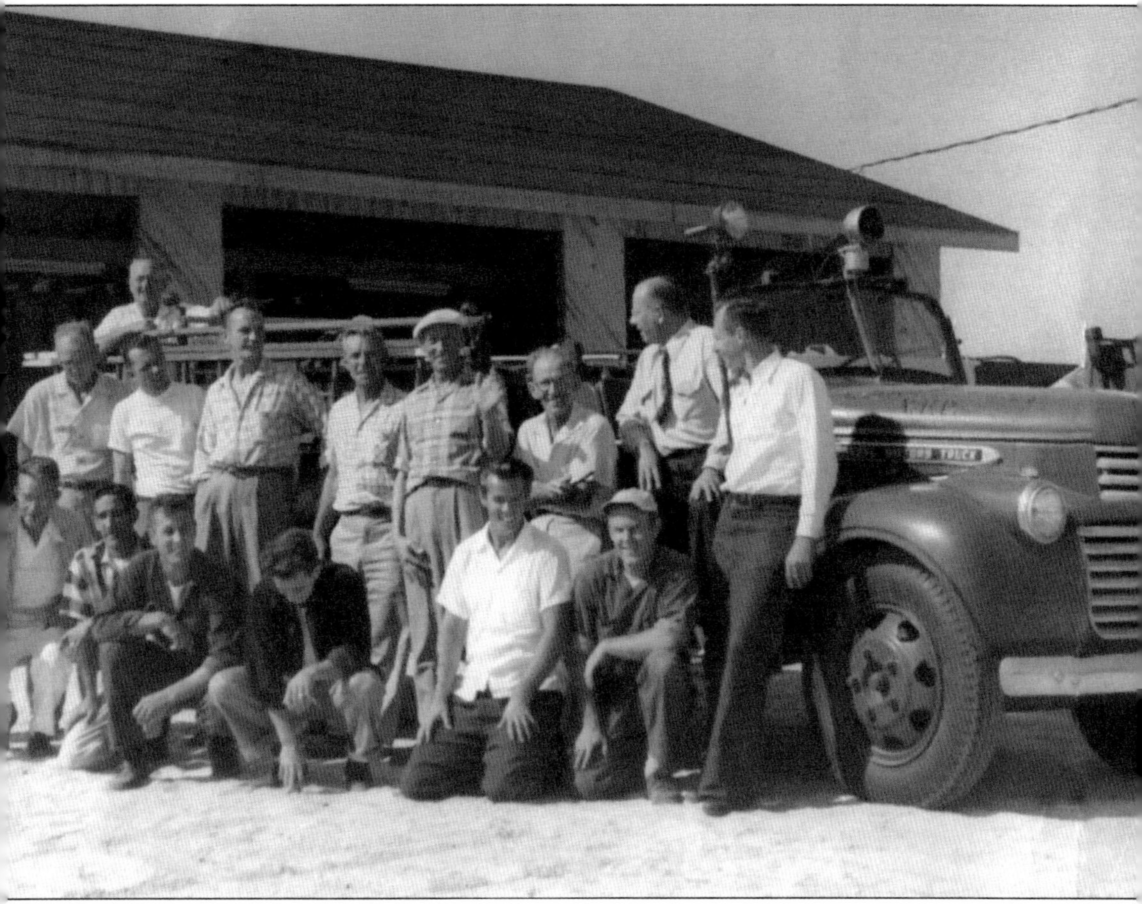

Members of the all-volunteer Anna Maria Island Fire Department gather for a photograph with the engine at the firehouse in Bradenton Beach. The firehouse still serves the West Manatee Fire Rescue District volunteer service organization and houses an old fire engine that appears in parades. (Courtesy of the *Islander*.)

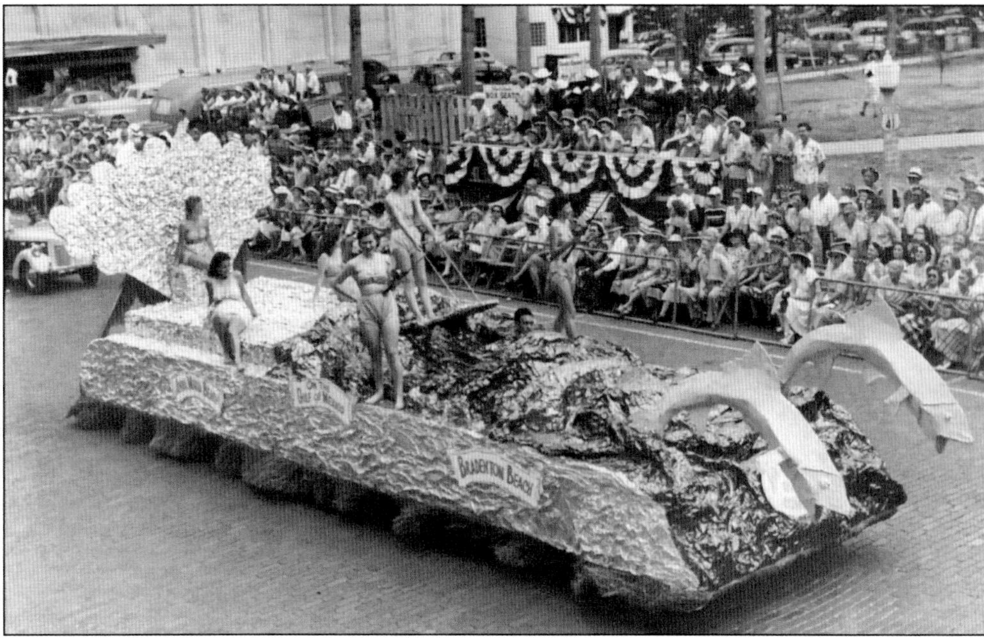

Jeanne Roat of Bradenton Beach "rides" a surfboard in a wake in the center of the Anna Maria Island Chamber of Commerce float in the downtown Bradenton De Soto Celebration parade on March 25, 1949. In front of the Manatee Courthouse, the float is passing a review stand on Manatee Avenue that includes seats for dignitaries and float judges. With Roat are Carolyn Meeker, Carol Woods, Betty Sue Burton, and Charlene Miller. The float featured aqua "waters" with gold accents and two giant tarpon leading the way. (Both, courtesy of the *Islander* and the Roat family collection.)

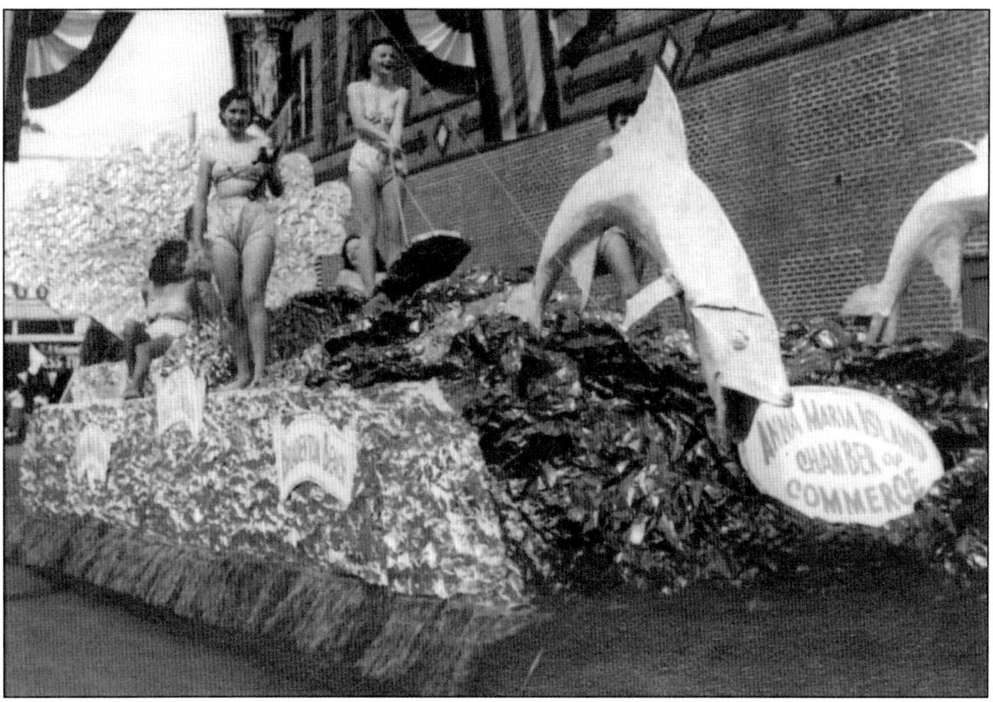

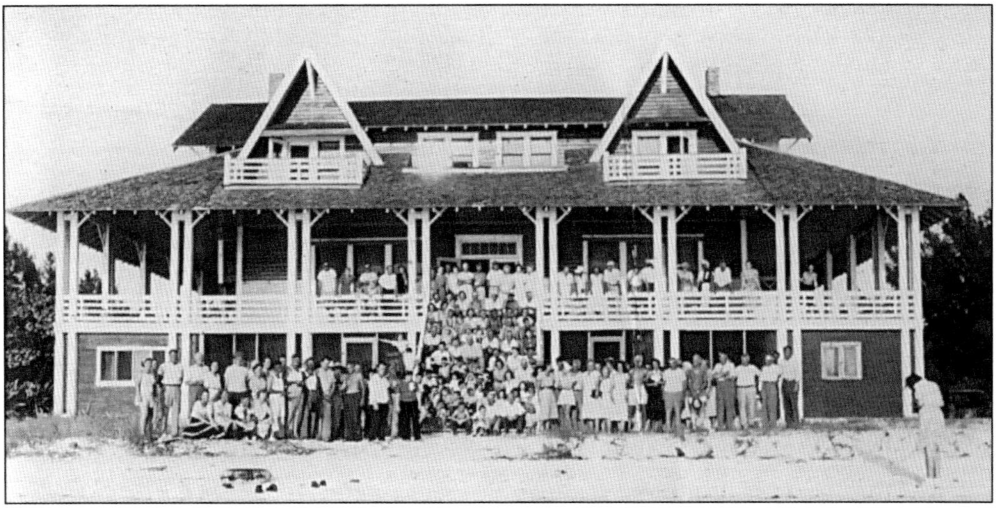

A large group gathers in the 1940s on the beachfront and porch of the Gulf Park Hotel on Gulf Drive in Bradenton Beach. The hotel was built in the early 1900s—before any bridges—complete with a dock on the bay for arrivals by boat. By the 1940s, the hotel had survived hard times and changed hands, as the Gulf Trailer Park began growing on the bayfront. It later became the Sandpiper Resort Mobile Home Park. The owners allowed the hotel bar to reopen as the Oar House in the 1970s on the ground level only, as the upstairs had been condemned. Loud music brought complaints from the retirees in the trailer park, but soon enough the remains of the Gulf Park and the Oarhouse were leveled by a fire.

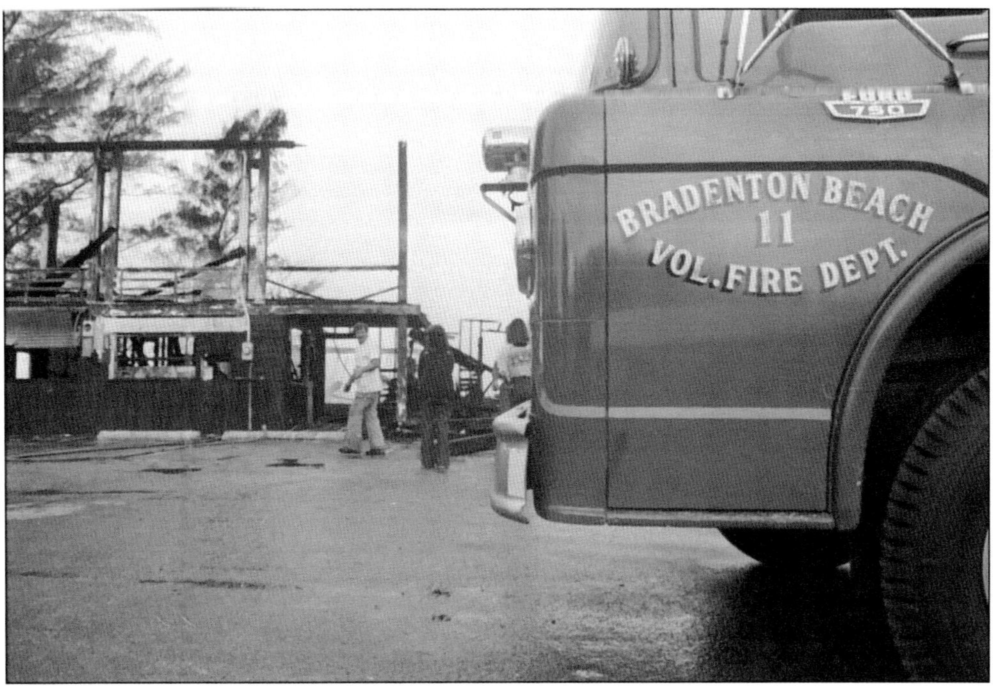

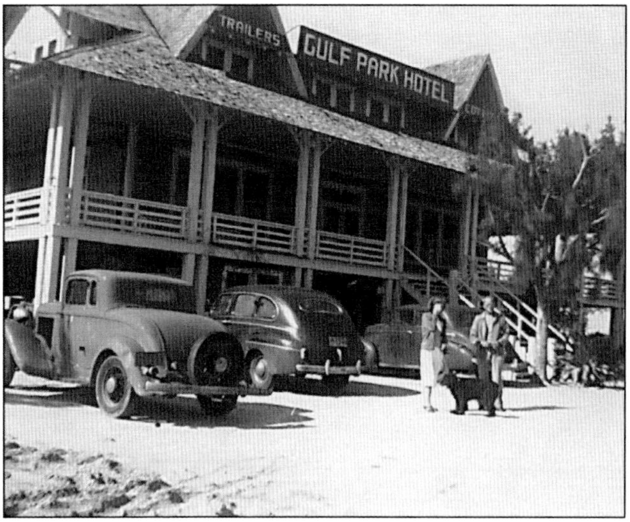

Guests arrive with their four-legged friend to the Gulf Park Hotel on the Gulf of Mexico in Bradenton Beach. The three-story building first opened in 1909 with a dining room, lounge, and beach showers on the first floor and guest rooms on the second and third floors. New owners and the growing need for accommodations in the 1940s–1950s prompted the development of the Gulf Trailer Park and some small cottages on the bayfront opposite the hotel. (Courtesy of the *Islander*.)

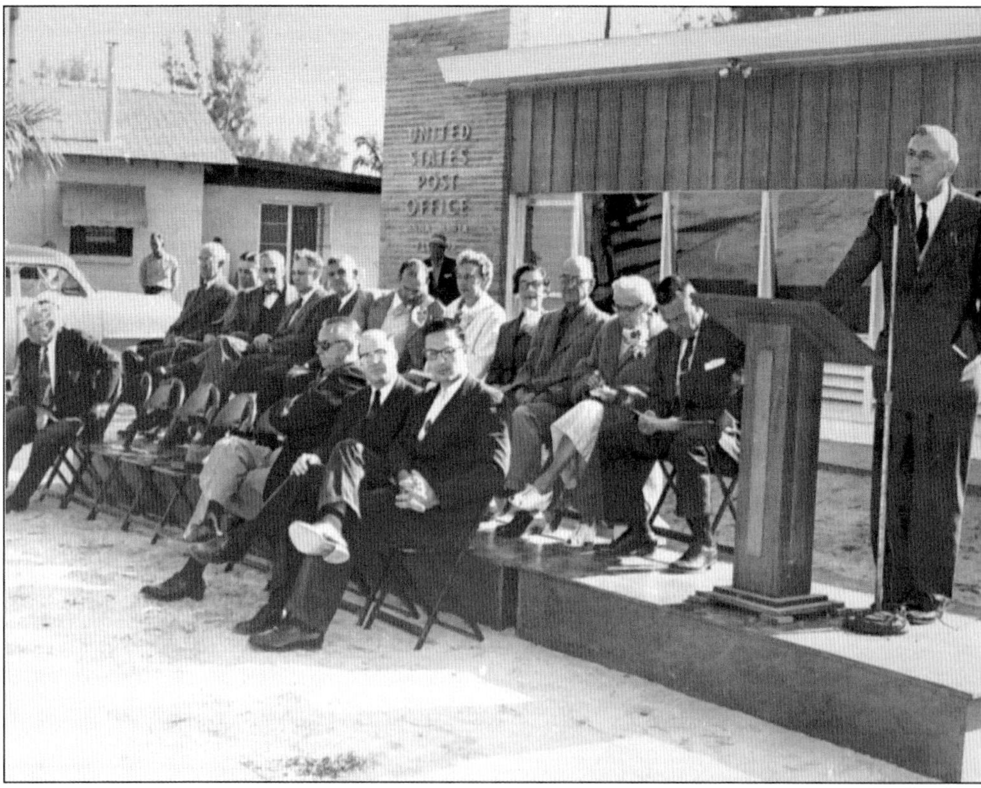

A man makes a speech to the dignitaries and other people gathered for the dedication of a new US post office in December 1955 on Gulf Drive in Anna Maria. It was the second post office to open on the island, the first being in Anna Maria in 1914. It was a long drive for delivery with only 30-plus mailboxes by the 1930s. The new building was dedicated two years before the bridge to the mainland in Holmes Beach opened, limiting automobile travel to and from the island to the mainland via the original wooden bridge in Bradenton Beach.

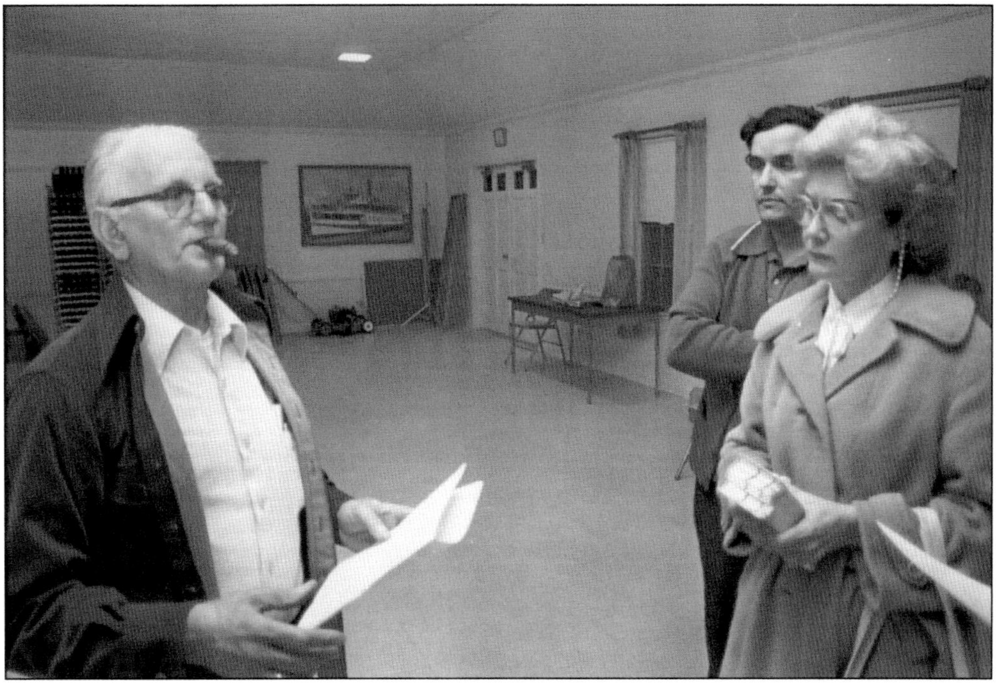

Mayor Ernie Cagnina (left), with his trademark cigar, meets at city hall on Election Day, February 14, 1978, with city clerk Mary H. Tebbetts, holding what appears to be ballot cards, and Commissioner John Chamberlain (rear). Tebbetts is the wife of major-league baseball's Birdie Tebbetts.

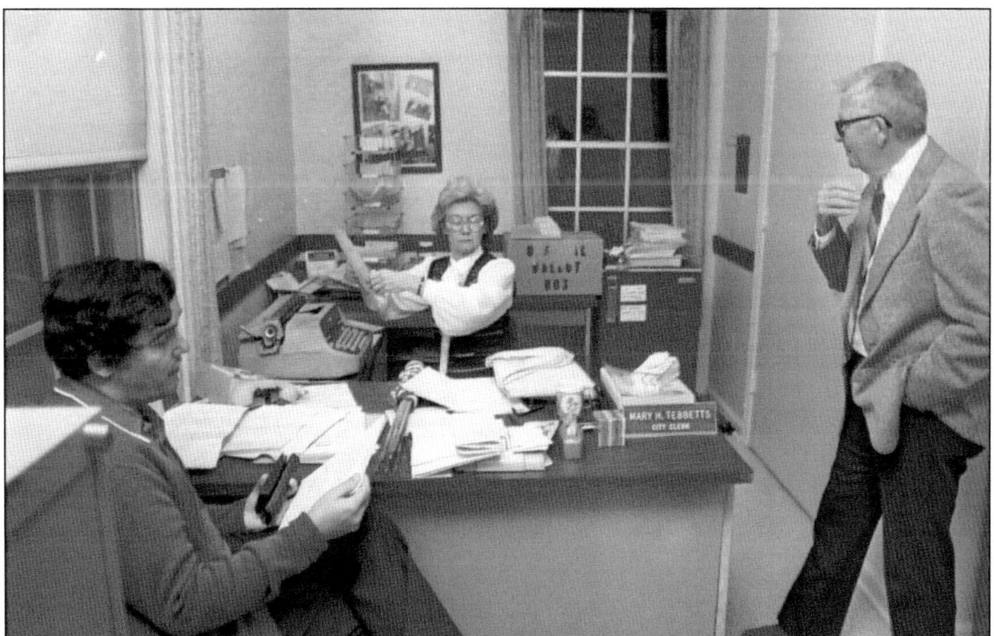

Anna Maria city clerk Mary Tebbetts (center) prepares to type a document, while Commissioner John Chambers (left) and commission candidate Bob McDonald carry on a conversation at Anna Maria City Hall on Election Day, February 14, 1978. The "Official Ballot Box" for the city election sits on a table behind Tebbetts.

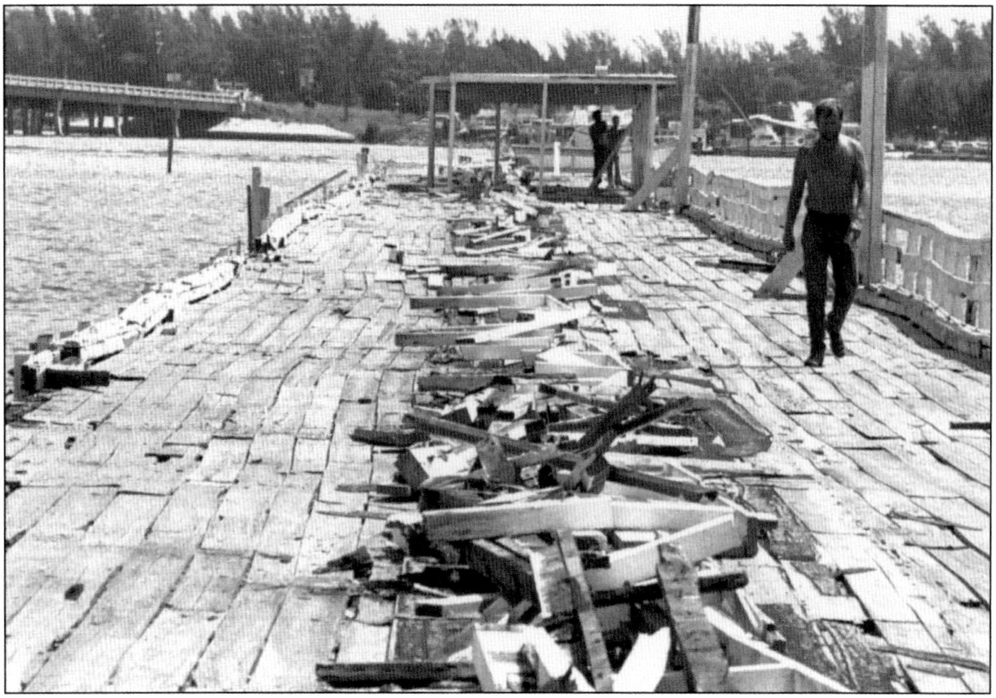

Demolition work is underway in 1977 on the original wooden bridge built in 1921, linking Cortez to Bradenton Beach. A new bridge built in 1957 is near the top left. The demolition work was the first step in reconstruction of the rickety bridge, which was transformed into a fishing pier in Bradenton Beach. A new shelter was built at the pier's terminus in Sarasota Bay, while much of the snack bar and a covered area for dining remained on the landward side of the pier.

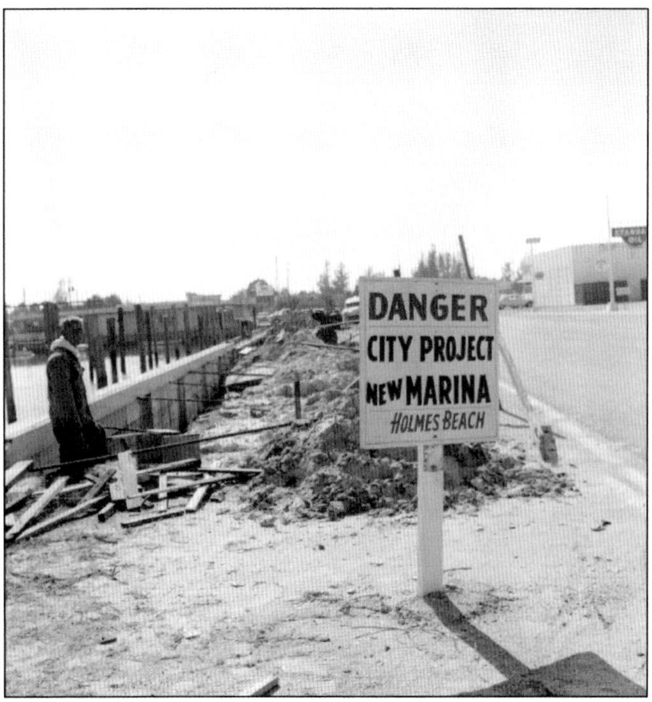

Construction on new docks in the basin once known as Watson's Bayou, opposite the landmark Pete Reynard's Yacht Club Restaurant on Marina Drive in Holmes Beach, is underway to replace old wood docks with new, and roadside angle-parking was removed to make way for a sidewalk adjacent to the concrete seawall. The former docks had served boaters since the 1950s. A commercial marina, not visible here, was added at the opposite end of the basin at Fifty-Sixth Street. Across the street on Marina Drive are Huffine's Standard Oil gas and service station and Rich's Drug Store.

A new post office in Bradenton Beach, then designated the 33510 zip code, is introduced in the 1970s with speeches from dignitaries and an audience of postal patrons. The postal service is still operating in the building today in Bradenton Beach, with the zip code 34217.

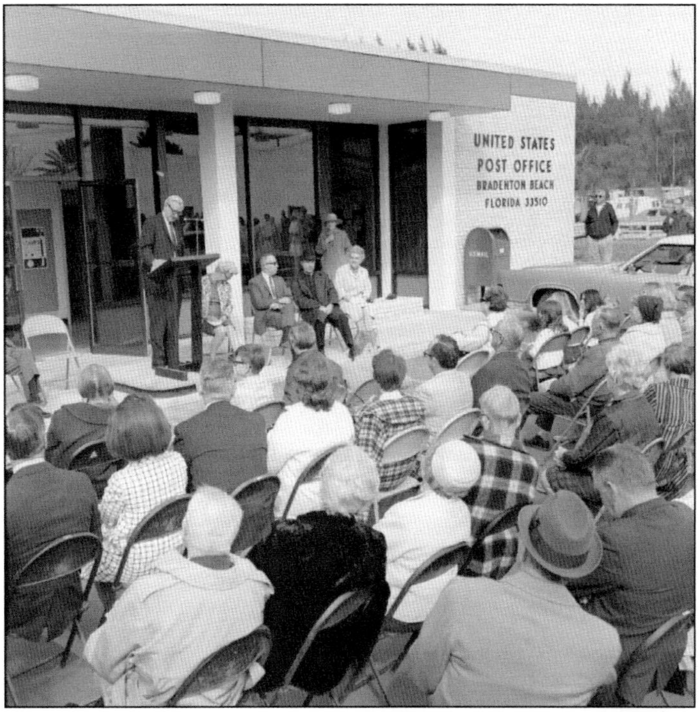

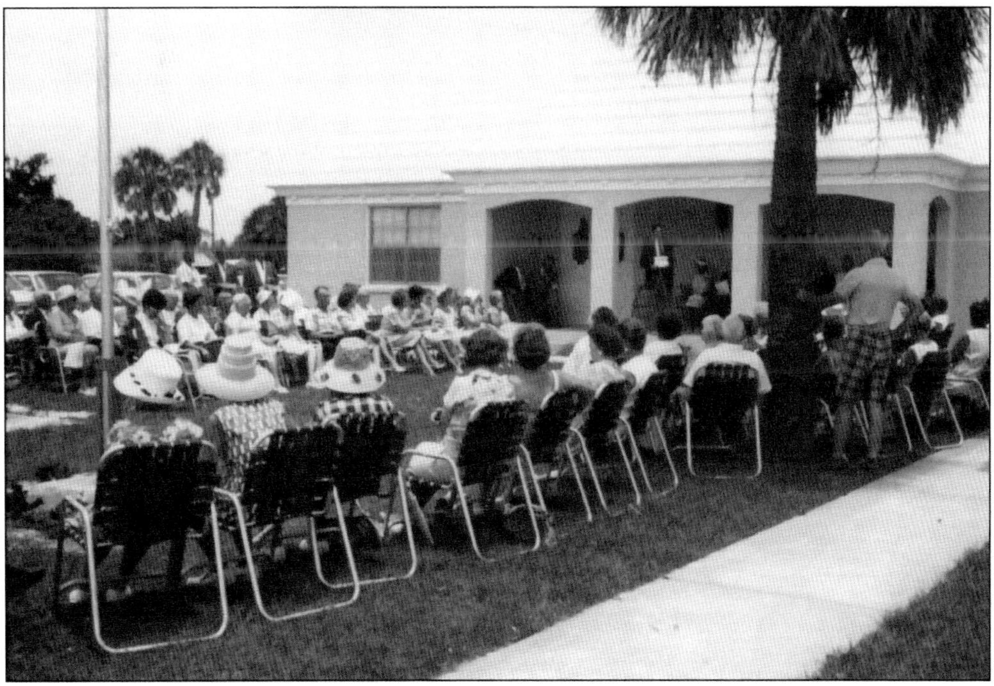

The present building housing Anna Maria City Hall, with modifications, is being dedicated in 1960. Seating for the ceremony is in lawn chairs—likely borrowed—and the day's attire features sun hats and shorts. The flagpole remains in the same position today, although the sidewalk was forfeited for shell paths, and native landscaping fills what was once a grass lawn. (Courtesy of the *Islander.*)

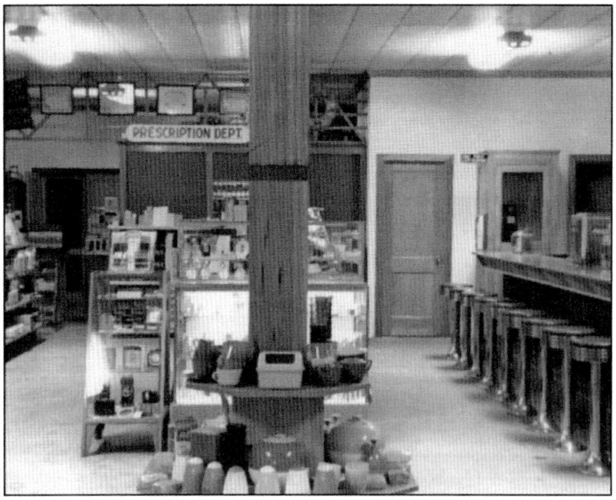

Rich's Drug Store is ready for business on May 17, 1949, at the Island Shopping Center in Holmes Beach. Food was available at a counter on the right side of the store, and a few booths were later added near the entry. The prescription department was in the back of the store, and a public telephone booth can be seen at the rear on the right. The store was stocked with pharmacy needs and sundry items, cameras, perfumes, dishware, and gift items, as well as beach gear. (Courtesy of the *Islander.*)

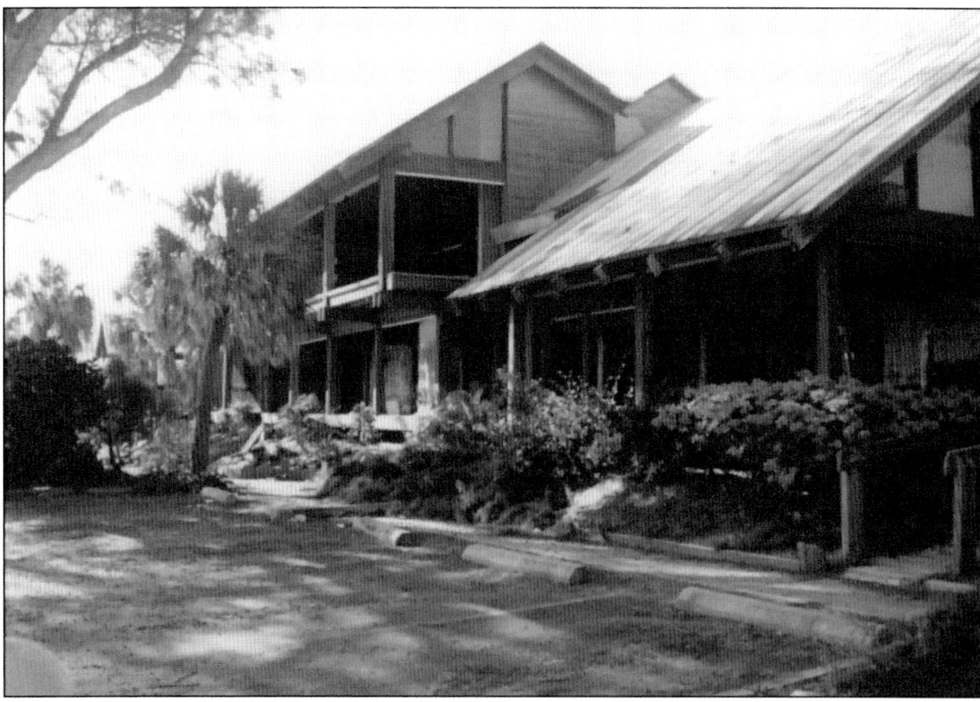

Fast Eddie's Place, a fast-rising seafood restaurant that expanded to other Florida cities before owner Ed Porter fell into tax trouble, awaits demolition in 1993. Porter started his enterprise at the Galati Marine docks, smoking mullet and selling it to the public. He eventually opened a kitchen and started serving meals under an awning on the dock. It grew to this location, at the corner of Pine Avenue and South Bay Boulevard, where the Anchorage Tavern had been for many years. The corner is now the site of a small shopping center and the Anna Maria Post Office. (Courtesy of the *Islander.*)

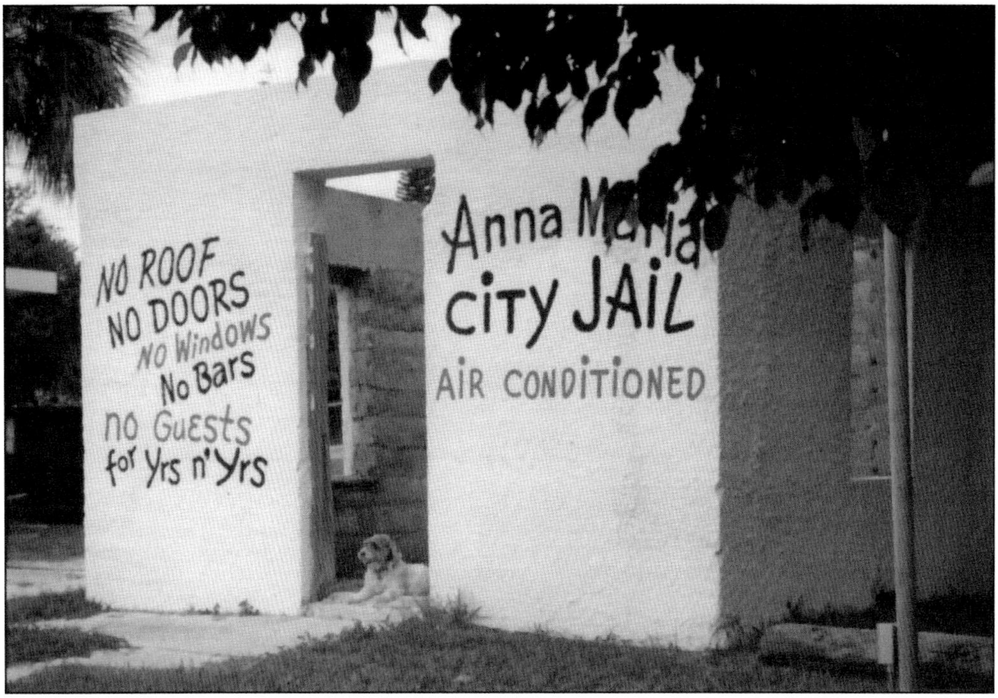

The first and only Anna Maria City Jail still stands as a visitor attraction and photo opportunity alongside the Anna Maria Island Historical Society Museum on Pine Avenue. As the sign says, "No Roof, No Doors, No Windows, No Bars. No guests for Yrs n' Yrs." The jail was built in the 1920s by the first mayor of Anna Maria, Capt. Mitch Davis. It soon burned, but the open-air jail has stood for "yrs n' yrs." (Courtesy of Lois Finley.)

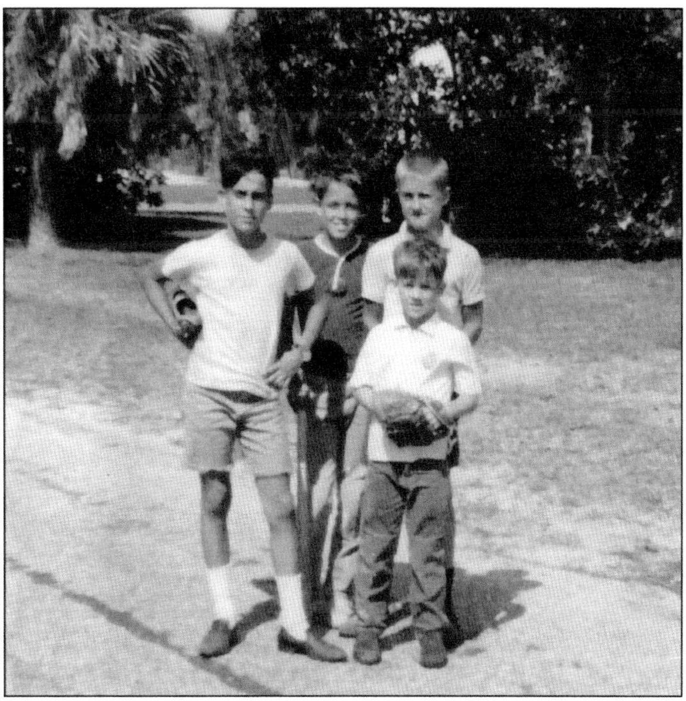

With their gloves at hand, boys of summer, from left to right, brothers Jim and Dan Herringshaw, Charlie Weaver, and George Tebbetts, are ready for a game of baseball sometime back in the 1960s. Jim Herringshaw, a FedEx delivery person on the island in the 1990s, and Tebbetts, the son of baseball great Birdie Tebbetts, still reside in the area. (Courtesy of the *Islander*.)

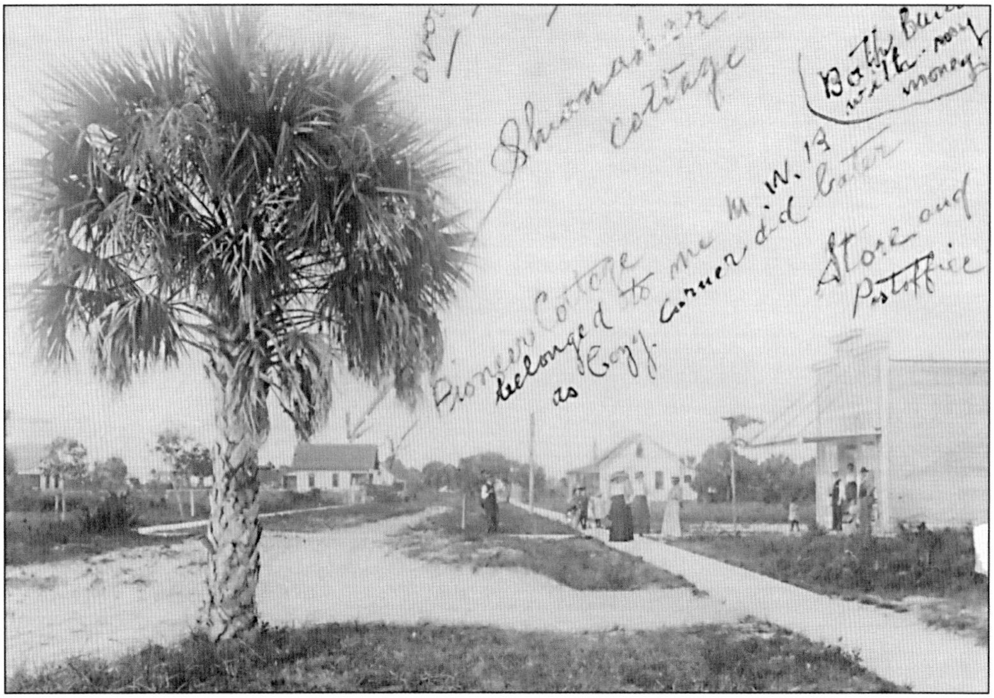

This view of Pine Avenue in 1914 shows the early development that came about thanks to a thriving development company that brought potential buyers to the island on steamer boats. It is intriguing for the writing, apparently scribbled by Mabel W. Bean. This original photograph also has writing on the back, including, "'It is me on bicycle,' Mabel Williams Bean." She also identifies the Anna Maria Post Office and Robin's Nest Cottage on the right. She notes that Cozy Corner and the house on "Bay Beach were built with my own money." (Courtesy of the *Islander.*)

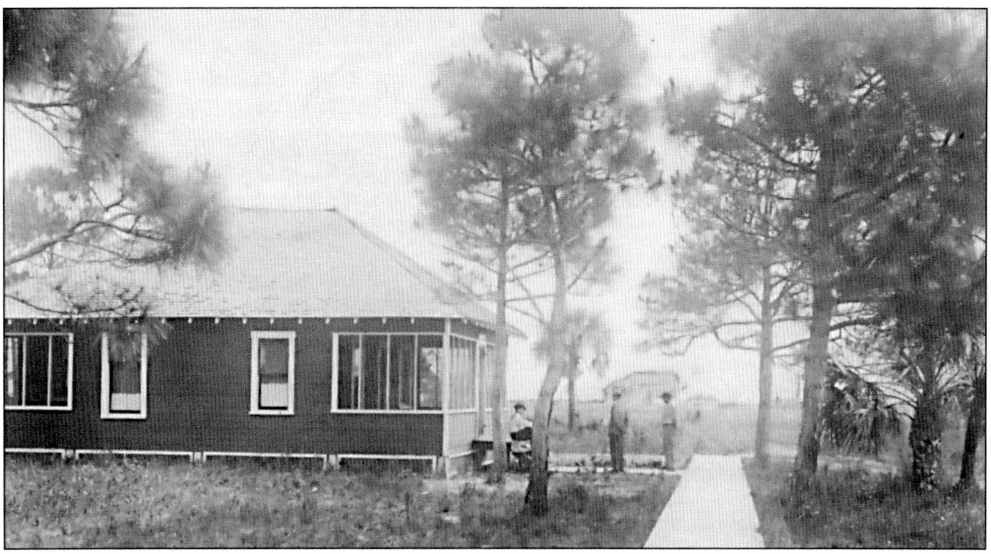

Mabel Bean labeled this photograph as the Parrish House, Keye's Cottage on Spring Street in Anna Maria near Cozy Corner. It appears two men on the sidewalk in front of the house are talking to people seated on the front steps. Behind the two men standing on the bayfront is a dock. (Courtesy of the *Islander.*)

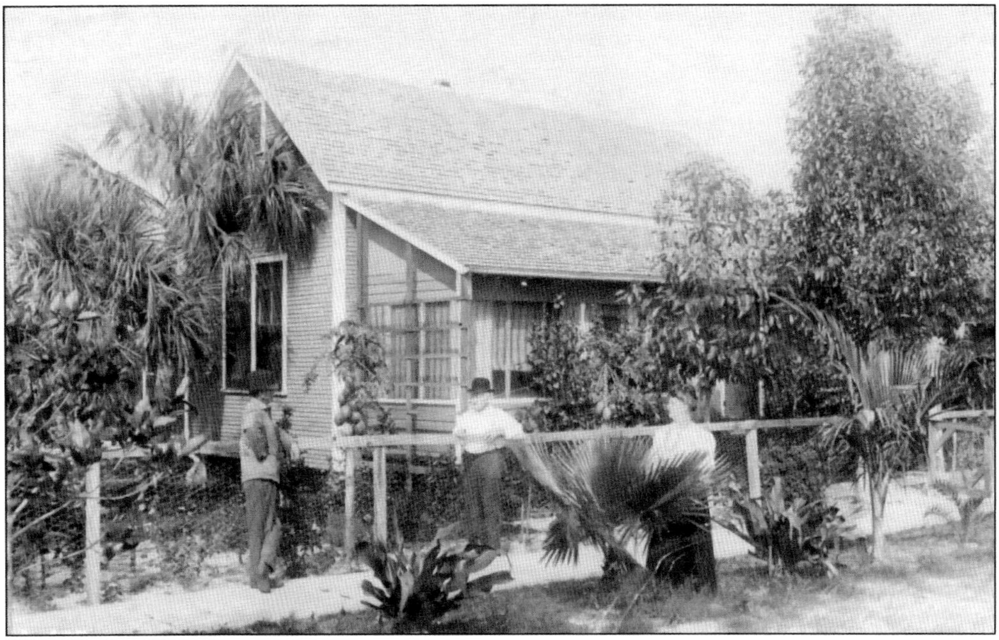

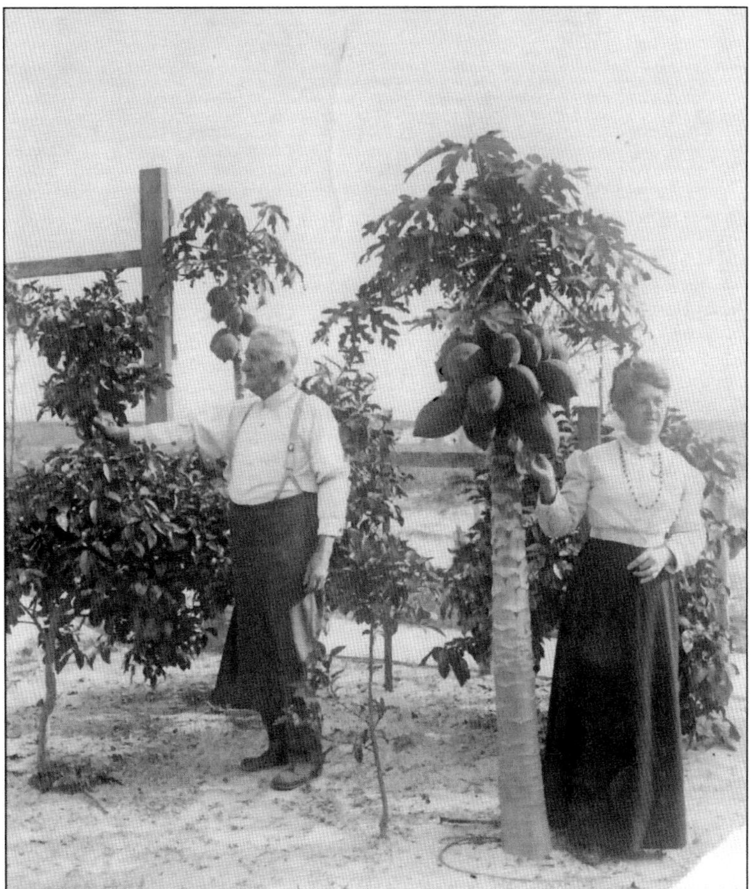

Around 1915, Professor and Mrs. Nichols greet a Mr. Tedder (left), a real estate man for Bean Development, who is leaning on the fence at their house on what old-timers call Snapper Street—the extension of Gulf Drive north of Pine Avenue—in Anna Maria. In the closer view, the professor and his wife show off their success with papayas in their garden. (Both, courtesy of the *Islander*.)

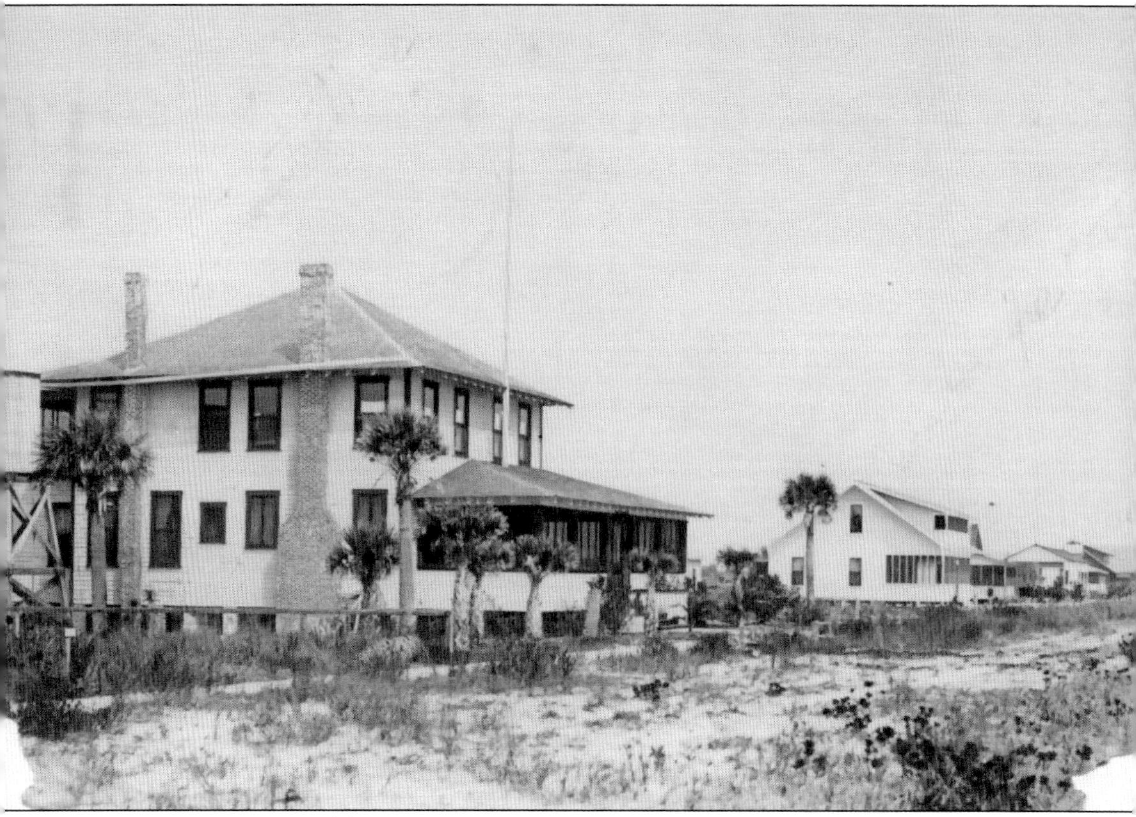

These homes, pictured here in 1916, were built facing the Gulf of Mexico on Gulf Boulevard in Anna Maria. The boulevard is one block west of Gulf Drive and still boasts some of the older homes, but it is now only one block. The homes continue, but the road is gone and only a public sidewalk remains. It is sometimes called the Secret Sidewalk, as it is somewhat hidden by landscaping. The house on the left with a water tower and two chimneys is labeled the Simonton House—later Paul Gilmore's home—on a similar photograph. The house to the right is the Vanderipe Cottage. (Courtesy of the *Islander*.)

In 1936, this Midwestern couple honeymooned in Florida. Janice and Carl Freeman made plans to return to the beach, and 16 years later, with their two young children, they did just that. They found a lot and started construction on their drive-in restaurant in 1952–1953. They offered full-course dinners, an ice-cream soda fountain, and curb service—the "going thing" in the 1950s. Now, grandchildren Estella and Clark, taking up where their parents and grandparents left off, continue the family tradition at Skinny's Place, opposite the Manatee Public Beach on Gulf Drive. (Courtesy of Skinny's Place.)

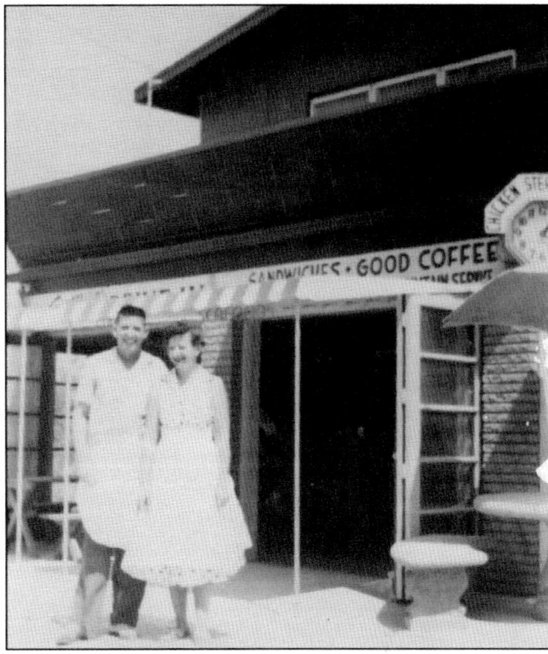

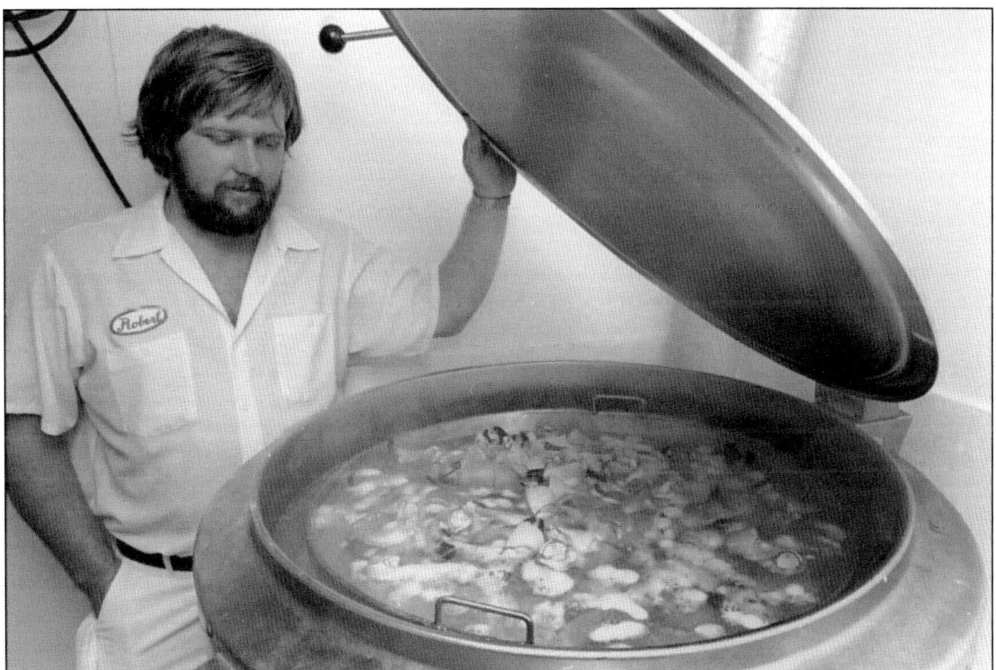

One of the cooks checks a whopping pot of stone crab claws at Moore's Stone Crab restaurant on the bayfront at the north end of Longboat Key. It came into popularity in 1967—about the same time *Flipper* was debuting on television. What helped Moore's stand out were two big docks extending into the bay and a connecting dock at the end. With some wood slats added, the Moore's created a pen for two pet dolphins and entertained its patrons by hosting feeding time for the dolphins until one escaped in a storm in the early 1970s. The second dolphin was then released. The restaurant was sold and closed in July 2015.

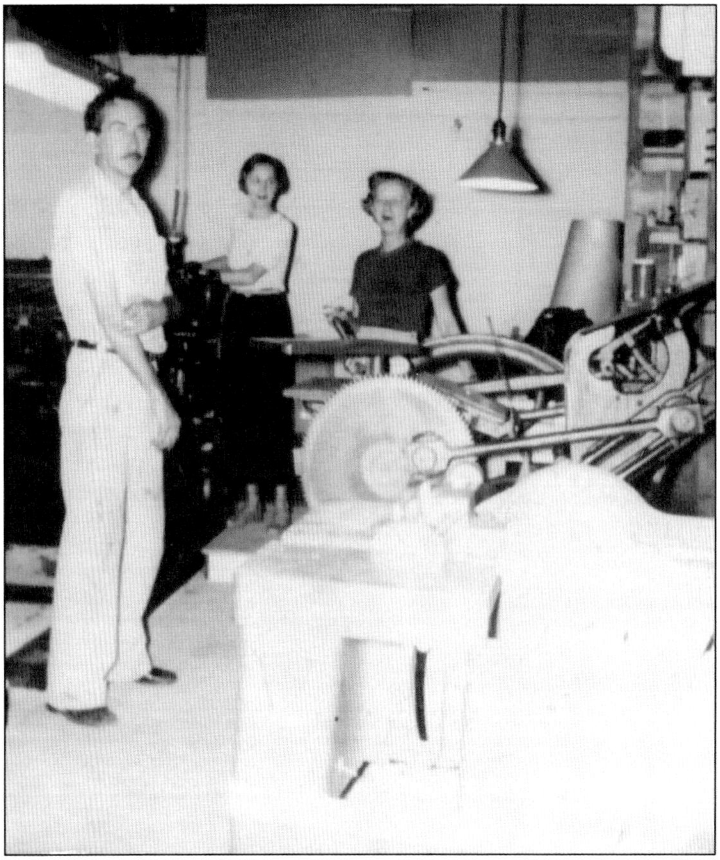

The pressroom of the *Anna Maria Key News* churns out newspapers in 1949 from its office in Holmes Beach on Marina Drive, opposite Watson's Bayou. With the pressman, Elmer Fenton, are owners/editors/writers Harriet (Blair) Williams (center) and Ellen (Brackin) Marshall. Marshall, born in 1908, remained on the island until her death in 2003. In the photograph below, taken in 1994, Marshall shows her surprise on finding a man pictured in a mural on the wall of the Home Hardware store in Holmes Beach reading the first edition of her newspaper, the *Anna Maria Key News*. (Both, courtesy of the *Islander*.)

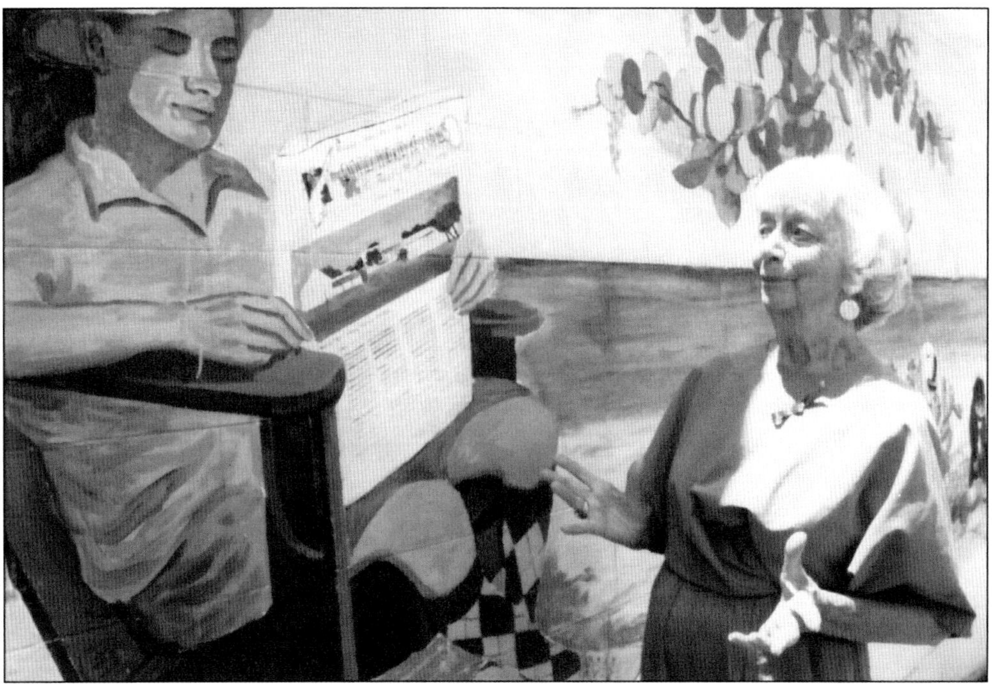

In 1957, Ellen and Jack Marshall of Anna Maria are dressed in their finest to attend the gala ribbon-cutting ceremony for the Cortez Bridge. Ellen Marshall was a key figure on the island in the 1950s. She reported on the early days of incorporation and the meeting where Holmes Beach got its name by a vote of some 30–40 citizens. The other choice? Cobb City. (Courtesy of the *Islander.*)

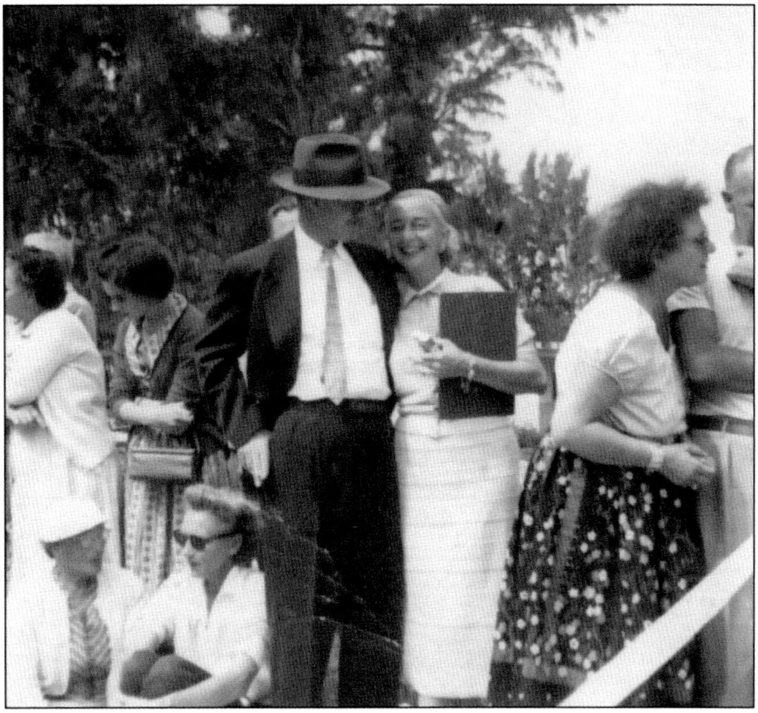

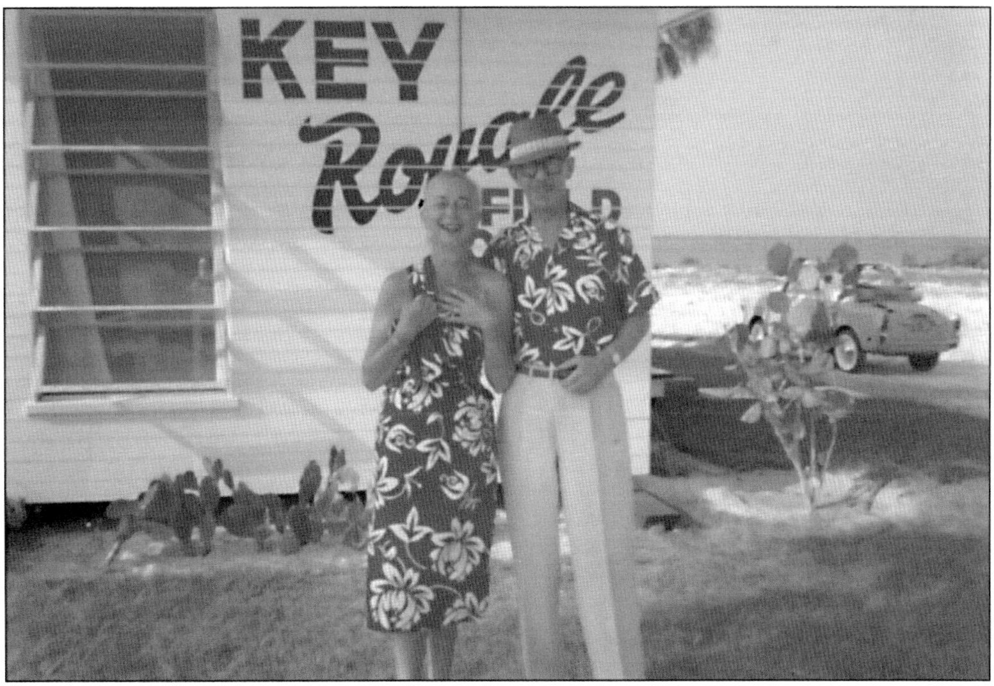

While the *Anna Maria Key News* was relatively short-lived, Ellen Marshall and her husband, Jack, found a career together in real estate sales. In June 1960, they opened a sales office for a new elite home development—Key Royale. They dressed in matching red tropical-print attire for the opening. Ellen's little sports car is pictured to the right of the small sales office they put up on the key to sign up their buyers. (Courtesy of the *Islander.*)

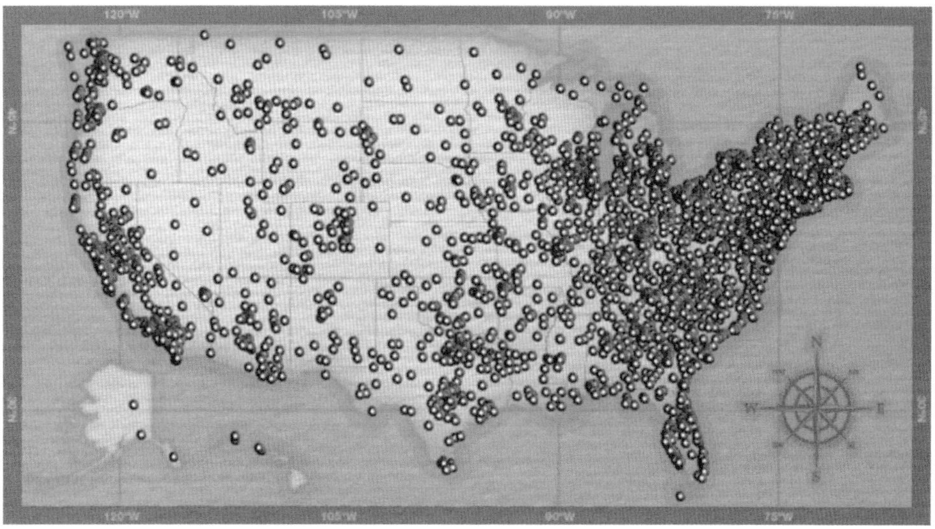